THE DESERT RATS

THE DESERT RATS

RATS

7th Armoured Division
1940–1945

Robin Neillands

Weidenfeld and Nicolson
London

940
542
nei

ISBN 0 297 81191 6

Printed in Great Britain by
Butler & Tanner Ltd,
Frome and London

Contents

LIST OF MAPS   vii

ACKNOWLEDGEMENTS   ix

FOREWORD BY MAJOR PETER VERNEY   xi

INFORMATION FOR READERS   xiii

INTRODUCTION   xv

1 The Coming of the Tank, *1914–1939*   3

2 The Western Desert Force, *1939–1940*   27

3 First Blood: Sidi-Barrani and Beda Fomm, *June 1940– February 1941*   40

4 Brevity and Battle-axe, *February to June 1941*   63

5 Crusader: The Battle for Sidi Rezegh, *July – December 1941*   80

6 Gazala and the Cauldron, *January – July 1942*   102

7 Alam Halfa, *June – September 1942*   129

8 Alamein   141

9 Alamein to Tripoli   163

10 Tripoli to Tunis   180

11 Italy and England, *September 1943 – June 1944*   195

12 The Battle of Normandy, *7th June – 31st August*   215

13 Belgium and Holland, *September – December 1944*   244

14 Germany, *13th January – 8th May 1945*   261

BIBLIOGRAPHY   277

INDEX   279

Maps

 1 The Western Desert and Cyrenaica
 2 The advance in Cyrenaica and the Battle of Beda Fomm
 3 Battle-axe
 4 The Crusader Battlefield
 5 The First Day of Sidi Rezegh
 6 Gazala
 7 The Cauldron
 8 Alam Halfa
 9 7th Armoured Division at El Alamein
10 7th Armoured Division's Advance from El Alamein to Tunis
11 7th Armoured Division in Italy, and the Volturno crossing
12 Normandy
13 The Pursuit to Ghent
14 Holland
15 Germany

Acknowledgements

My thanks go first to everyone who has contributed to this book. I have attempted to include as many contributions as possible, but I would like to acknowledge my thanks to all those whose accounts cannot appear but were nevertheless useful to me in filling in the background or as a check on other stories. To obtain these contributions we contacted many Old Comrades' Associations, together with a large number of national and regional newspapers, all of whom published an appeal for stories about the 7th Armoured Division during the Second World War. The eventual response to this was some 700 hundred letters, tapes, diaries, photographs, and poems, which were then followed up with telephone conversations and interviews.

Thanks must also go to the staff of the Imperial War Museum, the Tank Museum at Bovington, Thomas Cook's for their help in Egypt, and various museums in France, especially the *Musée de la Paix* in Caen, and the *Bataille de Normandie* museum near Bayeux. Within this general thank you, some particular acknowledgements are due. First, to Major Peter Verney, son of General Verney, who commanded 7th Armoured in North-Western Europe. Major Verney, himself a military historian, kindly agreed to write a foreword to this book, read it in draft and made many helpful comments, which I have not hesitated to adopt. He also passed on to me some of his father's papers and a personal account from General Harding, of his time in 7th Armoured Division, which forms the basis of the Alamein and Tripoli chapters. I am grateful to Major Verney for permission to use these accounts in this book. Captain Roddy de Norman of the Royal Hussars at Tidworth loaned me a wealth of information, particularly on the 11th Hussars and was a constant support and encouragement throughout. I look forward to reading his own book on the actions of 53rd (Welsh) Division on the Aller in April 1945.

Other people who must be thanked include Joe Cartwright, an old

Royal Marine friend of mine, who rounded up contributions from Southern Africa, especially those from the 4th South African Armoured Car Regiment. Thanks to Major Neville Gillman MC of the 4th CLY and his comrade Bobby Bramall MM, for his account of Villers-Bocage and to Field Marshal Lord Carver. Major General Shan Hackett and Brigadier C.E.F. Turner, with particular thanks for the loan of his wartime letters and scrapbook, and Colonel Duncan Riddell of 550 Company RASC for the loan of his Unit diary and his excellent taped account of 550 Company's time in the Desert. I would also like to thank Derrick Watson for his entertaining accounts of his time as an infantry officer in the Queen's Brigade.

I have been at particular pains to collect stories from the NCOs and private soldiers of the 7th Armoured Division, who are largely neglected in so many accounts. I have before me at least one history which mentions no one under the rank of Captain, which seems, to say the least, a trifle unfair. Thanks therefore to: Sergeant Rick Hall of the RASC; Arthur Waites of the 7th Hussars; Ron Haslam; Ronald Mallabar of the 9th Durhams; A. Flanagan of the 2nd RTR; Harry Upward of the 5th Royal Tanks; Rex Wingfield of The Queen's; Arthur Medler of the 5th Tanks; Alan Barnes of REME; Alan Austin; E.D. Johnson of the 2nd Royal Gloucester Hussars; Peter Forbes of the RASC; Barney Finnigan of the 6th Royal Tanks; John Allan; Philip Knowles; George Waddington of 146 Field Regiment, Royal Artillery; Harry Ireland; Harry Blood of the RASC; George Clark of The King's Dragoon Guards; R. Godwin of The Royal Gloucestershire Hussars; Harry Buckledee of the 11th Hussars; Gerald Milner of the RASC; and many, many more, whose stories appear in this book.

I am sure that all the contributors to this book will join me in thanking Estelle Huxley for typing so many drafts and to another Royal Marine, Terry Brown, for drawing the maps.

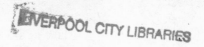

Foreword

BY

Major Peter Verney

I asked a distinguished commander of the last war about his experiences
in World War I. What was as incomprehensible to me about that – as
the last contest is now to the present generation – was what it was that
kept them going. In that War and time after time, one knew that one-
third of those sitting round the mess table would be killed or wounded
within the day. Field-Marshal Alexander, for that was who it was, said
with the simple clarity which was his hallmark – Well, what could we
do? If we were going to be killed, we would be killed. We couldn't run
away; that would be letting the chaps down.

This is the story of the 'chaps' of the 7th Armoured Division, the
famed Desert Rats, told largely in their own words, a distillation of taped
interviews, letters and diaries, accumulated with painstaking care by
Robin Neillands. What had started as a piece of extended research
turned into a labour of love which encompassed the remembrances of
nearly 500 veterans of the most famous armoured division of the last
war, and all 'Rats' will be delighted to know that the entire collection
is going to the Royal Armoured Corps Museum at Bovington to add to
their growing archives.

From the comfort of a post-war armchair men will justifiably and
proudly declare that in the last War they were fighting for King and
Country, for Liberty and Freedom. On the field of battle the reality is
somewhat different. Whether in the deserts of North Africa, the bocage
of Normandy, or on the 'Gallop' through Northern France – and many
still remember how painful unripe fruit can be when aimed with loving
accuracy by people rapturous with liberation – through the marshes of
northern Holland or at the final triumphant entry to Hamburg, and to
the end of the War, the most enduring memory, and one which comes

through in this book, is one of comradeship. The Desert Rats were really fighting for their mates, their 'muckers', who would no more let them down than they would let their muckers down. Their's, too, was a pride – pride in themselves, pride in their units and, above all, pride in wearing the celebrated *Jerboa*, the Desert Rat. This pride shines like a beacon through the many accounts in this superb book.

Commanding the Desert Rats in their 'Gallop' across the Seine to Ghent and beyond was certainly the proudest time of my father's military career. As I write this, his own model *jerboa* is sitting before me. I rather think that it, too, is winking approval at Robin Neillands' great achievement in assembling these splendid tales of a great fighting division. Now, as I write these lines, by a remarkable coincidence, the Desert Rats, in the form of the 7th Armoured Brigade, will be seeing active service again in the Gulf. All readers of this book will wish them well and rest confident that if called upon to do so, they will aquit themselves in the incomparable tradition of their distinguished pre-decessors.

Peter Verney
November 1990

Information for Readers

With the ending of compulsory Military Service, many aspects of Service life have become unfamiliar to the public at large. The reader is therefore advised to read the Foreword and consult the maps and the Orders of Battle for the Division as they appear from time to time throughout the book. This will help to clarify some of the more complicated parts of the story, but some further explanation at this point may help the general reader.

The 'Order of Battle' is not the order in which the Units of the Division engage the enemy, but a list of Units under direct Divisional Command at that time. The Order of Battle is rarely static, as Units are detached to aid other Units, while other Units are attached or 'taken under command' from time to time and on a temporary basis. Though it may vary, an infantry brigade usually consists of three battalions with supporting arms, and a cavalry or armoured brigade consists of three regiments. A cavalry regiment being the equivalent of an infantry battalion. Please note, however, that the Rifle Brigade is not a brigade but a regiment and, for example, the 2nd Rifle Brigade is the 2nd Battalion of that regiment. As the soldiers say, 'This is done to confuse you.'

A division will usually consist of three brigades with supporting arms; a corps of two or more divisions; an army of two or more corps; an army group of two or more armies. In this book I have aimed for clarity as well as following Service practice, which is by no means always clear to the lay reader, and where I have used Service abbreviations, they are explained in full at least once in the text. The 2nd Royal Tank Regiment is usually described as 2nd RTR, the King's Dragoon Guards as the KDGs, the County of London Yeomanry as the CLY, and so on. There are, as ever, exceptions. That illustrious regiment, the 11th Hussars is usually referred to by other members of the Division as the Cherry Pickers, while members of the Regiment tend to refer to it as the PAO

(Prince Albert's Own). With a view to making what follows as clear as possible, I have had the manuscript read by a non-Service reader, Paul Reynolds, and expanded on any term which he feels to be unduly obscure. Any failure on this point remains mine.

Introduction

This is the story of an armoured division, perhaps the most famous armoured division in the history of warfare, the British 7th Armoured Division of the Second World War, the Desert Rats. This book tells the story of that great fighting division and follows their tank tracks from the desert of North Africa to the streets of Berlin. This is a long tale, told as far as possible in the words of the men who served in the Division, of every rank from private soldier to general, and from as wide a selection of units and arms as possible. I have to make it clear that this is not an 'Official' or even an 'Authorized' history. Still less is it an attempt to recount the daily doings of every unit of 7th Armoured throughout the Second World War. Rather it is an attempt to paint a picture in words of life in an armoured division during the Second World War, and those in search of further detail are referred to the books listed in the Bibliography.

Among my first contributions was a letter from R.M. Wingfield, himself an author, who served with 7th Armoured in the Queen's Brigade and therefore knows about writing and soldiering. 'The best of luck in what you are trying to do,' he wrote, 'but you are on a hiding to nothing. Everyone will look up his unit, troop or company and if they are not there on every page, heaven help you.'

This is very true, so in fairness to myself, let me point out that in a work of this nature the writer is very much in the hands of his contributors, for as a general rule, the writer was not present during the actions described. I was ten when the Second World War ended. That apart, an armoured division was a considerable force, consisting of some 15,000 men in scores of different units. Each should have a say but each is part of the whole. I have restricted the contributions included to those who wore the Jerboa flash on their vehicles or battledress, and in doing so I am conscious that I may have been less than fair to other units who shared the battles with 7th Armoured and to other Services like the Desert Air Force, the gallant defenders of Malta, and the ships and submarines that harassed Rommel's supply lines. I have thought it worth while, and have found it necessary in the interests of clarity, to start the book with an account of the development of tanks and armoured warfare in the early days of the Great War, and included a certain amount of technical detail. History has a way of repeating itself and today, nearly fifty years after the Desert Rats rolled forward at Alamein, tanks of the British Army bearing the famous red jerboa flash are once again deployed for action in the Middle East, but the outcome of this current confrontation in 1990 has yet to be resolved and must await some other historian. The aim of this book is to tell the story of the 7th Armoured Division in the Second World War, told in the words of those who served in it. The Desert Rats are growing old now, and their numbers are shrinking, but they remain proud of their famous Division and rightly so. This is their story. It ought to be remembered.

> To famous men, all the earth is their
> sepulchre. Their deeds shall be recorded
> not only on stones at home but in all lands.
>
> *Pericles*

... and the Lord was with Judah,
and he drove out the inhabitants of the mountains;
but he could not drive out the inhabitants of the plain,
because they had chariots of iron.

Judges I: 19–20

1

The Coming of the Tank

1914–1939

> There is nothing more difficult to take in hand, more
> perilous to conduct, or more uncertain of success,
> than to take the lead in the introduction of a new
> order of things.
>
> *Niccolo Machiavelli*

At 7.30 on the sunny morning of 1st July 1916, 120,000 British infantrymen climbed out of their trenches on the rolling chalk downland of Picardy, to begin the series of actions known to history as the Battle of the Somme. By the end of that fatal day, half of them were lying out between the lines and almost 20,000 were dead. July 1st 1916 witnessed the greatest disaster inflicted on a British Army since William met Harold at Hastings in 1066. More men were killed or wounded in the first week on the Somme than now serve in the British Army, and by the time the Battle of the Somme petered out in November 1916, losses on both sides had exceeded one million men. In return for their share in this catastrophe the British Army had advanced exactly six miles.

The prime reason for the horrific death toll on the Somme, and on many other battlefields of the Western Front during the First World War, was that the tactics of the time were dominated by defensive weapons, most specifically by a combination of barbed wire, artillery and machine-guns. Against this combination the infantry hurled themselves in vain. Even when confronted with this fact on numerous occasions, at Ypres, the Somme, Loos and other battlefields since the war began in 1914, the futility of such assaults went apparently unrecognized. The generals were unable to win the war and the politicians were unable to end it. This is not to say that the problems of breaking through on the Western Front were not appreciated by inventive minds and higher authority.

A possible solution to the problem was first put down on paper four months after the outbreak of war, on Christmas Day 1914 by Lt. Colonel Maurice Hankey, then Secretary of the War Council and the Imperial Defence Committee. In a memorandum to the Prime Minister and the Cabinet, Hankey summarized the situation which had developed on the Western Front since the armies dug in for the winter in 1914 and pointed out that since the situation there was now deadlocked and likely to remain so, there were only two ways out: (1) to attack the enemy at some other point and so outflank the Western Front, or (2) devise some method or means of overcoming the defensive combination of artillery, machine-guns and barbed wire. Both Hankey's solutions were eventually adopted. The first led to a holocaust among the British, Australian and New Zealand troops landing at Gallipoli and the Dardanelles in 1915. The second led to the tank.

Armoured fighting vehicles were not new, even in 1914–15. Armoured trains had been used during the Boer War of 1899–1901, and in September 1914 the Royal Naval Air Service (RNAS) had started to use armoured cars – actually Rolls Royce civilian cars covered with boiler plate – to patrol the flat country east of their base at Dunkirk, in order to harass the enemy and recover any shot-down pilots. Their more aggressive patrols were suggested by the Director of the Admiralty Air Division, Commodore Murray Sueter, who introduced the armour plate. These armoured cars did good work during the 'Race to the Sea', when the opposing armies each marched hard for the West, each hoping to outflank the other. When the trench line settled in after First Ypres in October and November 1914, the opportunity for mobile action disappeared. Apart from any other considerations, the wheeled armoured car was road-bound, and in June 1915 the remnants of this little Naval force were handed over to the Army. Armoured cars were sent later to the Middle East and there used by, among others, Colonel T.E. Lawrence and his Arab army in the fight against the Turks, and against the Senussi in Libya. Those historians of the tank who wish to go back even further, have referred to Hanibal's elephants, the chariots of the Ancient Britons, or the plate-armoured medieval knight, as the first begetters of the armoured fighting machine.

No man claims to have invented the tank and, indeed, in the true meaning of the term, the tank was assembled rather than invented, for the basic elements of engine, armour plate and caterpillar track already existed. However, if anyone can claim to have initiated the early development of what eventually came to be the tank, then that man is Winston Churchill, then First Lord of the Admiralty. Churchill picked up Hankey's memorandum and pushed for the development of a tracked armoured vehicle which could cross trenches, flatten barbed wire entanglements and so provide close support for the embattled infantry. The rest is history.

This is the story of a fighting division, perhaps the most famous division to serve in the British Army during the Second World War. In telling the story of 7th Armoured Division, it is not my intention to follow every step taken in the early days of the tank. These first steps can be followed in detail by reading Captain B.H. Liddell Hart's excellent book *The Tanks* (Vol. 1), the history of the Royal Tank Regiment and its predecessors. A brief outline of the development is still necessary, partly because it will introduce characters who feature in the story of the 7th Armoured Division, partly because it will explain the origin of different theories governing the tactical use of an armoured formation in battle, which led, as we shall see, to many of the difficulties the Division came to face during the Second World War.

At this point it may be necessary to explain to a section of the readership that the successful development of a new weapon is far from being the end of the story. The weapon will have a designed range of technical features and benefits, but at least half the effectiveness of any weapon in battle will depend on how it is used, manned, serviced and deployed in battle. Indeed, a weapon may be developed for one purpose and used quite differently in the field. To give one modern example, from the Falklands War, the Milan wire-guided anti-tank weapon was used with great effect against Argentine heavy machine-gun posts which the British infantry had no other means of overcoming. How a weapon is *used* is therefore as critical to its success as its designed technical performance.

In the early days the tank was a Naval project, and therefore referred to as a 'landship'. The orginal landships ordered by Winston Churchill in 1915 were armoured vehicles, 40ft long and 13ft wide, with 6mm of roof armour and 8mm of side armour, designed to carry storming parties of fifty men armed with machine guns. This project foundered when Churchill was driven out of office following the failure at the Dardanelles expedition in 1915, but the idea was then followed up by the Minister of Munitions, David Lloyd George.

One of the earliest advocates for something like the tank was Lt-

Colonel E.D. Swinton, an officer of the Royal Engineers. Sent to France as a war correspondent in 1914, he had seen the war of movement stop with the creation of the Western Front, which now ran from the Channel Coast to the Swiss frontier, and there conceived the idea of tracked armoured vehicles which could crush barbed wire and trundle over trenches, impervious to mud and machine-guns. He saw them as based on an agricultural machine, the Holt Caterpillar Tractor. Swinton first put these ideas to his then chief, Lt-Colonel Hankey, and so sparked the thoughts which led to Hankey's Christmas memorandum. In June 1915, Swinton produced a memorandum of his own, entitled 'The Necessity for Machine Gun Destroyers', which he suggested might be 'petrol tractors of the caterpillar type which can travel at up to 4mph, cross a ditch up to 4ft wide and scramble over heathland. They should be armoured against German steel-cored bullets and armed with two Maxims and a 2-pounder' gun.' This was a step forward from the troop-carrier of the previous year.

A specification was drawn up by the War Office and sent to the Landships Committee, who ordered a prototype called the 'Triton'. Construction began in August 1915, the work proceeding rapidly as the main elements, the tracks and the engine – a 105hp Daimler – were readily available, though the design was changed constantly as the work progressed. The name 'tank' was first used to preserve secrecy about the weapon during transit, and gradually drifted into accepted usage. The first completed model, christened *Big Willie*, crawled into daylight on 8th September 1915.

Work continued throughout the autumn and winter and on 2nd February 1916 '*Big Willie*' was formally introduced to the Government and senior Army officers, including the Chief of the Imperial Government Staff, the formidable Lord Kitchener. By now, *Big Willie* had grown. The complete vehicle was 31ft 3ins long, 8ft high and 13ft 8ins wide, weighing over 28 tons when complete with men and ammunition. It carried a crew of eight, and either machine-guns or a naval gun in the side-sponsons. The demonstration took place in Hatfield Park, where *Big Willie* successfully negotiated a series of trench obstacles. This success in the trials met with a varying response. Commodore Sueter thought the Army should order 3,000 of these monsters at once; Lord Kitchener was rather non-committal and the first order was for just forty machines, later increased to 100. This order was placed on 11th February 1916, less than five months before the start of the Battle of the Somme. In that time there was a lot to do, men to recruit and train and the problems of tactical deployment thrashed out by the powers-that-be.

Lt-Col Swinton was appointed to raise and train the infant tank force, but it was at once made clear that he should not – must not – expect to command or lead it later in battle. Once convinced of the potential usefulness of the tank, the commanders in France began to agitate for their swift deployment in the field, a move Swinton attempted to resist. He also produced a series of 'Tactical Instructions', both as a guide to battle training and, he hoped, a blueprint for the way tanks would later be employed in action. In this, his main proposal was that the tanks should not be tied to the infantry and, above all, should not be used in driblets but deployed in large numbers, as part of one great combined operation with the infantry, artillery and airforce, employing the great advantages of surprise in the assault and speed in the subsequent exploitation.

In the months which followed Swinton's appointment, the tanks were built and the embryo Tank Corps took shape. The latter began life as 'The Armoured Car Section of the Machine-gun Corps', which later became the no-less-unwieldy 'Heavy Section, Machine-gun Corps', and then in November 1916, the 'Heavy Branch, Machine-gun Corps'. The name 'Tank Corps' was not adopted until June 1917, and the first commander of this infant arm was Lt-Col Swinton. Men who were felt to have a relevant aptitude for machines were recruited or transferred, many coming from the RNAS or the Machine-gun Corps. The tanks first went into action, commanded by Lt-Col Bradley, at the Battle of Flers on 15th September 1916, one of the many engagements in the five-month-long Battle of the Somme.

For the assault at Flers, between Albert and Baupaume, where the tanks were employed in battle for the first time, it was decided that tanks should advance with the infantry companies, operating in pairs to overcome German strongpoints. The fifty-eight tanks available were therefore distributed among the assault divisions, though in the event only thirty-six tanks made it to the Start Line.

The effect of the tanks on the Germans was immediate and dramatic. They rolled over machine-gun nests and crushed the barbed wire emplacements, sending the enemy scurrying in panic to the rear. Flers fell within the first hour when an air observer reported: 'A tank in the main street of Flers with large numbers of troops following it.' This message was later translated by the British Press into: 'A tank is walking up the High Street of Flers, with the British Army cheering behind it.'

In fact, the advent of the tank on the battlefield was rather less successful. Several were knocked out by artillery fire, others broke down, many became ditched in the trenches and shell-holes. In addition, although startled by these monsters rumbling up on them out of the mist, the German soldier is a resourceful fellow, as he was to prove time and again in this and a later war. Field guns were swiftly manhandled into position to engage this new invention, and by mid-afternoon the British assault at Flers had been halted. How much more might have been achieved had more tanks been available, or had those which were there had been used as a concentrated armoured spearhead rather than in penny packets, remains a matter of speculation.

It is not my intention here to follow the tank through every engagement of the First World War. At Flers it achieved a great deal, not least in convincing both sides that a new force had appeared upon the battlefield. General Haig, who commanded the British Armies in France, told Swinton that although the tanks had not achieved all that had been hoped for at Flers, they had saved many lives and amply justified their employment, adding, ' ... wherever the tanks advanced we took our objectives, and where they did not advance we failed.' Haig followed this up with a request for a thousand tanks to be delivered as soon as possible.

With Lt-Col Swinton still kept from a field-command, a new Commanding Officer had to be found, and in September 1916, at Swinton's suggestion, Lt-Col Hugh Elles was appointed to command the Heavy Section in France, and in October 1916 Swinton was relieved of his duties with the tanks and transferred back to the War Cabinet Secretariat, the first of many tank enthusiasts who were to be removed just when their experience could have been most useful. It was not until 1934 that Swinton's great contribution to the development of the tank was finally recognized with his appointment as Colonel-Commandant of the Royal Tank Corps.

The Somme offensive petered out in the rain and mud of November 1916. The next major action took place in April 1917 at Arras, further north, in the rolling country of Artois. In the preparations for this attack, the Tank Corps expanded first to four battalions, and then as more men and machines became available, into three full brigades. One of the staff officers appointed to this force was Major J.F.C. Fuller of the Oxfordshire & Buckinghamshire Light Infantry, an intelligent, far-sighted officer, who was to be the mainspring in the development of tank tactics. Even though most of his recommendations were ignored at home, his advice was carefully heeded abroad, but during 1916–17 Fuller revised the training schedules, and among a long series of Training Notes, devised a manual of tank tactics.

At this point we must return again to the matter of deployment. Even if the original specification is splendid and the resulting weapon capable of the designated task, it will not achieve this potential unless those who use it are properly trained and those who deploy it have some idea of its use and capabilities – this combination being covered by the term 'tactical employment'. With a new, even a revolutionary weapon like the tank, the *tactical* use of the weapon was a matter of heated debate, and this argument began with an attempt to define exactly what sort of weapon the tank was. Was it a mobile fort, fitted with machine guns, which supported the infantry in the assault, or was it really, if used in force, actually armoured cavalry, capable of thundering through the enemy lines into the open country beyond, and so restoring mobility to the battlefield? This argument was not academic. Depending on the view taken, so the tactics for employment would vary, and so the specification for new tank models would be drawn up, specifications affecting their speed, armour, armament. Tank tactics also had to consider where tanks, in whatever role, could be successfully deployed, and what type of terrain permits their best employment. This may seem a blinding glimpse of the obvious, but this question of tank deployment, in penny packets to support the infantry or as an armoured spearhead to break the enemy front, went to the heart of the argument about this new and revolutionary weapon. Even by November 1916, two months after Flers, the idea of a 'Tank Army' was already being mooted, armies which would operate against other tank armies, rather like fleets of ships at sea. Other, more conservative soldiers, saw the tank as a passing phenomenon, a solution only to the problems of the Western Front. By now there were enough tanks in France to form a full tank brigade under Hugh Elles, and in December 1916 Major J.F.C. Fuller joined Brigade HQ as a Staff Officer.

By April 1917, some sixty tanks were available for the Arras offensive. The Germans had not been idle since Flers and all their front line troops had been supplied with armour-piercing ammunition. After a number of breakdowns and delays only twenty-six tanks were available for the assault east of Arras on 9th April 1917. Here again, they were deployed in penny packets, but they gave useful service all along the front and played a major part in whatever gains were made, quelling enemy machine-gunners and supporting the attacking infantry.

During the summer months of 1917 the tanks were also employed, this time disastrously, in the fateful Battle of Third Ypres – better known as Passchendaele. Over 200 tanks were employed at various times, but all were rendered ineffective in the sea of mud. In July, the tank force was inspected by H.M. King George V and on 27th July received both a fresh title – The Tank Corps – and a distinctive tank badge together with a set of colours. The Colours were hurriedly manufactured from the small selection of silks available in a dress shop in Cassel, and those chosen, brown, red and green, were interpreted by Fuller as symbolizing 'From Mud, through Blood, to the Green Fields beyond.'

At Passchendaele, the use of tanks was largely negated by the flooded terrain, and so the story of the tank must move swiftly to 20th November 1918 and the Battle of Cambrai. Here, for the first time, the tank came into its own, operating in the van of the battle, leading, not supporting, the assault infantry and operating over dry, open terrain. Colonel Hugh Elles issued a special Order of the Day to his tank crews, an order which bears repeating.

Special Order No. 6

1. Tomorrow the Tank Corps will have the chance for which it has been waiting for many months – to operate on good going in the van of the battle.
2. All that hard work and ingenuity can achieve has been done in the way of preparation.
3. It remains for unit commanders and tank crews to complete the work by judgement and pluck in the battle itself.
4. In the light of past experience, I leave the good name of the Corps with great confidence in their hands.
5. I propose leading the attack of the Centre Division.

Hugh Elles
Brigadier General – Commanding Tank Corps

At dawn on 20th November, which is now the Regimental Day of the Royal Tank Regiment, Colonel Hugh Elles duly led his men into the attack. Three hundred tanks, deployed on a six-mile front near Cambrai, led five divisions of British infantry in an assault on the strong defences of the German Hindenberg Line. By noon the tanks had broken through the four 'tank-proof' trenchlines and penetrated to a depth of four miles, shattering two enemy divisions, capturing over 100 guns, taking over 4,000 prisoners. Total British casualties on 20th November amounted to 4,000 men killed and wounded, compared with 60,000 on the First Day of the Somme. In Britain the church bells rang to celebrate this long-awaited victory, as they were to do after the Battle of Alamein a quarter of a century later.

For the next ten days, the British enjoyed a success unequalled in the painful years of the Great War, but there were no reserves to exploit the breakthrough. The British infantry reserves had died or drowned in the mud of Passchendaele, and although five divisions of horse cavalry were available, just one machine-gun could bring their advance to a sudden halt. On 30th November the Germans struck back and the Battle of Cambrai finished as a draw, with the gains and losses equal on either side. Even so, the tanks had finally made their mark as an independent arm and shown that when used with the benefits of concentration and surprise, they could change the face of battle. Not all of this met with approval in the higher stations of the military establishment.

After Cambrai, the tanks increased in number and variety. New, light tanks arrived – Whippets – while both the French and Germans began to deploy their tanks on the battlefield. The first tank-versus-tank battle took place at Villers-Bretonneux in April 1918, and by the time the Great War ended on 11th November 1918, there were twenty-five tank battalions in the British Army alone.

The Armistice brought with it a revival of the horse cavalry and the resurgence of the pre-war mentality. Indeed, it is Fuller who first relates the tale of the Officer of the Old School, who emerged from his trench on the morning of Armistice Day and said, 'Thank God, now we can get back to real soldiering.'

Over the next twenty years, until the Second World War broke out on 3rd September 1939, the Tank Corps had a very difficult time. Apart from the disbandment of units and the loss of trained men as the armies shrank, their chief difficulties lay in (1) inadequate equipment, both in terms of quality and numbers, (2) disagreement over tactics and the employment of tanks in any future conflict, and (3) competition from the horse cavalry.

Once the Great War was over, it became popular in cavalry circles to claim that trench warfare of the Western Front variety had been a singular occurrence which would not occur again. This being so, the tank was already obsolete. In any case, it was increasingly vulnerable to armour piercing bullets. Tank devotees retorted that the machine gun and the magazine rifle had made the *arme blanche* cavalry obsolete for at least a generation, and reduced the cavalry role to that of mounted infantry, certainly since the time of the Boer War at the turn of the century. Some went further and suggested that the cavalry role would only arise again when all cavalry units were mechanized or someone could breed a bullet-proof horse.

The Tank Corps was finally put on a permament footing in September 1923, and in October of that year became the Royal Tank Corps, but even as late as 1925, seven years after the Great War ended, no less a person than the former Commander-in-Chief of the British Armies in France, Earl Haig, could write, 'Some enthusiasts today talk about the probability of horses becoming extinct and prophesy that the aeroplane, the tank and the motor car will supersede the horse in future wars .... I am all for tanks and aeroplanes, but they are only accessories to the man, and the horse.'

This opposition at the higher levels of the Army naturally had a detrimental effect on the tank forces. After the War the number of horsed cavalry regiments fell from twenty-eight to twenty, while the number of tank battalions dropped from twenty-five to two.

The story of Britain's tank forces in the years 1919–1939 is, therefore, one of a long struggle to convince the Government of the necessity for strong tank forces, and long arguments within the Army as to how these forces should be employed.

Even after the final decision had been taken to retain a tank element in the army, there was great dispute between those who saw the tank simply as an infantry support weapon, most useful if deployed in ones and twos among the foot soldiers, and those who dreamed of the Armoured Division, a fully mechanized force of tanks, infantry and artillery, supported by aircraft, that would sweep around the flanks of static enemy forces and destroy their depots and bases, cut their supply lines and restore mobility to the battlefield, acting more like battle fleets than traditional military formations. This latter view did not prevail in the British Army until the Second World War was well under way. The strategic use of armoured formations, though pioneered and argued in Britain by Swinton, Fuller, Liddell Hart, and their supporters, and publicized in their books and essays, was first grasped by the Germans and used with devastating effect by their Panzer Groups under generals like Guderian, in the *Blitzkreig* – lightning war – advances in Poland, France and Belgium during 1940–41. To this point we can now proceed, illustrating the story with a few steps taken along the way.

In 1926, to test the various tactical theories concerning the tank, the Chief of the Imperial General Staff (CIGS), General Milne, decided to permit the establishment of an Experimental Force, or Mechanized Force, which assembled for trials on Salisbury Plain in May 1926, on lines suggested by Fuller. This Force was the mother of all the armoured divisions of the world, and consisted of the 3rd and 5th Battalions of the Royal Tank Corps, equipped with armoured cars and light tanks, some Vickers Medium Tanks, plus a battalion of the Somerset Light Infantry carried in lorries and equipped with machine guns, and two artillery units, 9th Field Brigade, Royal Artillery and the 9th Light Battery RA, equipped with howitzers. Divisional Troops included a Field Company of the Royal Engineers. The total Force consisted of 280 assorted vehicles, tanks, armoured cars and lorries. The exercises of the Experimental Armoured Force were watched with great interest by military men in Britain and abroad, and the undoubted success of the Force in exercises against units of infantry and cavalry was beyond dispute (though not undisputed), even by the pro-cavalry officers. After this the gradual conversion of horsed cavalry to tank or armoured car units could only be a matter of time and the first steps were taken in 1928, when two cavalry regiments, the 11th Hussars and the 12th Lancers were converted to armoured car units, together with a number of Yeomanry Regiments of the Territorial Army. Two of these regiments, the 11th Hussars and the County of London Yeomanry (The Sharpshooters), were to play a leading part in the later actions of 7th Armoured Division.

In 1931 the first complete Tank Brigade was briefly formed for summer manoeuvres at Tilshead Camp on Salisbury Plain, with a fighting strength of eighty-five medium and ninety-five light tanks. Among other technical advances made at this time was the introduction of radio telephones to control the movement of the tanks, and although this Brigade only remained in being until 30th September, it proved so successful in the maneouvres that the Tank Brigade was reconstituted in the following year and reinforced with fifty of the new Mark II light tanks, which brought the Brigade's total strength up to 230 machines. The development of armoured forces became more critical after Adolph Hitler became Chancellor of Germany in 1933.

'The Army were well aware of the need for different types of tanks,' says Field Marshal Lord Carver, who joined the Army in 1933. 'The decision was made to opt for heavy armoured infantry tanks, 'I' tanks like the "Matilda", which need not be fast or have a great range as they were to operate with the infantry. All they needed was thick armour and a gun. For the Cavalry role, the decision was to choose a lightly armoured fast tank, later the Mark VI, which would take on the old Cavalry role of reconnaissance. The gap was the need for a well-armoured, adequately gunned cruiser tank, which eventually led to the development of the A9, A10 and the A13 Cruiser at the end of the '30s and during the early days of the war. These were not reliable and mounted only a 2-pdr gun – until the 6-pdr Crusader came along in 1942.'

The state of Britain's tank forces did not improve to any great extent during the Thirties. The Tank Brigade was not reassembled for the summer manoeuvres of 1933, but in November of that year it was finally decided to form a tank brigade, on a permanent basis, and Colonel P.C.S. Hobart, later Major General Sir Percy Hobart, KBE, CB, DSO, MC, was appointed to command it, combining his appointment as Brigade Commander with his role as Inspector of the Armoured Corps.

Percy Hobart, 'Hobo' to his admirers (and they were many), was a genius of armoured warfare, an innovator, a leader of men and, above all, a brilliant trainer of armoured forces. In the exercises of 1934 he showed the British military establishment what a well-trained, well-lead, armoured force could do. 'Hobart was a single-minded man, very intolerant of those who did not share his views, and a great trial to his superiors,' says Field Marshal Lord Carver. 'On the other hand, his subordinates adored him and he was certainly without equal as a trainer of armoured forces.' The Tank Brigade made sweeping advances by day and night, and these manoeuvres were studied carefully by General Guderian and his embryo German Panzer forces.

Various marks of cruiser tank were now becoming available by the end of the thirties, the Mark I (A9), the Mark II (A10) and later the Mark III (A13). These were fast – up to 30mph on roads, and the A13 had thick frontal turret armour, but all were inadequately armed with a two-pounder gun and a single Vicker's .303 machine-gun. The Light Tanks, for reconnaissance, were the Mark VIs. These had a range of 130 miles and a top speed of 35mph, but had only thin armour and one light .303 and one heavy .5 machine-gun as armament. Other nations were producing heavier machines intended for deployment in massed formations.

The Germans formed their first Panzer Brigade in 1934. By 1935 this had expanded to three brigades, which were then incorporated into a full-scale Panzer Division, a mixed force of tanks, artillery and panzer-grenadier infantry. By the end of 1935 Germany had three of these divisions. In Britain, on the other hand, very little happened. To give one telling example, in the 1935–36 Army Estimates, the sum allocated for horse fodder was £400,000, the total allowance for petrol just £121,000. Even so, there was a slow but growing awareness of the German menace and Britain slowly began to re-arm. In 1936 the Army decided to mechanize eight more horse cavalry regiments, the first since the 11th Hussars and 12th Lancers had been mechanized eight years previously. In 1939 it was finally decided to mechanize the whole of the Regular Army cavalry and form all the armoured formations, both former cavalry regiments and the battalions of the Royal Tank Corps, into a new organization, the Royal Armoured Corps. The horse, however, was still a significant force, especially in the Territorial Yeomanry, and still attracting Regular recruits, like Arthur Waites, who joined the 7th Hussars in 1934.

'It was the 7th day of December 1934. A cold, wet, dreary day, but that didn't deter me from carrying out the promise that I had made to my mother, and that was to try and find work. Since leaving school at the age of fourteen I had been working on a farm, and in my young days, whenever a lad went to work for a farmer he was 'hired' for a whole year, from one November to the next. In mid-November, 'Martinmas', the farmer would come and ask if you wished to stay on for another year. On the other hand, if he didn't want you to stay he would pay you off and you had to try and get employment elsewhere.

'So, on this wet December morning I found myself at the Army Recruiting Office in Hull. Once there, I asked the Officer in charge if I might join up. "Which regiment would you like to join?" he asked. I hadn't the foggiest idea, so he produced a long list of units requiring recruits. Scanning the names of all those famous regiments – Guards, Gunners, Signal Corps, Infantry, Cavalry ... my mind was made up the instant I saw the name, 7th Queen's Own Hussars ....

'In the first few weeks we went through the usual routine of square bashing, rifle drill, and always plenty of fatigues, but as yet no horses. I was looking forward to being with my four-legged friends once again. Then one day it happened; we were paraded down to the stables and got our first glimpse of a horse – a wooden one! We were told the basic things, such as how to saddle a horse and, more importantly, how to sit on one correctly. Some of the lads found things very difficult indeed, but it was no bother to me, having done the same thing hundreds of times before, when on the farm.

'At last the day came when we were introduced to a real horse. Each man was given a mount to ride and then he had to look after that animal. Our riding lessons were taken on Hounslow Heath, and very entertaining they were too. Most of the men hadn't a clue how to ride, and when the time came to do a bit of trotting and galloping, most of them fell off. Many's the day the horses would return to their own stables riderless! I really did enjoy myself, and when at last we came to a halt, Major Pelly asked me my name. He said, "Well done lad, keep it up."'

The development of new, more advanced tanks, was still hindered by the attitude of the pro-horse generals, a chronic shortage of money, which affected every arm of every Service in the inter-war years, and indecision on exactly what type of tank, or tanks, were required. All models required an element of compromise between the three elements of a battle tank; speed, armour, armament. A heavily armoured tank would be slow, a lightly armoured tank vulnerable. The one point which was, or should have been, beyond all doubt, was that any tank should carry a gun capable of out-ranging the gun and penetrating the armour of any enemy tank. Curiously enough, although the British eventually produced well-armoured tanks like the Matilda Infantry Tank, and later in the War, fast tanks like the Crusader and the Cromwell, British tanks remained undergunned and relatively under-armoured until the end of the Second World War.

By 1939, the British had various tanks available, but only one, the famous Matilda, was in any way suitable for modern warfare. The Infantry Tank Mark I, introduced in 1938, weighed eleven tons, had a crew of two and was armed with a single .303 Vickers machine gun. The Mark II, the Matilda, was much more formidable, weighing twenty-six tons, carrying a crew of four and being armed with a two-pounder gun as well as the Vickers. The Matilda was heavily armoured and therefore slow, with a top road speed of fifteen miles per hour and a fuel consumption of one filling for every seventy miles.

The question of how tanks should be employed in a future conflict also remained unsettled, at least in Britain. In Germany, followers of the doctrines of Fuller and Captain Liddell Hart had created highly mobile Panzer Divisions, which could sweep round obstacles, overrunning defences, creating havoc in the rear, while in Britain, tanks were still generally regarded as an infantry support weapon, providing mobile gun support for the advancing infantry battalions or to fight off incursions by enemy tanks into their defensive positions. For this reason, the popular Matilda had a top speed of about 5mph across country, or 10mph on roads, quite sufficient to keep up with heavily loaded infantry, but nothing like sufficient to overrun or outflank large enemy formations.

Meanwhile, with war and rumours of war in the air, men were drifting to the Colours or into the Territorial Army. One of these was Rick Hall, who owned a Morris 8 car, and therefore joined the Royal Army Service Corps, the RASC.

'I used to do a lot of cycling and in 1936 a group of us cycled all the way to Germany to try and see the Olympic Games. We didn't get in, having no tickets, so I didn't see Jesse Owens or Hitler, but I did see a group of Nazi Brownshirts smashing a Jew's head against a wall ... terrible, and I thought, "Right, one of these days this lot are going to need sorting out." I came home convinced there would be trouble, because people like that have to be stopped. I kept telling people there was going to be a war, and they kept asking me, "What are you going to do about it?" So I joined the Emergency Reserve in 1938 as a driver. You did no training but you were for the high jump as soon as war broke out – and you got 7s.6d. (37.5p) every three months. I got called up on Friday, 1st September 1939, and by teatime was at Bulford Camp. There was a terrible thunderstorm that night and our tents were flooded. Then on the Sunday I heard Chamberlain say we were at war. I then joined 10 Coy of the 2nd Echelon, 1st Heavy Armoured Brigade, and went to France.'

Neville Gillman was studying accountancy when he joined the Territorial Army in May 1939. 'This was the Sharpshooters, the County of London Yeomanry, later the 4th CLY. We then had Rolls-Royce Armoured cars of the 1914–18 vintage, but we lost those in September 1939 and got light tanks, Mk IVs. At the time there was no love lost between the Cavalry and the Tank Corps, I can tell you. I can remember one officer complaining, "Bloody smelly tanks ... give me horses any day." The 3rd CLY wore a curious mixture of dress; long puttees, riding breeches and spurs, topped off with the black Tank Corps beret. "The Second Line" of the 3rd, became the 4th CLY, with Bill Carr of the 12th Lancers as the C.O. We also had berets, a very sensible headgear for tank crews, but Bill Carr wouldn't have his men in Tank Corps berets and we had to wear side caps, which were a damned nuisance. It's a small thing, but he was never popular after that.

'Promotion was rapid on the outbreak of war. We formed up at Lords Cricket Ground, because one of our officers, Ronnie Aird, was Secretary of the M.C.C. Then we were billeted at St Margaret's, a girls' public school at Bushey, and in 1940 we moved to Clandon Park near Guildford, the home of my troop commander, Viscount Cranley, later the Earl of Onslow. I had, meanwhile, been to the Gunnery School at Lulworth and returned as a Corporal Instructor, and became a Sergeant in January 1940 – not bad in three months. We were all quite untrained. You did a course and came back to pass on what you had learned. I became SQMS – Squadron Quarter Master Sergeant – in 1941, and in July we sailed from Merseyside to the Middle East.'

General Sir John 'Shan' Hackett was at university when he first took up the profession of arms.

'I joined the Supplementary Reserve of Officers in 1931, with the 'Queen's Bays'. It was clear to me even then that war was coming and we would all be killed in it, either as amateurs or professionals, so I finally joined my family regiment, the 8th Hussars. My great-grandfather had served with that regiment in 1782 or thereabouts, when they were Light Dragoons. I joined them at Hounslow in 1933 and I was very sad to transfer to engines and tanks, because, like many others, I joined with an eye for horses. I was in Egypt by 1935, first with the Cairo Cavalry Brigade, where we were hurriedly mechanized, not into tanks or armoured cars – we didn't have enough of those, so we had Ford V8 trucks. It was good fun though ... you knew everybody. In war it is always as well to head for the front line – you will meet fine people there and enjoy better company than you will at the base.'

Some units of what was to become 7th Armoured were already in the Western Desert, more notably the 11th Hussars, who had sailed for Egypt in November 1934. The 11th Hussars who were to make an outstanding name for themselves in the Western Desert, were one of the youngest, yet one of the most distinguished, cavalry regiments in the British Army. Raised as Light Dragoons in 1715, they had fought at Culloden, during the Seven Years War, and throughout the Napoleonic Wars, during which time they served in Egypt with General Abercrombie. After Waterloo they went to India and stayed there until 1838 when, on returning to England, they became Hussars and were given the task of escorting Prince Albert of Saxe-Coburg, when he arrived to marry Queen Victoria. The Queen then directed that the regiment should be designated The 11th Hussars (Prince Albert's Own), and wear a new uniform with distinctive red overalls, which gave the Regiment a new nickname, 'The Cherrypickers'. At this time they also acquired a new colonel, that imperious lord, the Earl of Cardigan, who in 1854, during the Crimean War, led the 11th, the 8th and the 4th Hussars, with other units of the Light Brigade, into the fatal charge at Balaclava. Lord Cardigan commanded the 11th for eight years and even today the regiment's successor, The Royal Hussars, sound Last Post at 9.50 pm, the time of Lord Cardigan's death.

A.S. Prosser was a trooper in this regiment: 'I joined the 11th Hussars (PAO) as a Band Boy on 17th February 1934 at the age of sixteen. They were stationed at Tidworth, equipped with Crossley Armoured Cars, and the regiment consisted of 408 officers and ORs. Although I was keen on music, I never made the grade as a Bandsman, devoting my time to education, exams and first-aid.

'On 23rd November 1934, we embarked at Southampton, en route to Egypt to replace our sister Regiment, the 12th Royal Lancers, who were coming home. We disembarked at Alexandria and went by train to Cairo; not a very comfortable journey on wooden seats. On arrival in Egypt I joined the Quartermaster's Staff and became a clerk in the transport section.

'From 1936 onwards, we had spells in Palestine, stationed in Jerusalem and Tel Aviv. In January 1937 I was promoted Lance Corporal (unpaid) and posted to 'C' Squadron No. 4 Troop. I trained as a motor mechanic and passed my driving test on Sollum Hill, one of the steepest hills in Egypt. I took part in several night patrols between Jerusalem and Nablus, keeping the roads open after Arab attacks. In June 1939 I was granted leave to the U.K., with £10 for the trip home and £10 for the trip back. I enjoyed my leave but knew that war was coming. I arrived back in Egypt the day war was declared. We were put on new footing and I was promoted Corporal that day.'

The 11th took to the desert at once and soon learned to master it. The Regiment had a strength of 23 officers and 408 NCOs and men, mounted in 34 Rolls Royce armoured cars, divided into Regimental Headquarters (RHQ) and three 'Sabre' Squadrons, 'A', 'B', and 'C'. Squadrons were divided into an H.Q., and three (later four) Troops, each consisting of three armoured cars. They later acquired Crossley armoured cars, equipped with wireless, and these were allocated to RHQ and Squadron Leaders as command vehicles. The 11th Hussars trained relentlessly in the Desert until they felt completely at home there, and one of their tasks, which was later to benefit the entire British Army, was the preparation of a 'going' map, showing all the passable tracks and deep sand places in the Western Desert east of the Italian frontier. This frontier with Libya was marked by a thick wire fence, 200 miles long, which ran from near Sollum deep into the desert. While the 11th Hussars were exploring the desert, other units of what was to become the 7th Armoured Division were training in Britain.

R. Godwin joined another 7th Armoured unit, the Royal Gloucestershire Hussars (RGH) in 1937: 'We who survived have just enjoyed a dinner to acknowledge the fiftieth year since the outbreak of war and the formation of the Cheltenham Squadron 'H' Squadron of the 2nd Royal Gloucestershire Hussars, a Territorial Unit.

'I joined one evening shortly before the outbreak of war with a colleague and friend from the office (a local firm of Architects and

Quantity Surveyors), and soon discovered others from school and play – even way back to infants' school. This is the reason why Lt-Col Birley, appointed as our Colonel early in 1940 from the Regular Army and late of the 17th-21st Lancers (The Death and Glory Boys), never understood the difference between his Regular Army units and ourselves. Our Troopers would obey NCOs without question when NCOs would say Please would you, or Just do this or that. The discipline was an integral part of a whole Squadron of friends and colleagues who were together to do a job and then return to their more normal occupations – comradeship which exists as strongly today as then. However, when the Colonel was mortally wounded in the Desert, he understood us and declared that he was proud of us.'

A. Flanagan was called up for Service on 15th July 1939: 'I did my training at Warminster (Salisbury Plain), for approximately five months, on guns, lorries and tanks etc., passing out as a Tank Driver. In January, with others, I was transferred to the 2nd Royal Tanks and stationed in civilian billets at Ringwood, Hampshire. Meals were eaten in a school taken over by the Army. Two of us were billeted in a room in a private house, for which I recall they received 5s.0d. (25p) per night for the two of us. The Battalion left Ringwood for France in May 1940.'

Another 7th Armoured Division veteran, Reginald Powell, came from a Tank Corps family: 'My father served in the Forces for twelve years, serving in India and South Africa, and also the First World War, earning himself a DCM.

'I myself followed in his footsteps and joined the Royal Tank Corps on 11th January 1937, doing my Basic Training at Bovington and Lulworth, Dorset. I then went for a brief period to Dereham Downs and was then drafted to Egypt in the following November as a Driver Operator on medium Tanks. There were a number of light tanks to train on, and these were all we had up to 1939, when the Second World War started.'

John Bainbridge joined the Tank Corps in 1935: 'Unemployment was very high and many young men were enlisting in the Services. A close friend had met a trained soldier serving with the Royal Tank Corps, to whom he introduced me, and after a great deal of discussion we came to the decision that this was the branch for us. Within seven days we were on the way to Bovington Camp.

'By the time the train reached Wool Station we had become a small party of four: Tommy Law from Spennymore, Co. Durham, Harry Game from Southend, Albert Higgins, and myself from Cheltenham. We walked the three miles and reported to the Guard Commander. On learning that we had come to join the Army, we were greeted with the welcome, "Thank God Britain has a Navy."

'A conducted walk to the Store, where each of us were issued with our full kit, and then to a hut which was to be our home for the next twenty-two weeks. We formed part of No. 442 Squad. There were then twenty-five recruits in the hut, and a further five joined later in the day to complete our Training Squad, under the instruction of Sgt. Port and Cpl. Paul. From now on we marched everywhere, sometimes at the double. A slovenly, undisciplined, motley gathering of untrained men. After a short lecture and some marching instruction, we marched to the M.I. Room for examination and vaccination. The first five weeks consisted of Drill, Physical Training, Lectures, Revolver practice. By the end of that time the Squad was reasonably well turned out and a co-ordinated, disciplined unit.

'During the next seventeen weeks, more complicated Square Drill was undertaken, including the use of Flag Signals; Driving and Maintenance, Educational Instruction, Revolver and Rifle Instruction, and practice Gas Drill, and many lectures. On completion of this training and satis-factory Passing Out, seven days furlough could be taken. I was an entirely different person from the one who left home twenty-two weeks previously.

'The time came for overseas postings and I was delighted to find myself on the draft for the 6th Bn RTR in Egypt. We sailed from Southampton in late February 1937 on *HMT Lancashire*, and arrived in Alexandria on 2nd March. Disembarkation completed, a march round the town to get our land legs, enjoying the warmth of a Mediterranean sun in completely different surroundings from any previously experi-enced, was most pleasant. We then entrained for Cairo and arrived at Abbassia Rail Siding about mid-day. We paraded on the square of Main Barracks, Abbassia and were greeted firstly by RSM Stannard, the Adjutant, Capt. Cooper and the Commanding Officer, Lt.-Col. Morrough. We were then informed of the companies to which we were to be posted and handed over to the Company Sergeant Major and an orderly, who installed us in our respective barrack rooms. Soldiering became a very pleasant occupation.

'There was so much leisure time, it was compulsory to spend a fortnight each summer under canvas in Alexandria. Home leave could be taken every 2nd year, travelling by troopship at a cost of £10 return. Holidays could be taken elsewhere and Cyprus, Lebanon, Syria and Palestine were popular. This leisurely life continued, and troops became lethargic about their military duties.

'This began to change after the arrival of Major General P.C.S. Hobart, who came to form a Mobile Division. There was a great deal of activity, such as conferences, indoor exercises, tactical exercises without troops (TEWTS), sand table exercises, cadre courses. The wish for intensive training became infectious. Tank Commanders gave intensive instruction to their crews. All members of the crew interchanged duties and functions. All members became fully conversant with all the duties of a crew, even that of Tank Commander. We all became inter-dependent, not only were we partners at work, we became partners socially. Off duty hours, which incidentally became shorter, were spent together with your crew. This spirit made the 7th Armoured Division an *Esprit de Corps* which continued throughout the war years and to the present day. Our Adjutant, Capt. G.P.B. Roberts (later Maj-Gen Roberts) frequently took out small parties into the desert and gave meticulous instruction in map reading, navigation, including the use of the sun compass. This training became invaluable in the months and years that followed.'

Another veteran, Harry Kirkham DCM, came from a military family and enlisted in the RTR in 1936: 'I grew up in and around the army from the age of one year, and in view of its many attractions I enlisted into the Royal Tank Corps on the 2nd November 1936 at the age of 18, and went to Bovington Camp for training.

'On the completion of my 18 weeks training I was posted to the 2nd Battalion RTR at Farnborough, and found myself in a light tank section commanded by 2nd Lieutenant Mike Carver (now Field Marshal Lord Carver). The adjutant was Captain "Tinny" Dean, better known for his rugby skills.

'After only a few months here, I was posted to the 6th RTR in Egypt. I was a reserve replacement and as one person deserted I was ordered to fill the gap. I sailed for Egypt at 11 am on 11th November 1937 for a two year tour, which became a 6 year tour because of the North Africa Campaign.'

Arthur Waites of the 7th Hussars continues his story: 'Our routine life of stable work and parades now had a few manoeuvres thrown in. We used to go into the desert and stay out for a few days, but we were always glad to get back to the comfort of the barracks, as we found out very quickly that the desert at night time is a very cold and inhospitable place.

'Now I come to one of the sad episodes in my life. There had been rumours floating round for some time that the 7th Hussars would become a mechanized unit. Well, now it had happened. Our dear old horses were taken away from us and where they went to I never knew. I didn't want to know! I only knew that never again would I sit astride my beloved William, never again would I feel the hot wind in my face as William and I raced across the desert, round Coombe Hill, on past Virgin's Breast, and rested near the Remarkable Rock. I was heartbroken at the thought of someone else taking over William, and I can only hope that he went to a good home.

'Now William had gone, and sadly the stables were empty and bare. No more grooming, no more saddle-soaping, no more the making of straw whisps, and no more the polishing of saddlery, or burnishing of bits, and stirrups. The only good thing about the whole affair was the fact that there would be no more night guards on the stables. So farewell to those marvellous Cavalry days. In the days that followed, we entered a new phase of our army life, while we awaited the arrival of our new mounts, the Tank.

'Please don't think me too sentimental in the love and esteem which I had for my regiment, or for the men who played such a vital role in my life; not just one, but all of those who served with me in the 7th Queen's Own Hussars.'

To continue the story of 7th Armoured we must now return briefly to the United Kingdom. In February 1937, Brigadier Hobart had to relinquish his command of the 1st Tank Brigade, which had shrunk over the years as new vehicles and equipment were still not available. He returned to a Staff appointment at the War Office, where his unorthodox views and unflagging advocacy of armoured forces soon made him plenty of enemies. This number increased when he became Director of Military Training at the end of 1937. At about this time, in October 1937, the decision was taken to form a 'Mobile Division', and in March 1938 it was decided to reorganize the entire British Army on the basis of two types of division, a Motorized Division, based on infantry equipment with the light machine gun, the Bren, carried in lorries or tracked Bren-gun carriers, and an Armoured Division, based on the tank.

By now Europe was moving at increasing speed towards war. The Munich crisis of 1938 spurred Britain to re-arm swiftly, and when the Germans occupied Czechoslovakia in March 1939, the pace of re-armament quickened still more. On 4th April 1939 the Royal Armoured Corps came into being, but five months later, on 1st September 1939, German tanks rolled across the Polish frontier. The Second World War had begun, and two days later, on Sunday, 3rd September 1939, Great Britain declared war on Nazi Germany.

THE WAR IN NORTH AFRICA

1939–1943

After the War, when a man is asked what he did,
it will be sufficient for him to say,
'I marched and fought with the Desert Army.'

Winston S. Churchill
Address to 8th Army
Tripoli. 3rd February 1943

2

The Western Desert Force

1939–1940

Who is the happy warrior? Who is he
That every man-in-arms would wish to be?
It is the generous spirit who when brought
Among the tasks of real life, has wrought
Upon the plan that pleased his childish thought,
Whose high endeavours are an inward light
That makes the path before him always bright.

William Wordsworth

The German attack on Poland, which began on 1st September 1939, did more than mark the opening moves of the Second World War. It introduced a new concept – *blitzkrieg* – or 'lightning war', an overwhelming combination of tank, artillery and air-power which successfully overran or outflanked infantry or cavalry forces before they were able to put up more than a token resistance. The essence of *blitzkrieg* was mobility. The highly trained German Army advanced with great speed, overwhelming the Polish infantry and cavalry with tanks, calling in dive-bombers, the formidable Stukas, to attack strongpoints, deploying lorried infantry – the Panzer Grenadiers – to assault entrenched positions after they had been softened up by devastating air attacks and artillery bombardment. Above all, the German Army kept moving, and the Panzer generals led from the front. Within days they had broken the gallant but obsolescent Polish Army (which attacked the German Panzers with cavalry charges, sword and lance), into fragments.

A year later the Germans were to repeat this successful strategy in the West with another lightning advance through the Ardennes, splitting the French and British Armies, forcing the abrupt collapse of Belgium. On 4th June, 1940, the British Army withdrew from the beaches of Dunkirk, leaving most of its equipment behind, and on 25th June 1940, France surrendered. British tanks, notably the Matildas, had done well in France, checking the German advance around Arras, but their success was limited by technical defects and various failures in command and maintenance facilities.

Brigadier Pope of the Tank Brigade summed up their shortcomings in a letter to the War Office in terms that were to be repeated frequently in the years ahead: 'We must have thicker armour on every tank and every tank must carry a cannon. The 2pdr gun is good enough now, but only just good enough. We must mount something better behind 40–50mm of armour. All of our tanks must be simple to maintain and reliable. 75% of our losses were due to mechanical breakdown and slow repairs. We want the highest road speed compatible with the above. The A12 MkII is too slow, the A13 all right. Armoured cars are invaluable for recce and 12th Lancers have done wonders, but the Morris car is not good enough. The armour need not be too thick but the car must mount a gun. The 2pdr will do.'

Hitler had swept to the Channel in a few weeks, but with this much accomplished he paused. His ambitions were now checked by the outcome of the Battle of Britain and the formidable obstacle of the English Channel. The land battle between the British Commonwealth and the Axis Powers now shifted south and east, to the bleak deserts of North Africa, where the British and Italian Armies had been watching each other carefully since the outbreak of war with Germany.

Although the Second World War began in September 1939, Italy did not declare war on Great Britain until 10th June 1940. The Italian dictator, Benito Mussolini, was too cautious to join a war while the outcome was still undecided, and his advisors were rightly aware of the influence on Mediterranean strategy of the powerful British Mediterranean Fleet. However, the startling successes of the German *blitzkrieg* in France encouraged Mussolini to enter the war swiftly so that he might gain some share of the spoils of victory. That this wish was to be so swiftly frustrated was due in no small part to a single British force – the 7th Armoured Division, the Desert Rats.

The British had deployed small armoured forces in the Western Desert of Egypt and Cyrenaica for many years. British armoured cars had first operated in the Western Desert towards the end of the Great War, when they had been used to fend off attacks on the Egyptian frontier by Senussi tribesmen from Cyrenaica. Between the Wars, Cyrenaica. Tripolitania and eventually Ethiopia came under the rule of Mussolini's expanding African Empire, and after the Munich crisis in 1938, the British in Egypt decided to increase their forces in Egypt and so protect the vital link of the Suez Canal in the event of hostilities.

To this end a 'Mobile Force' was established on the coast at Mersa Matruh in 1938, 120 miles west of Alexandria. This Mobile Force consisted of the Cairo Cavalry Brigade, made up of three armoured regiments, the 7th, 8th and 11th Hussars (PAO), the famous Cherry pickers, and the 1st Royal Tank Regiment (1 RTR), supported by the 3rd Regiment, Royal Horse Artillery (3rd RHA) and, as Divisional troops, a company of the Royal Army Service Corps (RASC) and a Field Ambulance unit. This scratch force was the nucleus of what was to become the mighty 7th Armoured Division.

For equipment, the Mobile Force had nothing of very recent vintage. The 11th Hussars, the reconnaissance element, still operated in Rolls Royce armoured cars dating from the Great War, plus some Morris armoured cars. The 1st RTR had only recently arrived from Britain, bringing with them light Mark VI tanks, which were already worn out and armed only with Vickers .303 machine guns. The 7th Hussars had light tanks of an even earlier vintage and the 8th Hussars had no tanks at all, being mounted in 15cwt trucks equipped with .303 Vickers machine guns. The RHA had 3.7ins howitzers. In October 1938, this force was joined by an infantry unit, the 1st Bn., The King's Royal Rifle Corps (KRRC), commanded by Lt-Col W.H.E. (Straffer) Gott. This Mobile Force was regarded with some amusement in Cairo and often referred to as the 'Immobile Farce'. Fortunately, soon after its formation in Mersa Matruh it received considerable encouragement when Major General Percy Hobart DSO, MC, arrived from England to take command of what was now called the Mobile Division, and start an intensive and effective training programme in the Western Desert.

However, if Hobart's arrival gave a great boost to all ranks in the 'Mobile Division', his arrival was greeted with something less than enthusiasm by the local Powers-that-Be, for Hobart was not popular. His views on the organization and employment of armoured forces had met with increasing opposition at the War Office, where many people considered that he wished to turn the entire army into one vast armoured formation. This was not the case; Hobart was well aware of the need to co-ordinate all arms into an effective whole, employing tanks, infantry, artillery and aircraft, but using them to restore mobility to the battlefield, and avoid static warfare. His expressions of these views might have been more tactful, and he made many enemies. After the Munich Crisis of 1938, when it was decided to transform the Egyptian Mobile Force into a Division and give the command to an experienced RAC Officer, the War Office mandarins regarded this as a chance to get Hobart out of the way. He arrived in Egypt on 27th September, and was greeted by the GOC, Lt-General Sir Robert Gordon-Finlayson, with the words, 'I don't know what you've come here for and I don't want you anyway.'

From then on, discussions between the GOC Egypt and his principal subordinate, took the form of protective memoranda, while day-to-day requests were met with what Liddel Hart has described as, 'No help and no lack of hindrance.'

Even so, aided by a brilliant staff officer, Major C.M. Smith, RASC, Hobart went to work. With the help of willing hands and the arrival of the 6th RTR, he rapidly organized his Division into three brigades:

1. **The Light Armoured Brigade:**
   7th Hussars
   8th Hussars
   11th Hussars

2. **The Heavy Armoured Brigade:**
   1st RTR (Light Tanks)
   6th RTR (Light Tanks plus A9 cruisers)

This Brigade lacked a third regiment of tanks, and in spite of the title, was still in light Mark VI tanks, the Mk I and II cruiser tanks of the 6th RTR being left in Cairo for security duties.

3. **The Pivot Group** – later the Support Group:
   3rd Regiment RHA
   F. Bty 4th RHA
   1st Bn KRRC

The Pivot Group existed to supply the tanks with their essential artillery and infantry support. The KRRC, supposedly a motorized battalion, had no transport and no anti-tank guns.

The Division had no HQ staff, but fortunately Hobart had also been appointed to command the Abbassia District as well as the Mobile Division, and he was able to divert Service Corps troops to the Division for exercise purposes. Sergeant Alec Lewis recalls this time in Egypt:
'I was on the first draft of RASC clerks and tradesmen which arrived

at Alexandria on 29th November 1939, and within a week, myself and another clerk were posted to 7th Armoured Division HQ. The Division was just arriving back in Cairo after a few months in the Western Desert and Div. HQ Sqn, and the 1st and 6th Battalions RTR were put in Main Barracks, Abbassia.

'As a "rookie", I was impressed to meet these tanned, tough-looking men, all Regulars, of course, in their sand- and sun-bleached khaki drills, and I was glad to know I was joining an elite unit. It was about this time that the men were pleased to be officially recognized as 7th Armoured Division instead of the Mobile Division. HQ was administered from the offices at the old Remount Depot and I was allocated to G Branch – Operations, already staffed by a staff-Sergeant and a clerk. The chief clerk at HQ was WOI Dolly Gray, who was later commissioned. We used to work each day from 8am till noon, then from 5–7pm. Nobody in Cairo seemed to work in the afternoons!

'Nearly all the army units in Egypt were on a peacetime basis and it was interesting to see how the majority of the troops wore their "blues" when going into the city off duty. Very smart they were too; the 11th Hussars in their "Cherrypicker" maroon trousers, the "Tankies" in their navy-blue uniforms and berets, the gunners with their dress caps, blues and red braid, the Rifle Brigade and the KRRCs in their dark green tunics and black facings.

'I found work at "G" Branch very interesting. There was much typing and duplicating of reports and operation orders for training schemes, and so on. The Division had two or three exercises that winter, one went on for three days in the Western Desert – not a long way from Cairo – when I realized how cold it could be. The water for the General's morning wash, left out overnight in the canvas wash-bowl, froze about two inches thick! Incidentally, one part of the desert we covered had numerous petrified trees laying around; they must have been there for thousands of years.

'For operations, "G" Branch had a 15cwt office truck with an RTR driver. It was canvas topped and open sided, with a double sided desk to hold the two typewriters (the only typewriters to keep working in sand); there were racks to hold stationery and, of course, seats for the clerks. At a location, canvas extensions were rolled down from each side over tubular frames to provide additional office space for staff officers.

'In mid-May 1940, when it seemed war with Italy was becoming a real possibility, most of the Division moved up to the Western Desert again and Div. HQ was established at Gerawla on the coast. "G" Branch

31

work continued, only now a very strict watch was being kept on the Italian frontier – "The Wire" – by the 11th Hussars and there were plenty of reports, appreciations etc. to keep us busy. On the night of 10th June, when Italy declared war, the 11th Hussars wasted no time in cutting 'The Wire' (which stretched from Sollum to Fort Maddalena) and proceeded to carry out their observations in Libya.'

During the winter of 1938–39, the Mobile Division pulled itself together in Cairo, where the staff worked out their ideas in discussions, lectures and TEWTS (Tactical Exercises Without Troops). Then, in May 1939, Hobart took them into the Western Desert to put his ideas into practice. Hobart intended to make his men desert-wise, able to live, fight and win battles in the wastes of the Western Desert.

John Bainbridge was in the 6 RTR: 'All ranks became fanatical about training and volunteered to devote most of their leisure time to practising and becoming more efficient. The Regimental Education Sergeant, Sgt. Watkins, who normally only taught academic subjects, was also an excellent driving instructor. He gave up his leisure time, teaching, training and improving the driving standards of Company and Regimental non-combattant staff until he was satisfied they were competent drivers of both tanks and lorries. Sergeant Watkins recalls:

'Several NCOs gave off duty instruction in the use and theory of firearms. The Regimental cooks became excellent marksmen and conversant with the maintenance of such firearms, confident that the additional skill would be available should need arise.

'The railway siding in Abbassia now became a hive of activity. Railway flats were brought into the garrison and a great deal of practice in boarding the tanks onto the flats took place. As tanks were strictly limited in the number of miles they were permitted to cover, it was necessary to transport them to as near the front as possible by means other than under their own power. As the width of the tank was about the same as the width of the flat, the skill of the driver and that of the person guiding him was most testing. Training in this art continued until the precision of the task became second nature. My Regiment became a very formidable, fit, well trained fighting unit, ready to face anything that came our way, as come our way it did.'

The Western Desert is not the rolling, golden, sand-dune desert of the popular imagination, or the Hollywood Foreign Legion epic. It is a stony, arid plain, of sand and rock, gently rolling, searingly hot in the summer, bitter cold at night, a quagmire after rain and a paradise for flies. To the west, south of Benghazi, the rolling desert gives way to the hills of the jebel country, rocky and virtually impassable except on a few bumpy tracks. There is a great shortage of water and what little exists lies in deep, brackish wells – *birs* – most of which date back to Roman times. The main feature of the Western Desert in Egypt and Cyrenaica is a great escarpment some 600 feet high, which dominates the coastal plain from a few miles inland, and curves round like a great wall down to the sea at Sollum. This escarpment can be climbed near Sollum, where the coast road swings up a series of hairpin bends to the neck of the Halfaya Pass – or Hellfire Pass as the troops came to call it. A close study of map 1 will be helpful at this point.

This inhospitable terrain was empty except for roving Arabs, and all the towns lay along the coast. Some, like Benghazi, were of considerable size, and had trains and cinemas, while others, like little El Alamein, were just halts on the coastal railway line which itself terminated at Mersa Matruh. There were only two roads, one along the coast, which had a twenty-mile gap in the stretch between Alexandria and Mersa Matruh, another south from Matruh to the Siwa Oasis. West of Sidi Barrani the coast road was little better than a track as far as the wire fence which marked the Italian frontier and Cyrenaica. The other main feature which was to have a crucial effect on the Desert War was the great impassable salt flats of the Qattara Depression, which ran from the escarpment south of Alamein down to the Sand Sea. This whole area was plagued by flies and periodic sand storms, sometimes the suffocating *khamsin*. All in all, the Western Desert was a hard place to live, but mechanization, tank tactics, and desert lore had to be learned together. Arthur Waites of the 7th Hussars, having given up his horse, was just one going through this process.

'After returning to Abbassia, we continued our approach towards becoming mechanized. Most of us had already passed our 3rd-class certificate of education and now we were in the process of punching up, to try and obtain our 2nd and ultimately our 1st. We had nearly got half through when things came to a halt, as our tanks, lorries and motor-bikes had arrived, and so now our driving lessons could begin.

'Our instructors came from that famous unit, the 6th Royal Tank Regiment, but first we had to be sorted out into squads, and once this was done we set off one day into the new world of driving and maintenance. I was very apprehensive indeed, and wondered if I could come to terms with my new mount, as never in my life before had I been near the cab or steering wheel of a vehicle, let alone driven one, but all my worries seemed to vanish as soon as I met our instructor, for Cpl Roy was a very likeable chap and very capable in his handling of

33

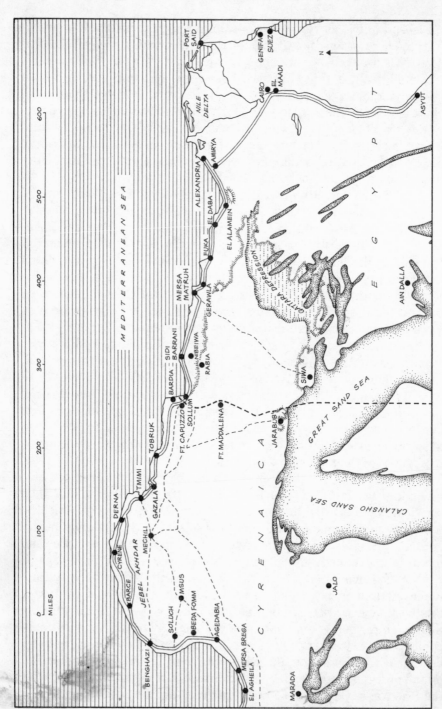

1 The Western Desert and Cyrenaica

his crew. When my turn came around to take the wheel for the first time in my life, I listened intently to what Roy told me, and so I put the lorry in motion and did my best. After my turn was over, Roy turned to me and said, "Are you sure you have never driven before?" I told him that was so. "Well you did remarkably well – keep it up," he said. I was very chuffed at that, and truth to tell, in the days and weeks that followed my driving improved by leaps and bounds, so much so that when we finally did our test on all the vehicles, tanks, motor-bikes and lorries, which took us a full week (not half an hour as today), I was as good a driver as anyone in the regiment. I'm afraid I used to show off a bit when it came to parking the tank in the garage, for with the tanks we had the old Mark 6 and I could sit on the front flap with my legs dangling inside, looking to the rear of course, and then by pushing the steering sticks in any given direction with my feet, I could put the tank into its garage with no bother.

'One night all the names were published in regimental orders, as to who was sent where. There was one mad rush to have a look at these orders, and I was astonished but highly delighted when I read my name – Tpr Waites to be the Squadron Leader's driver in tank No 1651. As if that wasn't enough, I got another thrill, for also published were the names of men chosen to go on a driver mechanics' course, and mine was among them.

'So, for the next few weeks I was busy on that course, and when it was over we were all tested as to our ability, and I am glad to report that I came out with flying colours. I was now a Mechanic Group Three, Class One. In view of this, and being the Squadron Leader's driver, I was asked to take a stripe and become a Lance-Corporal, which I accepted gratefully, for as I wished to make the army my career it was futile to refuse.

'A few weeks later, most of the drivers were taken down to the railhead, and there, waiting for us, were some new tanks. I was given the then latest model, the "A19", and I drove it back to barracks a very proud young man. Since becoming mechanized, we were doing more and more manoeuvres and staying out in the desert for longer periods, and we soon became a very efficient unit indeed, mastering the art of desert warfare really well. This did not go unnoticed by the Brass at HQ, and they instructed our Colonel to convey to all the troops their thanks and their praise. However, the most important thing was the way we had all taken to this new lifestyle.'

Desert navigation was never easy for inexperienced troops, but the desert was being steadily mapped and marked. Lt. Mike Carver recalls spending three months based at Mersa Matruh, training drivers in desert navigation and carrying out a 'going' reconnaissance of the desert from Mersa Matruh to the Italian frontier wire, south as far as Siwa Oasis. 'There were tracks of a kind, eventually marked with numbered barrels – rather like buoys at sea – so that you could usually have some idea of where you were when you came upon one.' The 1st Royal Tanks had already served in Egypt in 1936 under Lt-Col 'Blood' Caunter, who was still their CO in 1939. Although they had only just returned from the UK, they too had already built up considerable desert experience, but the most experienced and desert-wise unit in either the British or Italian armies was undoubtedly the 11th Hussars.

Apart from carrying out tactical exercises and improving desert lore, Hobart's aim was to make his division a soundly knit, desert-wise formation, used to the terrain. The desert had to be somewhere the troops could live, if not comfortably, at least in a battle-ready state, able to fight while coping with heat, flies and, above all, a shortage of water. Much time was spent on learning desert navigation, the use of the sun-compass, and on vehicle and equipment maintenance. Dust and sand can play havoc with mechanical and electrical equipment. All vehicles, including tanks, had to be fitted with sand-filters, improved water pumps and other devices before they were able to operate in desert conditions. Tanks could *not* be driven off the ship and straight into action. They had to be serviced and checked, guns and radios calibrated, sand filters fitted, and crews trained. It took time. Given good leadership, good troops can learn quickly and adapt to almost any conditions, and it was at this time, under General Hobart, that the Mobile Division 'got its knees brown' and became accustomed to living in the desert.

On the outbreak of war against Germany, on 3rd September 1939, the Mobile Division moved up to the Egyptian-Libyan frontier, taking up positions along the frontier wire, which was to play so great a part in their lives in the years to come. However, it soon became apparent that Italy was not keen to join Germany in all-out conflict by declaring war on Great Britain or France, and field training was soon resumed. The first blow received by the Division came not from the Axis Power but from the War Office. In November 1939, General Hobart was relieved of his command, having fallen out with the new G.O.C., General Sir Henry Maitland Wilson. Hobart drove away from his command, his route lined by men of his Division, cheering him to the echo. The War Office clique had, it seemed, finally pulled Hobart down, and by the summer of 1940, this dedicated and inspiring soldier was serving his country in the only way then left open to him, as a corporal in the Home Guard. This book must follow the fortunes of 7th Armoured, the Division he helped to create and which owed so much to his initial leadership and training, but it is pleasant to recall that Hobart was eventually rescued from military oblivion by Winston Churchill and went on to raise and train two other great Armoured Divisions during the Second World War, the 11th Armoured Division, which did outstanding service in 1944–45, and the 79th Armoured Division (the Funnies), which played such a great part in the D-Day invasion and the advance into Germany. Seventh Armoured Division never forgot their first commander, and in his appendix to the history of the Division, General Sir Cecil Smith recalls that Hobart's views were often quoted during the war, and remembers other officers recalling the many things that 'Hobo always used to say.' General Hobart eventually became Colonel-Commandant of the Royal Tank Regiment.

In December 1939, Major-General Michael O'Moore Creagh MC, a Cavalry Officer, arrived to take command of the Mobile Division and they continued with field exercises, while more and better equipment continued to arrive throughout the winter. During this period the three component Brigades changed their names. The Light Armoured became the 7th Armoured Brigade under Brigadier H.E. Russell, and the Heavy Armoured became the 4th Armoured Brigade, now commanded by the ex-Colonel of the 6th RTR, Brigadier J.A.L. Caunter, while the Pivot Group became the Support Group, and came under the command of a great desert warrior, Brigadier 'Straffer' Gott. Each tank regiment of the Division now had fifty-two tanks. The Support Group expanded with the arrival of the 2nd Bn., the Rifle Brigade, a fully motorized infantry battalion.

On 16th February 1940, the Mobile Division became the 7th Armoured Division and at about the same time received a new Divisional sign, the leaping hardy rodent, the *jerboa* or Desert Rat. The Mobile Division sign was a plain white circle on a red background, but Mrs Creagh, having inspected a jerboa closely in Cairo Zoo, produced a design of a desert rat that met with general approval from all the officers and men. Her design was then drawn up by Trooper Ken Hill of the 50th RTR, who was then serving with the Division and was later killed in a booby-trapped tank at El Adem. The men of the Division took to the jerboa and adopted the nick-name of The Desert Rats with considerable alacrity. This original emblem had a decidedly rat-like shape, quite unlike the kangaroo-style creature which now decorates the Divisional

History. When the Division left Italy in 1943, a Staff Officer was sent to England and ordered to produce a Desert Rat shoulder patch for the troops. Thousands were duly delivered, looking more like a kangaroo than their familiar rodent, but the men duly sewed them on their battledress and many retain them to this day. It is worth pointing out here that the term 'Desert Rat' is often used to describe any soldier of the Desert Army or the men who fought in Tobruk – the Australians have a Rats of Tobruk Association – but the only true 'Desert Rats' are the men who served in the 7th Armoured Division, whose shoulders or vehicles wore the jerboa emblem.

In April 1940, it became clear that the Italians were moving troops up to the frontier wire near Sollum, and so at the end of that month the 7th Armoured Division began to deploy. The 11th Hussars and the Support Group moved up to Mersa Matruh, and from there the 11th moved out to reconnoitre to the wastes of the Western Desert, taking up that position in the van of the division they were to occupy until the end of the war.

The Division now formed part of the Western Desert Force, under the command of Lt-General Richard O'Connor. The new GOC Middle East was General Sir Archibald Wavell, who had under his command Sir Henry Maitland Wilson's forces in Egypt, and the Western Desert Force under O'Connor. General Sir Archibald Wavell was a typical British officer of the period, in that there was more to him than there appeared. A professional soldier, he was also a poet. During the Desert Campaigns of 1940 and 1941, when not commanding armies, he was actually producing an anthology of poems, *Other Men's Flowers*, which is still in print fifty years later and a model collection of verse. Wavell was a thinking soldier and one with a steady nerve. He needed a steady nerve, for his responsibilities embraced the whole Middle East theatre from Egypt to Iraq, from Palestine to Kenya, and as time wore on, they expanded to include all the territories, including Greece and Syria at the eastern end of the Mediterranean and beyond. His chief concern however, was with the Italian 10th Army in Cyrenaica, and here he was lucky in his chief subordinate, that perky, birdlike and indomitable general, Richard O'Connor. O'Connor was another fighting soldier, with the MC and the DSO from the Great War as well as, ironically, the Italian Silver Medal for Valour, won on the Piave in 1918. O'Connor had been mentioned nine times in despatches and was now in command of a small force in an apparently desperate situation.

Seventh Armoured were virtually O'Connor's entire Force, for the only other troops immediately available were an infantry brigade, the Cairo Brigade, garrisoned in Mersa Matruh. The Division had an attached RAF contingent, 208 Squadron, forerunners of the famous Desert Air Force. The Western Desert Force also included another great division, the 4th Indian Division, which had recently arrived at Suez, while the 6th Australian and the 2nd New Zealand Division were already training in the Delta. For the moment, the defence of the Western Desert rested on O'Connor's small force of desert-trained troops, and most particularly on the 7th Armoured Division. Against this tiny force the Italian commander in Cyrenaica, General Balbo, could muster the Italian 10th Army, consisting of six divisions containing more than 250,000 men.

On 10th June 1940, Italy entered the war, and the 11th Hussars, who had been patrolling the wire for months, promptly crossed the Libyan frontier.

3

First Blood
Sidi-Barrani and Beda Fomm

JUNE 1940—FEBRUARY 1941

> We are not wont to ask
> how many the enemy are, but
> only where they are.
>
> *Agis: Apothegems*

The entry of Italy into the war against Britain in June 1940, though not unexpected, brought all the problems facing Sir Archibald Wavell sharply into focus. To maintain a British presence here against any threat, he had at his disposal some 50,000 poorly equipped troops, and although men and equipment were arriving all the time, none was of much use until men and machines had been trained for desert warfare. He faced some half-a-million Italians on two fronts, with their German allies hovering in the background, though not as yet directly engaged. A lesser man, faced with such wide responsibilities and such odds, might have been overwhelmed by the difficulties, but Wavell was not subject to doubts. He had already made his dispositions and he elected to attack the Italian army to the west before they could advance upon him.

Just across the frontier wire in Cyrenaica, Marshal Balbo, the Italian commander, could muster an army of six divisions, now totalling 300,000 men. Marshal Balbo, the commander of the 10th Army, had no wish to engage the British, in Africa or anywhere else, but on 28th June his aircraft was shot down by Italian anti-aircraft batteries when returning from a recce flight over Sidi Barrani, and this reluctant warrior was killed. His replacement was Marshal Rodolpho Graziani. Graziani was more aggressive but a survey of the troops at his disposal revealed that their equipment was inadequate and their training lamentable. He, like Balbo before him, requested help from the Italian mainland, in particular an increase in transport and aircraft, but Mussolini was insistent that he should at once advance upon the British with the considerable forces already at his disposal. The Italians believed that the British forces were much more numerous than they actually were, an impression confirmed by the raids and patrols mounted by the British forces within hours of war being declared. These British forces were neither complete, suitably equipped nor, with the exception of 7th Armoured, as yet well trained. Alec Lewis, then a Sergeant in Cairo, remembers some incidents at this time.

'Most of the staff officers were from cavalry regiments and their off-duty conversation (which we could not help but overhear) was usually about horses and hunting. One officer, Colonel Morrison from Leicester, the CRAMC, was, in fact, writing a book on hunting, and he used to get me to type the chapters as he completed them, for which he would reward me with a cigar! At times, when our Gloster Gladiator biplanes were overhead, perhaps chasing a Savoia bomber or a CR42 fighter, the officers would be watching with keen interest and shouting, "Tally-ho" and other hunting terms. At Gerawla, on the Sunday before Italy declared war, a gymkhana was held "on National Hunt lines", complete with a Tote. The competitors were various units' tanks, Bren carriers, vehicles and motor cycles – an enjoyable "break":

'Brigadier Jock Campbell of the 7th Support Group was a frequent visitor and was one of the first, if not the first, to introduce the casual style of Desert Army dress with silk neckerchief, light cord trousers, suede desert boots, and in the cold weather a goatskin coat from Afghanistan or Persia or somewhere like that, with some embroidery on the outside and hair on the inside.'

Fortunately the Italians made no move to invade Egypt for another three months, and in that time the British position improved considerably. More and better equipment arrived, more units came forward to join the Western Desert Force, bringing both the 7th Armoured and 4th Indian Division up to strength. Some of these men, like Herb Lassman, came up from Rhodesia.

'The Rhodesia contingent arrived in Egypt in 1940, and were split up and seconded to various regiments. I had the honour, being in the Artillery, of going to F (Sphinx) Battery, 4th Regt. RHA, my Rhodesian No. CR2 (civilian registration) being changed to 1095639. Our first job was outside Mersa Matruh. I had left the guns (one split-trails 18 pounder converted to 25-pounder) to go down the waggon lines and check the ammo. The chaps were all on "easy", washing, shaving etc., when a flight of planes flew over, flying high. Someone remarked, "Pretty, they look just like silver birds," when the birds laid their eggs! Len Bell (Rhodesian) was standing in his unlaced boots, shorts unbuttoned, scraping the lather off his face, when the first stick exploded, 400 yards away. We all got a shock. Len went straight up, out of his boots and shorts, and hit the slit trench in his birthday suit.

'We were split up, 4 guns, 11th Hussar Armoured Cars (Cherry Pickers) and a couple of trucks, mounted infantry (with usual signal, ambulance vehicles etc) did hit-and-run behind Graziani's lines. We also took Fort Capuzzo. I think we were the forerunners of Long Range Desert Group, who were often recruited from our blokes.

'The Italian advance caught us bending and someone either passed on an incorrect message or didn't interpret one correctly. On the guns we heard it as, "Hold the position to last man!" Very cheerful. We had the range and were knocking their trucks off the road as they came down the escarpment by Sollum. They didn't appreciate our attention, and although none of our casualties was fatal, we were brought down to four men per gun, including officers and drivers. Suddenly, in a cloud of dust, General Wavell drew up just behind our tanks. "What the hell are you doing here? Get the hell out of it." The order to limber up must have been our quickest ever. Apparently we were only supposed to delay, not attempt to take on the Italians.'

Graziani did not make his move into Egypt until dawn on 13th September, three months after the declaration of war, and although he succeeded in advancing as far as Sidi Barrani by 16th September, he did so in the face of fierce opposition from the tanks, guns and armoured cars of 7th Armoured. On arriving at Sidi Barrani, Graziani's army halted and were still there when the British struck back. During this period the British – especially the men of 7th Armoured Division – established a great moral superiority over their Italian opponents. This process began on the night of 12th June 1940, when the armoured cars of the 11th Hussars pushed their way through the frontier wire and advanced into Cyrenaica, where the Italians had garrisoned their various frontier forts in considerable strength.

The 11th Hussars (PAO) now took on that aggressive reconnaissance role which they kept up to the end of the war and which gave them such a glorious reputation. Every old soldier of 7th Armoured still freely admits that the 11th Hussars were the most remarkable unit of their Division, although the finest acknowledgement of their military prowess came later from their most deadly and distinguished opponent, Field Marshal Erwin Rommel of the German Afrika Korps. Berating some subordinate for a tactical error, Rommel finished his rebuke by remarking, 'The 11th Hussars would *never* have made an error like that.' A. S. Prosser and Harry Buckledee were both in the 11th Hussars and Sgt-Major Smith was then serving with "A" Squadron.

A. S. Prosser recalls his time in the desert: 'I was a car mechanic, junior in rank. Before the war started and in the time before the Italian advance, we carried out extensive training, scouting patrols and map reading. We also carried out night exercises using a compass and the stars (there were no signposts). We also did a lot of target practice, moving vehicles against moving targets. Our main recreation was sport on makeshift football pitches, and swimming. When Italy declared war we moved over the border to attack their forts, and although Intelligence said they were only lightly guarded, we soon found they were on full alert. I was engaged in several minor battles, where the enemy were routed. The Italians surrendered en-mass and we could not cope with the numbers. On one patrol our armoured car was blown up on a land mine and was a write-off, but with no serious injuries among the crew.

'Our main enemy at these times came from air attacks, which scored some successes in the early days, concentrating on the Troop leaders who only had wireless sets. As time went by we were equipped with South African made cars, Marmon Harringtons, which gave quite good performance but their armoured plating was too thin.'

Harry Buckledee also remembers the desert: 'The 11th Hussars were at Maadi in June 1940, just outside Cairo. We moved up to the Libyan border and waited for the Italians to declare war. The 11th was the first regiment to attack when war was declared. Water was in very short supply in the early days, with strict rationing of four pints per man per day. Not very much when you consider the heat and that vehicle radiators had to be topped up out of the ration. The order was given – no washing or shaving – so we all grew beards and were filthy. However, after four or five weeks supplies of water improved and we were soon ordered to get ourselves cleaned up. We learned to shave and have a wash down in a pint of water.

'We were never short of food. I cannot speak too highly of the organization in the regiment for getting supplies up to us in difficult conditions and over long distances. We were also well equipped with cooking utensils, every vehicle had a frying pan, kettle and a dixey, all supplied by the regiment's PRI. Our mainstay was corned-beef and biscuits, with potatoes, onions and an oxo cube for flavouring. We survived mainly on "Bully stew", with tinned bacon, sausages, soya bean sausages, tinned fruit, and always enough tea, sugar and good old Carnation milk to make a brew whenever we wanted one or when we could make one. Sometimes we had boiled rice with sugar or jam and milk. There was flour available on the ration wagon if needed. When we had the time, which wasn't often, we made pastry with the flour and margarine, using a map-board for rolling it out on and a beer bottle for a rolling pin. Small pasties were filled with apricot jam and fried in deep margarine. So we didn't starve, although there were many days when we had little time to eat. It was essential to get a brew made on our primus stove inside our armoured car before it got light, because it might be night before we got another chance.

'Our shooting was mainly against enemy transport. We hadn't got the fire power to take on anything big. In 1940 we had one Morris and two 1924 Rolls Royce armoured cars to a troop, armed with a Bren gun and a Boyes anti-tank rifle, which was not a very effective weapon. Fighter aircraft were our greatest hazard. With the Italians it was their CR42s firing .5 inch armour-piercing bullets which penetrated our armour plating. Against the Germans it was the Messerschmitt 109 and 110. After the defeat of the Italians, the regiment was sent to Cairo for new vehicles. We were equipped with South African 'Marmon Harrington' armoured cars with Ford V8 engines. The armour plating of these cars was thin and of poor quality, easily penetrated by the armour-piercing 'needle bullets' from the Messerschmitts. One afternoon in June 1941 I saw three 110s attack one of our troops and in about two or three minutes they had destroyed all three cars. Our troop was sent to their assistance. I was anxious as I knew my mate, L/Cpl Bob Ramshaw, from West Stanley, Durham, who had joined up the same day as me, was in that troop. All but two of the crews were dead or wounded. Bob was badly wounded but recovered from his wounds, although he had a leg amputated.

'This was something different from our usual job of keeping the enemy under observation, getting information and shooting them up whenever the opportunity arose. Although there were long periods when the main force was inactive, the 11th Hussars were always in action. Each troop would be out on three-day patrols with one day's rest in between. In spite of the heat, the flies and the dust, we actually liked the desert.'

Squadron Sgt-Major Smith was then a Trooper in the 11th Hussars: 'When Italy declared war in June 1940, I was already in Egypt, and our forces were mobilised and ready to move up to the "wire". The "wire" refers to the boundary fence between Libya and Egypt, a fence some ten or fifteen feet thick. We used to spend nights cutting the wire and making an entrance into Libya so that we could carry out raids on Italian convoys of vehicles which serviced the various forts scattered along the frontier, then return back to Egypt after inflicting maximum damage on the convoys. Their escorting tanks were of little trouble to us, as they were slow and the crews were no match for the "super fast tactics" of the 11th Hussars. One such fort which did worry us a little was Fort Maddalena. It made our left flank quite insecure, so it had to go. The general plan was for the RAF to send Blenheim bombers in to soften the target; we would attack from the front and crash-bang, the job would be done. However, it did not go quite like that. Hour "X" arrived, no bombers. "X" + 15, no bombers; "X" + 30, no bombers, so we decided to attack alone. After a struggle we took the fort and we were rounding up the prisoners when the bombers arrived – and yes – they bombed us! We tried all forms of recognition, Very lights and so on, but nothing worked. I was standing by an 80ft high watch tower when I saw a plane release a bomb above me. I knew it was mine but I continued watching it fall, when it hit the side of the watch tower and bounced off, exploding outside the fort perimeter. I had a fag.

'During the first night that we were cutting the wire, it was necessary to cut the telephone wires as well. The poles were wooden and about 20 feet high. One of our very agile lads shinned up the pole to cut the wires with a pair of pliers. Unbeknown to us, one member of the troop had procured a chain-saw which was operated with both hands, sawing the pole in a flash. "Ticker" Emmett was still up the pole; that is to say, he was, until the pole collapsed, and "Ticker" with it. One thing that could be said in defence of the chap with the saw was that it was a very dark night, and we were in a hurry. We found out why "Ticker" was so called.

'During a desert patrol we were out looking for tank movement somewhere south of the coast road, when suddenly we ran slap into about twenty Italian tanks. We were only 3 armoured cars, so we had no option but to get out of these quickly. They started firing at us like mad and we got hit in the engine compartment. The shot blew out the petrol tank and there were flashes but no hazardous fire to make us bale out. The car still ran for 3 or 4 miles, enough to get us out of danger. I often think I had good cause to thank the people of England who made the Humber Armoured Car.

'This happened later, but I'll tell you about it now. At one time in the

45

desert campaign, the 11th Hussars were equipped with an armoured car called a Marmon Harrington. The armoured plating was only a little more than an eighth-inch thick. Our orders were that if we saw 109s approaching to strafe us, we were to bale out of the cars as they offered no protection, being such thin metal. Later on the 109s introduced their "Needle Bullet" which would pierce almost anything. We had just had a beer ration – one bottle of beer per man per week. We had it nicely stowed so that we could drink it that night when we rested. 109s were spotted and they spotted us. One could tell from experience when a plane was going to strafe us, so we all baled out. That is to say, except "Snub" Pollard. He couldn't find his beer to take with him. His reward? He was shot through both cheeks of his backside by a needle bullet.'

On the outbreak of the war against Italy, Lt-Colonel John Combe of the 11th Hussars was ordered to take his regiment forward through the wire and dominate the open desert between the main Italian positions at Fort Capuzzo and Fort Maddalena. As the above accounts show, the 11th were soon having a high old time, ambushing Italian patrols, shooting up convoys and sending back scores of prisoners. On 14th June the 7th Hussars took a hand. In their light Mark VI tanks, accompanied by a company of the KRRC and a battery of the Royal Horse Artillery, they assaulted the fort at Capuzzo, killed or captured the garrison and destroyed the installations. On the same night the 11th Hussars overran Fort Maddalena, and two days later, in the first tank battle in the Western Desert, the 7th and 11th Hussars engaged a force of Italian tanks and lorried infantry, knocking out twelve tanks and taking an entire battalion of prisoners.

These Italian tanks, the M13, provided no real opposition, even to the 2pdr British tank guns. The M13 weighed 14 tons, had frontal armour, 30mm thick, and a maximum speed of just 20 mph. With a crew of four, the M13 mounted a 47mm gun and three 8mm Breda machine guns. Fairly slow and used in the main as infantry support, the M13 proved no match for the British tanks or guns. Sgt. H. Roberts of the 7th Hussars recalls these early battles.

'I was in the 7th Queen's Own Hussars, who arrived in Egypt in 1935 as horse cavalry, and were eventually mechanized in 1937 with the light tank Vickers Mark VI. The forerunner of the 8th Army was the Western Desert Force which, when the Italians came into the War in June 1940, was under the command of General O'Connor. The recce regiment was the 11th Hussars in their armoured cars; and after the declaration of war by the Italians, the 7th Hussars crossed the Libyan wire and attacked Fort Capuzzo, which I consider to be the first tank attack of the Desert War. In the action we lost a tank blown up on a mine, and the driver was killed, so he would be the first casualty of the Desert War in which thousands would die. Also, later in the month, the 7th Hussars intercepted a convoy of lorried infantry supported by Italian tanks, and in the ensuing battle the A9 Cruisers of A Squadron knocked out the Italian tanks and captured the lorries and the infantry, so I would consider this to be the first tank battle of the many that took place in the desert. The regiments who formed the original 7th Armoured Division were the 7th Hussars, 8th Hussars, 11th Hussars and the Tank Regiments, indeed all who had the famous Jerboa sign on their vehicles. So when you read in various books about the 8th Army described as Desert Rats, this is quite wrong; only those who were in the 7th Armoured Division were entitled to be called that.

'In 1941 I transferred to the 4th Hussars and my tank was eventually knocked out at Knightsbridge in June 1942 in the tank battles in the Cauldron, where I was wounded and captured by the Afrika Korps and spent two years as a POW before being repatriated from Germany in May 1944.'

The Italians re-garrisoned Capuzzo in July, but this made no difference to the raids and probing patrols of the Hussars and the light tanks of the 4th and 7th Armoured Brigades, who now roved at will in the open desert and never attempted to hold any fixed position west of the wire. These early actions had both good and bad effects. On the one hand they gave unit commanders at all levels valuable experience in desert warfare and desert navigation, and led the Italians to over-estimate grossly the strength of the British forces. On the other hand, this free-range soldiering introduced 'column warfare', where small groups of mixed detachments roved the desert harrying the enemy, supported by their own 'B' echelons. This was great fun, and the Unit Diaries are full of cheerful accounts of good times, 'swanning about in the blue,' but this lack of concentration had unfortunate effects later when the Germans came on the scene. Before then, however, there were victories to celebrate.

Probing forward, often well behind the Italian lines, the 11th Hussars sent back a constant stream of reports and prisoners throughout the hot months of that 1940 summer. General O'Connor was therefore well aware of what was happening across the wire when, on 13th September, the Italian 10th Army finally lumbered into action and began an advance into Egypt. The 10th Army included six fully-equipped divisions plus a battalion group of 200 tanks and infantry. Fortunately, the Western Desert Force had also received reinforcements, including three armoured units, the 2 RTR, the 7th RTR with Matilda tanks, and the 3rd Hussars, equipped with cruiser tanks. These were mainly A9s and 10s. A number of Rhodesian troops and a squadron of RAF armoured cars had also been added to the 11th Hussars, who had Morris armoured cars as well as their antique Rolls Royce models. This reinforcement enabled General O'Connor to have a cruiser tank squadron in every tank regiment with guns capable of knocking out the main Italian battle-tank, the M13. In spite of air attack and constant harassing from the 11th Hussars and the Support Group of 7th Armoured, by 16th September the Italians had captured the town of Sidi Barrani, on the coast, sixty miles east of the 'wire'. There, as we have seen, they halted and dug in, and made no move to attack deeper into Egypt.

Then, on 28th September, Italy declared war on Greece. With the Italians working round his northern flank in Greece, Wavell decided to attack the 10th Army before his situation became even more critical. Having taken Sidi Barrani in September, the Italians were still sitting there at the end of November, hemmed in by the 11th Hussars, and 7th Armoured's Support Group, and harassed by more of those ad-hoc formations, the famous "Jock" Columns of armoured cars, artillery and infantry put together originally by Lt-Col Jock Campbell of the 4th RHA. Rifleman T.T. Smith took part in some of these operations.

'I joined the 1st Battalion KRRC at Mingalordon in Burma in 1936, joining the Army on Boy Service. At the end of 1938 the Battalion embarked on HMT *Dilwara* and was transported to Egypt to be stationed in the Citadel, Cairo, where we were to be trained and re-equipped as mechanised infantry. Lt-Col. "Straffer" Gott (later General Gott) took over command of the Battalion. We had to be fully trained within six months and to be ready for active service. We were then in the Pivot Group, which became the Support Group, of what became the 7th Armoured Division. Originally the insignia was the red square and white circle; the desert rat was added when General Wavell was GOC and General O'Creagh commanded the Division. General Graziani, the Italian commander, said, "Like the rats of the desert they appear and then disappear."

'I took part in Wavell's offensive at Bardia. The Platoon I was with was positioned on the main track westwards from Bardia, with the Free Poles on the north, and the Free French on the south, cutting off the Italians' escape. I went as far as Tobruk, where I contracted jaundice. After being taken to hospital in Alexandria by hospital ship, I went to

El Arish convalescent camp. I returned to my unit at the Infantry Base Depot at Genifa and on being sent back up the line, carried out duties in the 7th Armoured Division Reinforcement Camp in the Orderly Room, before my return to my unit. Serving in the desert with "B" Company most of the time, I was on the "Jock" Columns, June, July and August they were codenamed, and we did two weeks on the columns and two weeks on rear duties, guarding dumps, the railhead etc. While serving on one column, we were withdrawing eastwards, and I was on one of three Bren carriers which were cut off by a German force and returned to my unit to find we were reported missing for ten days, presumed captured.'

Wavell first instructed O'Connor to attack the Italian Army in the area of Sidi Barrani, Sofafi, and around the saltpans of Buq-Buq, using the new heavily-armoured Matilda tanks which had recently arrived from England. The Western Desert Force began their attack on 8th December 1940.

The Italians had not been idle in the last three months and the Sidi Barrani position was now protected by another string of fortified camps. Three of these, Nibeiwa, Tummar East and Tummar West, lay just south of the main Sidi Barrani position. These were manned in strength by infantry, tanks and Italian heavy artillery – and Italian artillerymen always fought well and had already earned the respect of the British soldiers. It was estimated that the Italians had around 75,000 men in or around Sidi Barrani, with some 120 tanks and 200 guns. To match this, O'Connor could field the 7th Armoured and 4th Indian Divisions, amounting to 25,000 men and a total of 275 light, cruiser and Matilda tanks.

O'Connor's plan was for 7th Armoured to sweep west and mask the Tummars and Sidi Barrani from the main Italian army, while 4th Indian with 7th RTR in Matildas would hack north to overrun the camps and take the town. The attack was carefully rehearsed throughout November, and on 9th December 1941 the advance began. Major Harry Kirkham was then a Sergeant in 6 RTR.

'I was still in the Light Tank Squadron and my Squadron Leader was Major "Tinny" Dean (later to win the MC). All our tanks had very limited mileage before a major overhaul was required, therefore most training was done by TEWT's, but in the Light Tank Squadron we did long periods of border watches and observation. These were boring days with hardly any action at all.

'Limited action started in mid-1940, and the 7th Armoured Division were pushed back some 50 miles from the border. No serious action took place and no effort was made to push the Italian forces back. Daily patrols were made and reports made each evening. Each day the 'Flying Circus' passed overhead and we normally counted 18 bombers heading east at 25,000 feet and on their return would number anything from 12 to 16. The next day it would be back to 18. When the losses occurred no one could explain. We always heard them coming a long way off and kept an eye on them, because they did on a few occasions drop a stick of bombs. From one of these, the only casualty was a camel, and meat from this animal was served as an evening meal. It was too tough to really chew but at least it added flavour.

'When not on patrol, we would camp in a wadi we called Happy Valley. Each tank crew would find their own 'home' and be self-contained. Rations would arrive daily at a central point and all the Desert Rats would emerge from their holes and collect whatever was going. Sentries were posted at night, but during the day it was a case of tank maintenance, gun cleaning, cooking food, a daily conference at squadron level to obtain information and perhaps collect new codes, and then relax. I remained with the Mark VI Light Tanks, but our Vickers Medium tanks were replaced by Crusaders, still under-armed but much faster and easier to handle. The Mark VI Light Tank was fast but had only twin machine guns mounted in the turret. Should a track pin break when travelling at 40 mph, the metal track could be left 30 yards or more behind, and it was heavy going to drag it into position at the front of the tank. It was therefore a continuous task to check each pin and replace cracked ones.

'With Christmas 1940 not far away, all commanders were called to a briefing by the CO. Our first major offensive was to hand. Plans were explained, dozens and dozens of enemy positions were to be put onto our maps. We returned to our tank crews and passed on all information they were required to know. After twenty-four hours we were ready to move off in darkness to our forming-up positions. At the crack of dawn on 9th December we were already on our way to the first objective. In our case it was a camp area on the map made up of infantry and light artillery. It was a very mobile battle, being ordered to first one enemy area and, when under control of our infantry, moving off to yet another. It lasted two or three days, and at that stage the enemy were clamouring to give themselves up. At one stage we were five tanks together and Italians were all around us. All had arms of some sort but they did not want to fight any more.

'My troop of tanks entered one camp area, dismounted and searched each trench and dugout for any strays. We found cases of hand grenades and let off quite a few in holes in the ground. They were useless as a grenade and we ended up tossing them to each other. Provided you kept six feet away, they were harmless.

'In the search of officers' hideouts my driver, "Granny" Knott, found a cash box, locked but with the key in the lock. Inside was the payroll, including a separate package containing the pay of a general. In all it contained over 35,000 lira. That night we agreed it should be kept intact and put in the food storage bin inside the troop commander's tank. We were in for a lively time sharing it out between our troop for our next trip to Cairo.

'A conference was held for all troop commanders and NCOs that night, the 9th December, and we spent hours taking down hundreds of map references, relating to enemy positions, gun emplacements, minefields etc. Our squadron was to cross the frontier line south of Bardia and then head north. The remainder of the regiment would be close behind. Bardia had been under heavy artillery all day, but they obviously were not going to surrender so easily. There had been an infantry attack from the south, but they had been forced to call a halt. After a hurried conference it was decided to mount an infantry attack from the west of the town. For this purpose the infantry would be the Free French Forces, supported by the light tank squadron of the 6th Royal Tanks – us!

'We formed up about a mile from the enemy defences in the late afternoon, and waited for the Free French Forces to arrive. There was some delay before they appeared, and then they went to ground to await the signal. Shells were falling around us, but they seemed to avoid every target. At long last we were away. The French had requested that we go slowly, which we did. The shelling became heavier, but they were tracer HE (High Explosives), and they came towards us so slowly we were able to avoid most of them. Some tanks around me had halted at the halfway mark, and as we had no orders to stop, I looked behind at the Free French infantry, and there was not a man in sight. My Troop Commander reported back to the Squadron leader, Major Dean, and we withdrew. Once more we formed up and the French gave the signal and we advanced once more with the infantry behind. By now the enemy were turning on the heat, and with only machine guns to answer back, we were little more than nuisance value and a morale booster for the French infantry. Before we had reached the halfway point, the latter had again gone to ground. Almost as our troop leader began to report, his tank was hit and burst into flames. He began to scream and, no doubt because he was badly wounded, he was unable to lift the turret hatch. I began to think of my two long-standing friends inside the burning tank and – another thought – all that cash inside ... perhaps we should have shared it out last night.

'The tank in front was hit and the track blown off. The commander "Dingle" Rogers, was waving to me for help. By now all thought of infantry support had been forgotten. Roger's tank was being shelled hard now that he was stationary. I told "Knotty" my driver to head for Roger's tank so that we could tow him to safety. I popped my head out of the top to decide how to tackle the tow and I saw a shell heading towards me by the tracer. Unable to give any order in time, the shell landed on the front of the turret, and I thought that was it, but no, we were all alive and none was wounded. Looking outside I could see that the armour above the driver was blown in but not holed. I reported back what had happened and pulled up behind Roger's tank. His driver was ready with the tow rope and with shells passing over us we managed the tow rope. I realized that without the track the tank could not be repaired, so I jumped down, undid our tow rope, went round to the front of the damaged tank and hitched on my tow rope. I mounted my tank and pulled the damaged tank backwards. The driver then connected the tow rope to the broken track and pulled them back to HQ. Both crews got back without any loss or injury.

'The next day we were pulled out of action and sent back to Cairo for a rest. We had lost 4 tanks out of 11. Looking back I am still amazed that we were able to shout warnings and be in time to dodge several close shots. For this action I was awarded the DCM by General Wavell, the first DCM, I believe, in North Africa.'

The Order of Battle for 7th Armoured at the start of the battle for Sidi Barrani is shown on the facing page.

On 9th December, the 4th Armoured Brigade got astride the coast road west of Sidi Barrani, while 4th Indian Division attacked the Tummar Camps and isolated Sidi Barrani. The Italian collapse was dramatic. The Indians swiftly overran Nibeiwa and the Tummars, while 7th Armoured, sweeping west and then north, cut the coast road to isolate Sidi Barrani, from which the garrison was soon in full retreat. The 25-pounder field guns of the RHA and the awesome advance of the 7 RTR Matildas soon cracked the defences at Nibeiwa, but the Italian commander, General Malatti, emerged from his tent to engage the tanks with a light machine gun, firing until he was killed, his son falling wounded at his side. The Cameron Highlanders then swept through with the bayonet, killing several hundred Italians and taking over 4,000 prisoners. The British attack on the Tummars was reinforced by the

ORDER OF BATTLE NOVEMBER 1940

4th Armoured Brigade
7th Hussars
2nd Royal Tank Regiment
One Battery 3rd RHA
One Squadron 3rd Hussars

7th Armoured Brigade
3rd Hussars
8th Hussars
1st Royal Tank Regiment
One Battery 3rd RHA
One Squadron 2nd Royal Tank
   Regiment

Support Group
4th RHA
1st KRRC
2nd Rifle Brigade

Divisional Troops
3rd RHA
106th RHA
11th Hussars
Divisional Signals

Royal Engineers
2nd Field Squadron
141st Field Park Troop

RASC
No. 5 Company
No. 58 Company
No. 65 Company
No. 550 Company
4th New Zealand Reserve
   Company
1st Supply Issue Section RIASC

RAOC
Divisional Workshops
Divisional Ordnance Field Park
Divisional Forward Delivery
   Workshop Section
1st Light Repair Section
2nd Light Repair Section
3rd Light Repair Section

New Zealand drivers of No 4 Motor Company, who borrowed rifles to charge at the head of the British infantry to cries of, 'Come on, you Pommie bastards.' By the evening of 10th December, over 5,000 prisoners had been taken, and when the 7th Hussars finally blocked their retreat to the west at Buq-Buq, the surrendered Italian troops became so numerous that, unable to count them, a 7th Hussar officer reported, 'As far as I can see, we have captured about twenty acres of officers and about a hundred acres of men.' There were, in fact, some 20,000; total British losses were about 700.

More might have been achieved had not two brigades of the 4th Indian Division been suddenly recalled to Cairo on the second day of the battle and sent to the Sudan, where another Italian army had taken the field. This left the battle around Sidi Barrani to the 7th Armoured Division, and they swept on to secure the Rabia and Sofafi camps, which had been abandoned by the Italians and fallen to a troop of the 11th Hussars. This troop, commanded by 2nd Lieutenant Reid-Scott, had previously discovered a strong Italian force drawn up west of Buq-Buq, well dug in under the dunes and behind the salt flats.

A hastily assembled force, consisting of the 3rd Hussars with a squadron of the 2nd Royal Tanks, cruisers of the 8th Hussars, supported by C & B Squadrons of the 11th and a battery of the Royal Horse Artillery (RHA), all under Lt.-Colonel Combe of the 11th Hussars, attacked this force that same afternoon, and met stiff opposition from the Italian artillery, who stood to their guns and fought well. C Squadron of the 3rd Hussars was stopped by the fire of thirty guns, and the 'A' Squadron tanks coming in from the flank were swiftly bogged down and then knocked out on the open salt flats, just 300 yards from the Italian positions. The crews stayed in the tanks and continued to fire until, one by one, their tanks were set on fire. The Italians were finally overwhelmed by a flanking attack from the 2nd Royal Tanks in cruiser tanks, and B Squadron of the 3rd Hussars.

Stunned by these violent assaults and this rapid series of defeats, the Italian army was now in full retreat, harried again by 7th's Support Group and the roving Troops of the 11th Hussars, who chased them back along the escarpment and across the wire south of Sollum and back into Cyrenaica, leaving some 38,000 prisoners and a vast quantity of equipment behind, including 237 guns and over 70 tanks. Some of the Italian kit was not so useful as Ron Haslam recalls:

'Although I served in the Desert Campaign from the first day to the last, I am having great difficulty in recalling any worthwhile incidents. I think this shows how terribly monotonous life was. I can recall our spirits lifting on hearing rumours of a "big push". After entering "Buq-Buq", after the start of the first advance, we found the Italians had fled, leaving mess tins of food around their brew-up fires. Evidently we had interrupted their breakfast. We then looted their dugouts of blankets and pullovers, which we later bitterly regretted when we found out we had lice.

'I recall watching a dog-fight – two Germans followed a Spitfire down to a crash landing. As I approached the plane, the pilot (a South African) was walking along the wing, wiping his nose and saying, "I've got a bloody awful cold . . . is there a landing strip near here?" How's that for coolness?'

On 15th December, having chased the Italian Army out of Egypt, the

British paused to count their gains. During the rest of the month, both sides held their positions while the 6th Australian Division made ready for the assault on Bardia. The time was also used to bring up supplies for the next stage of the attack and to probe the enemy positions around Bardia, a town held by General di Corpa Bergonzoli, known to soldiers on either side as 'Barba-Electrica' or 'Electric Whiskers'. To defend Bardia he had a garrison of 40,000 men and over 400 guns.

There was also a great need to re-equip, for the tank strength of the 7th Armoured Division had dropped to 108 light tanks and 59 cruisers, and many of these had already outrun their designed track mileage. In a small way, where possible, the advance still continued. On 16th December, the Italian position at Sidi Omar fell to the 7th Hussars and the 2nd Royal Tanks, supported by the guns of the 4th RHA, where Captain Hobart of the 2nd RTR was seen 'steel helmet on, shooting away over the top of his turret cupola with a pistol'. The real battle during December was the battle for supply. Logistics were the great determinator throughout the Desert War, for the desert was a place that many considered 'Heaven for generals and hell for quarter-masters.'

Lacking suitable ports and adequate air cover, the replenishment of food, ammunition and, above all, water and petrol stocks, threw a great strain on the rear echelons and in particular on the drivers of the Royal Army Service Corp (RASC). Seventh Armoured had four companies of the RASC under command at this time, Nos. 5, 58, 65 and 550, plus the 4th (New Zealand) Reserve Company of Tummar fame, and the 1st Supply Issue Section of the Royal Indian Army Service Corps. Colonel Duncan Riddell was then a Captain in 550 Company.

'550 Company RASC was a Territorial Company, raised in Birm-ingham and joined 7th Armoured Division in October 1940, becoming Support Group Company to the Support Group. The front then extended over 60 miles of desert and because of the rough going, speed was restricted to 10 mph. The Company continued to support the brigade during the advance to Bardia, and across the desert to Beda Fomm during which, according to the Company Diary, "Commander, RASC, considered reducing the petrol allocation to the 11th Hussars, say-ing that otherwise they would be in Tripoli before anyone was prepared." 550 Coy built up a formidable reputation for reliability in these early days and their efforts were rewarded with a clutch of medals and mentions-in-despatches for some of the officers and men.'

These RASC drivers drove hundreds of miles, often by night, over open desert, to find and replenish the forward units, but all too often, by the time they reached the units, half their supplies had literally run into the sand. The inadequacies of British equipment were not confined to tanks and guns. Petrol, oil and water were conveyed in two-gallon cans, rightly called 'flimsies', or four-gallon drums which cracked and leaked, often losing half their contents in the course of the journey. The desert *birs* (wells) were quite inadequate, often salty and had sometimes been polluted with oil by the enemy to prevent them being used. It was now winter and in the open desert the nights were often freezing. Not all the units had received their warm battledress, and there was a considerable amount of sickness. Slight cuts and grazes, when irritated by sand, swiftly became deep, suppurating desert sores, while jaundice – Hepatitis 'A' – became all too common and was particularly prevalent, for some reason, among the officers. Water was always short, sometimes only half a gallon a day for all purposes. This included replenishing radiators, cooking, washing and shaving. Fresh food was rare, with bully-beef stew pepped up with tomato puré captured from the Italians at Sidi Barrani being the usual fare. By any standards it was a hard life, but there was a smell of victory in the air and that made up for all the difficulties and hardships.

On 1st January 1941, General O'Connor's Western Desert Force was renamed 13 Corps. The Corps began the year by moving 7th Armoured up to block the coast road west of Bardia, and on 3rd January the town was attacked by the 6th Australian Division. The town fell two days later, and while the Australians gleefully counted their prisoners, 7th Armoured was on the move again to carry out a similar blocking manoeuvre by hooking round south and west to isolate the town of Tobruk. The Australians captured most of the garrison and all the guns at Bardia, but General Bergonzoli and his staff had already slipped away to Tobruk. With Tobruk duly outflanked, the Australians came up again to assault the Italian positions, which fell after fierce fighting on 22nd January, yielding another vast haul of booty and some 30,000 prisoners, though to the great disappointment of the Diggers, General Bergonzoli had again slipped through their hands.

What the British and Australian troops were now achieving in the Western Desert was little short of miraculous. A Corp of two Divisions, one newly arrived, the other seriously short of tanks, was knocking the stuffing out of a well-equipped force ten times its size. With the forward airfields now in British hands, Wavell began to pour equipment and men up the coast road to garrison Tobruk and complete the route of the Italian 10th Army, which was now in full retreat through Barce and Derna, towards the town of Benghazi and beyond.

At this point another glance at the map will help. Tobruk lies on the North Coast of Cyrenaica, while Benghazi lies on the western shore of the Gulf of Sirte, over 200 miles away to the west by the coast road, but rather less, say 150 miles, directly south and west across the open desert. Given the successes already enjoyed by the Anglo-Australian combination of armoured hook and infantry assault, there was much to be gained by sending a force across the open desert to cut the coast road south of Behghazi, before attacking the town, but this desert terrain, south of the Jebel Akhdar, was unmapped, waterless and decidedly rough going. Even so, this was the course chosen by General Wavell. The Australians would pursue the Italians round the coast through Barce and Benghazi and keep up the pressure there, while 7th Armoured struck south-west across the desert through Msus and Antelat to hit the coast somewhere south of Benghazi, between Sidi Saleh and Beda Fomm. On 4th February, lead by the 4th Armoured Brigade under Brigadier 'Blood' Caunter, with the 11th Hussars in the front as usual, the 7th Armoured Division struck across the desert on one of the great adventures of the war.

The going was terrible and the advance of the tank regiments soon slowed to the point where it was decided to send the faster vehicles and infantry of the Rifle Brigade forward in Bren gun carriers to join the 11th Hussars, who were now ranging far ahead. This composite force was placed under the command of Colonel Combe and therefore called 'Combeforce'. Combeforce consisted of the 11th Hussars, reinforced by a squadron of the King's Dragoon Guards (KDGs) and the RAF Armoured Car Squadron, the motorized 2nd Battalion, The Rifle Brigade, with light anti-tank guns, and C Battery of the 4th RHA, with a section each of anti-aircraft and anti-tank guns attached. With this force of some 2,000 men, Colonel Combe hurried to cut the coast road. The Italians were already evacuating Benghazi, and if their Army was to be cut off, speed was now essential. The march began early on 5th February. Combeforce reached Msus, north-east of Beda Fomm, later that morning and hit the coast road near the village of Sidi Saleh about noon. They barely had time to take up their positions when at 1430 hrs the first column of Italian lorries came fleeing down the road from the north to find their way blocked by 'A' Company of the Rifle Brigade. The men of Combeforce had flung themselves in the retreating path of an entire army.

'A' Company of the Rifle Brigade, with rifle and machine-gun fire,

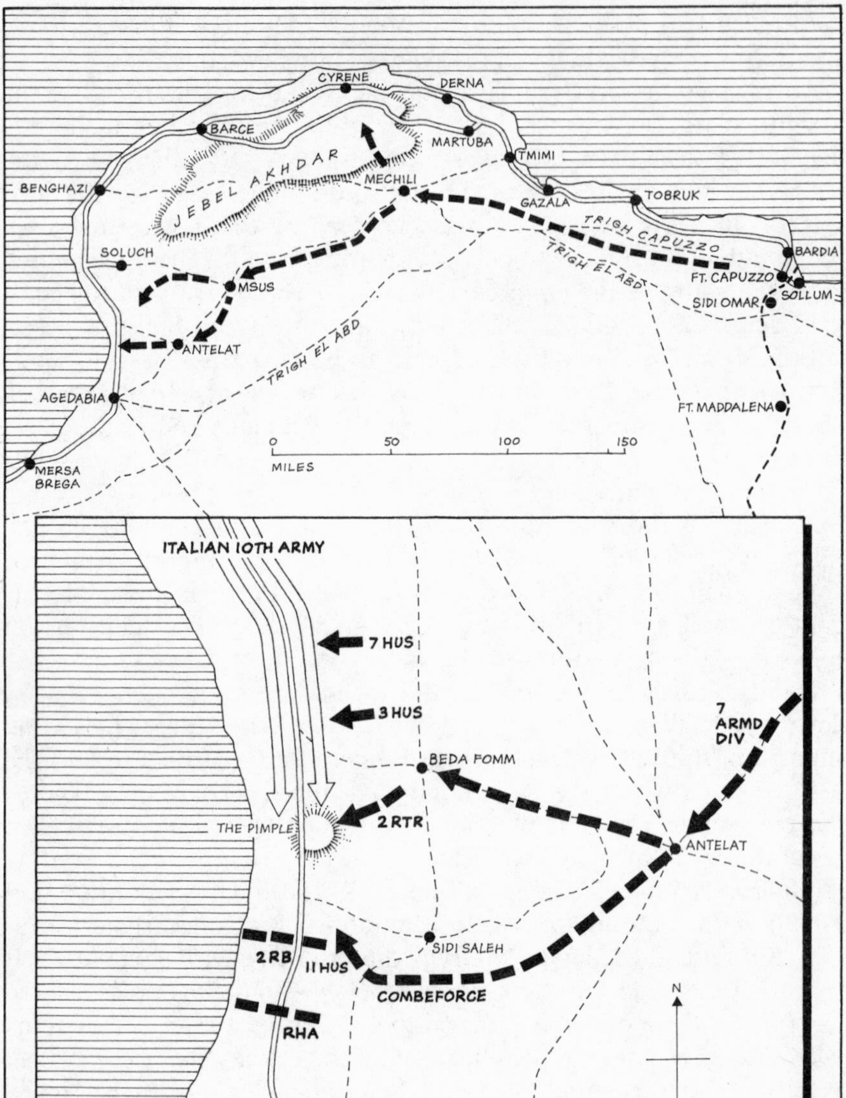
CYRENE
DERNA
BARCE
MARTUBA
TMIMI
JEBEL AKHDAR
MECHILI
BENGHAZI
GAZALA
TOBRUK
TRIGH CAPUZZO
TRIGH EL ABD
SOLUCH
BARDIA
MSUS
FT. CAPUZZO
SOLLUM
SIDI OMAR
ANTELAT
TRIGH EL ABD
AGEDABIA
FT. MADDALENA
0
50
100
150
MILES
MERSA BREGA
ITALIAN 10TH ARMY
7 HUS
3 HUS
7 ARMD DIV
BEDA FOMM
THE PIMPLE
2 RTR
ANTELAT
SIDI SALEH
2 RB
11 HUS
COMBEFORCE
RHA
N
0
10
20
MILES
AGEDABIA

2 The advance in Cyrenaica and the Battle of Beda Fomm

plus support from the artillery and 'C' Squadron of the 11th Hussars, soon brought the Italian column to an abrupt halt. As their traffic began to pile up, the Italians began to fan out west of the road towards the sea, and probing south, came to engage more of Colonel Combe's scanty command. Fighting now boiled up on either side of the road and continued throughout the day. In spite of the increasing pressure and a growing shortage of ammunition, the 11th Hussars and the Riflemen continued to block all movement down to the south. When the rest of 4th Armoured Brigade came up on 6th February to strike the Italians in the flank at Beda Fomm further north, the Italian rout was complete.

Even so, this was no quick collapse. The Italians pressed home their attacks with great tenacity and increasing desperation. They also had the advantage of numbers and an apparently inexhaustible supply of ammunition. Brigadier 'Blood' Caunter of 4th Armoured Brigade repeatedly asked for more supplies and for the support of 1 RTR from the Divisional Reserve at Antelat, but did not receive it until the battle was nearly over. Much of the tank-v-artillery fighting took place around a low hill called The Pimple, east of the coast road at Beda Fomm, and Colonel Binks of 4th Armoured Brigade described the scene there after the battle as 'An extraordinary sight, a two mile area of knocked-out tanks, abandoned tanks, ditched tanks, burned-out vehicles and dead or dying Italians, many roving about trying to surrender.'

F.W. Digby, MM, was with the 2nd RTR at Beda Fomm: 'Our Regiment was in the 7th Armoured Brigade, as were the 3rd Hussars. They were equipped with World War I Mark A5 tanks and we had A9s and A10s, and we interchanged one Squadron of theirs for one of ours. After a long drive over uncharted desert, we arrived south of Benghazi at Beda Fomm, where we met the Italian army in full retreat from Benghazi, and gave them battle there and defeated them. All regiments in the Division had exhausted their supplies and vehicles were in much need of repair. On the morning following the battle of Beda Fomm, we were put on burial fatigues, and were to use prisoners of war from the newly erected compounds, but the Italians refused to carry the dead and would only carry out the digging of the graves. These men were of local regiments and knew one another and some were related, which probably explains their reluctance to bury them. Some of the tank crews who were killed in their tanks had to be left as they were, as we could not remove them and these tanks were set fire to.

'The Regiment, after the defeat of the Italians, moved to Sidi Bish, outside Alexandria, to await more tanks. In the meantime the Germans had entered North Africa and advanced to regain most of the territory which had so recently been won.'

Seventh Armoured pounded the Italian 10th Army for two days, but by 11am on the 7th it was all over. White flags began to appear, the Italian Chief of Staff surrendered to the HQ of 4th Armoured Brigade, and the famous General Annibale Bergonzoli, 'Electric Whiskers' himself, surrendered a little later. With that, the rest of the 10th Army laid down their arms; twenty thousand men, six generals, and a vast horde of weapons, transport and supplies fell into British hands. The cost of the Battle of Beda Fomm to 7th Armoured Division was nine men killed and fifteen wounded.

A. Flanagan recalls this time: 'The A10 Cruiser tanks were unloaded from the ship and reloaded onto Egyptian railway flats and taken to a transit camp, where everyone suffered from dysentry for a few days. The day came when we were all sorted out – me to 7 Troop (3 Tanks), B Squadron, 2nd Tanks Regiment. Arriving in the Western Desert for the first time, somewhere near Mersa Matruh, we met the Italians. All that has been said about them being poor soldiers is correct. At Mikelia, the Italians had Heavy Artillery and tanks, so put up a good show, and although they outnumbered us in equipment we took thousands of prisoners.

'The 3rd Hussars were equipped with Vickers Light Tanks with .303 and .5 machine guns fitted. We had A10 Cruiser Tanks with 2-pounders and machine guns. it was decided to exchange B Squadron 2 Tanks for B Squadron 3rd Hussars, thus giving them extra fire power. Although we had some rough times, the 3rd Hussars looked after us very well considering the circumstances. After several battles at Tobruk, and Buq Buq Derna, the Italians retreated up the coast road towards Benghazi, then left towards Tripoli. General Wavell (great fellow) decided to send the Brigade diagonally across the desert. We travelled for three days and nights to cut off the Italians convoy, 7 miles long, consisting of tanks, lorries, shower caravan, mobile brothel and, I think, about a dozen women. That was the end of the Italian campaign at Beda Fomm.

'Each squadron was allotted sections to bury the dead, for which we used prisoners. I remember one particular Italian would not touch the dead, but insisted on making wooden crosses. I pulled out my revolver and threatened him many times. This did the trick. We gathered souvenirs – a Lancia lorry, Birreta motor bike, watches, Birreta automatics and so on. Leave was granted to Cairo at last.'

In two months, Wavell's forces had swept west for 700 miles, destroyed an army of nine divisions and captured 130,000 prisoners and over 400 tanks. The jubilation was considerable, both in Egypt and in Britain, but out in the empty spaces of the Western Desert the war went on.

As soon as the Italians surrendered at Beda-Fomm, the 11th Hussars swung their guns west and set off for Agedabia and El Agheila, but the rest of the Division was in too poor a shape to follow. The tank strength was now down to just twelve A13 cruisers and forty Mark VI light tanks. It was decided, therefore, that the 7th Armoured should withdraw to Egypt to rest and re-equip. The 11th Hussars were relieved on the van of the Desert Army by the King's Dragoon Guards (KDGs), and the 7th Armoured Division, replaced by the 2nd Armoured Division, newly arrived from England.

After Beda Fomm, General Wavell was anxious to continue the advance into Tripolitania and drive the Italians right out of Africa, but it will be remembered that Wavell had wider responsibilities in Africa and the Eastern Mediterranean. The Italians had ordered their forces in Eritrea to take the field and draw some of Wavell's fire, while in Greece the German army had now come to the rescue of the Italians, who had been roughly handled by the Greek army. Orders from London now compelled Wavell to halt the Desert Army and send precious men and equipment north across the Mediterranean Sea. The experienced 6th Australian Division, victors of Bardia, was sent to Greece, together with the tough New Zealanders, a full brigade of 2nd Armoured Division and most of the Desert Air Force. The defence of the newly conquered territory in Cyrenaica was left to one Brigade and the Support Group of the 2nd Armoured Division and another new arrival, the 9th Australian Division. Seventh Armoured withdrew to rest and refit in the Delta, where – in the words of the Divisional History – 'There was no reserve of tanks to re-equip the Division and as a fighting formation it rapidly disintegrated.' All the fruits of Sidi Barrani and Beda Fomm were about to be thrown away, and worse was to follow.

Before their withdrawal could commence, the 11th Hussars had a brief encounter with a new enemy. On 14th February 1941, one of their squadrons was strafed by a flight of fighter aircraft who pressed home their attack in a strangely aggressive fashion, sweeping in to attack at low level with cannon and machine guns. The Germans had sent help to their Italian allies. These aircraft of Fleigerkorp X were only the first part of a new force, the Afrika Korps, which was even now coming ashore in Tripoli under a great fighting general, Erwin Rommel. After General Rommel arrived in Africa on 12th February 1941, things were to go seriously awry for the British Armies in the Western Desert.

4

Brevity and Battle-Axe

FEBRUARY TO JUNE 1941

> The art of war is simple enough.
> Find out where your enemy is. Get
> at him as soon as you can. Strike
> him as hard as you can and as often
> as you can, and keep moving.
>
> *Ulysses S. Grant*
> On the Art of War

When General Erwin Rommel arrived at Tripoli in February 1941, the British were masters of the North African shore as far as El Agheila at the bottom of the Gulf of Sirte, which gave them control of Cyrenaica and the use of the vital ports at Benghazi and Tobruk. The Italians had been defeated, and for the moment Britain's fortunes in Africa were on the ascendant. However, before we follow the fortunes of 7th Armoured Division, it would be as well to consider again the plight of their Commander-in-Chief, General Wavell, for Wavell's responsibilities included Greece as well as North and East Africa. The British Prime Minister, Winston Churchill, had already offered to send troops to aid the Greeks against the invading Italians, but although the Greeks proved more than a match for Mussolini's legions, it now looked more than likely that the Germans would invade Greece and Yugoslavia, which in fact they proceeded to do at Easter 1941. The British were therefore compelled to send troops to Greece, and these troops could only come from Wavell's thinly stretched command, which, of necessity, compelled a halt to any further advance in Tripolitania – and all to no avail. The

Greek campaign and the debacle in Crete which followed, fall outside the scope of this book, but this sudden drain on his resources from February 1941 is relevant because it forced Wavell to halt the advance of 13 Corps towards Tripoli. This, in turn, provided the Germans with both a foothold in Africa and a breathing space to muster their forces.

General Erwin Johannes Eugene Rommel, the most charismatic commander on either side during the North Africa Campaign, began his military career as an infantry officer and commander of mountain troops. He saw the effective deployment of armoured units during the Polish campaign of 1939, and by May 1940 had obtained command of the German 7th Panzer Division on the Western Front. With this division he stormed across France in a fashion he was to repeat in the desert, and only came to a halt when his men arrived at St Valery at the mouth of the Somme, where they took the surrender of the British 51st (Highland) Division.

Rommel was a few months short of his fiftieth birthday when he arrived in Africa and made his enduring reputation. From then on, all accounts of Axis activity refer not to the relevant German or Italian units but to Rommel. It is always 'Rommel' who is advancing, or moving up, never the actual unit concerned, and even now, fifty years after he first stepped ashore in Africa, it is hard to write about the North African campaign without using that charismatic name. In recent years, Rommel's reputation has come under attack from the revisionist's school of historians, even in Germany, and he is sometimes portrayed as an opportunist, or simply a man who was lucky. Napoleon regarded luck as an essential requirement in any general, and the views of those who fought Rommel in the Western Desert seem more relevant than those coloured by hindsight. Stan Smith, who served in the 11th Hussars (PAO) expresses his views on General Rommel:

'An enemy will always be an enemy, but in some cases the enemy seems to carry a certain form of dignity and honour. In my opinion Rommel portrayed himself as a man of great compassion, though ruthless in his pursuit of victory in the Western Desert. I liken him to our own General Wavell who, in the early years of desert warfare, laboured against a great deal of inefficiency among the higher echelon, and only made a real impact in his early pushes against the Italians. Rommel's strategy of attack when he first entered the desert conflict showed him as a good tactician and as time went by, his confidence showed.'

George Clark of the KDGs recalls another soldier's view of Rommel: 'Rommel, the Desert Fox, we respected, a fine soldier and a good leader. He gave us the job of patrolling the wire which marked the boundary between Cyrenaica and Libya, and in the early misty mornings we hoped he wouldn't arrive unexpectedly out of the gloom. All we did see was a C41 Italian single engine biplane which didn't really give us any worry, only some target practice. One dark evening, a patrol was keeping a lookout near the front line, when a strange armoured car passed us. It was a new type of German armoured car, which had eight wheels. This one, we saw quite clearly, had four wheels on the side near to us. This was radioed to HQ but the question was, how could we be sure? We said, "Well, we can see four wheels on our side and can safely assume there are four on the other side." Hence the heavy eight-wheelers of Rommel's army, which rather upset the balance of power.'

Trooper R.G. Page of the KDGs actually met Rommel: 'I served in the Western Desert in the King's Dragoon Guards in besieged Tobruk for almost the whole of 1941. In early December, while driving an armoured car beyond the wired perimeter, we were captured by the Africa Corps and later interrogated by General Rommel. After giving him my name and number, he disclosed that he knew the names of the Regiments at present serving in Tobruk and the exact location of every gun position there. As it was Italian territory, he apologised that he would have to hand me over to the Italians. The following day, the Italians transported us to Benghazi, where we boarded a ship destined for Italy. However, it did not make Italy, because we were torpedoed somewhere off the coast of Greece and a large number of lives were lost, including many New Zealand personnel.'

Rommel had read all the books on the theory and practice of armoured warfare, including those written by Fuller and Liddell Hart and put their lessons into effect when the German Army attacked the Anglo-French forces in 1940. His swift success in France brought him to the attention of Adolph Hitler, and on 6th February 1941, the day the Italian 10th Army surrendered at Beda Fomm, Hitler offered Rommel command of a new formation, to be made up of the 5th Light Division and 15 Panzer Division and intended for operations in North Africa. This force was designated the 'Afrika Korps' and equipped with the latest Panzer Mark III and Mark IV tanks.

The Panzer III weighed 20 tons, carried a crew of five and mounted a 50mm gun and two 7.92 machine guns. The frontal armour was 30mm thick and the tank had a top speed of 25mph. The Panzer IV was altogether more formidable; weighing 20 tons and with a similar amount of armour it mounted a 75mm gun and one 7.92 machine-gun. This 75mm gun had good sights and outranged any British gun then in service. German tanks also had the advantage of wide turret rings which enabled the tank hulls to be fitted with larger turrets and easily up-gunned. To these advantages must be added excellent tank recovery services and a small but significant number of the formidable 88mm anti-tank guns. Rommel's force was small, professional, integrated, and he led it from the front.

Rommel arrived in Tripoli on 13th February 1941, followed by Naval transport bringing a crack Italian armoured division, the Ariete, and part of the German 5th Light Division. In spite of the name, the 5th Light was a strong tank force, equipped with 70 light tanks, some eight-wheeled armoured cars and half-tracks, and 80 of the formidable Mark III and Mark IV Panzers. This division also contained some anti-tank units equipped with a gun which was to bedevil the British and Allied tank forces until the end of the war, the 88mm dual-purpose gun and most accounts of tank fighting from then until the end of the war mention the whip-crack sound of the high velocity 88mm shell. Most of this force had disembarked at Tripoli by 11th March 1941.

After Beda Fomm, General O'Connor was convinced that even without further reinforcements, his force could have advanced to Tripoli and secured the Libyan shore, but the arrival of the Germans and Rommel put a swift stop to all that. By the time Rommel arrived in Africa, O'Connor had handed over command of 13 Corps to General Philip Neame, VC, and returned for a well-earned rest to Cairo. The British advance had stopped at the Mersa El Brega gap between the desert and the coast, just east of El Agheila, and Rommel struck here on 31st March. By this time, 7th Armoured Division had been withdrawn to the Delta and the forward positions of 13 Corps were occupied by scattered elements of the 2nd Armoured Division. The cutting edge of Rommel's advance was just 50 gun armoured tanks, but these were Mark III and IV Panzers, and supported by the Luftwaffe they cut through the British armour like a knife through butter.

For some reason the British seemed convinced that Rommel was attacking in overwhelming strength, and by concentrating all his tanks into one force, Rommel reinforced this impression. In fact, Rommel still had only a part of his force ashore, and only attacked because the British seemed reluctant to advance any further into Tripolitania. His force consisted of the 5th Light, with the 5th Panzer Regiment, with Panzer IIIs and IVs as its strongest element, and two Italian divisions, the Ariete and the Brescia. The British forces were well scattered and Rommel's solid punch soon had the British in full retreat. Advised by the 'Ultra' intelligence, which they were receiving daily from Bletchley Park in England, where scientists had succeeded in cracking the German wireless code, and could therefore read all the radio traffic between Rommel and his High Command, Wavell and Neame had supposed, not unreasonably, that Rommel would wait until all the Afrika Korps had arrived before attacking. In fact, Rommel attacked with what he had just one month after landing in Africa, and took the British forces completely by surprise.

The 2nd Armoured Division was soon forced out of Mersa Brega, and by 2nd April had withdrawn to Antelat, about 90 miles to the east, with Rommel's tanks and motorized forces hot on their heels. This was Rommel's way – to strike one immense blow with all his available forces, using the advantage of surprise. Then, having knocked his opponent off balance, Rommel kept him that way by relentless pursuit, bouncing the British out of any position before they had time to dig in. Rommel preferred to lead from the front, riding up in his staff car to urge the leading units on or getting an overview of the situation from his light Storch spotter-aircraft. By 3rd April, the British were in full retreat. Picking up plenty of petrol and transport from the retreating British, Rommel decided to press on and drive them out of Libya and – why not? – perhaps out of Egypt as well. In the British lines there was, according to the official despatch, 'considerable confusion'. Units coming up to join the fight were overrun, tanks ran out of petrol and had to be abandoned, while everywhere the Afrika Korps swarmed forward.

A good account of this period comes from the history of 550 Company RASC: 'March 1941 saw the Germans advancing along the coast road to Egypt. Refitment of 7 Support Group was speeded up. The unit received replacement vehicles from 5, 58 and 65 Coys, all of 7 Armoured Div. and an advance detachment was sent forward to the Western Desert to serve 1 KRRC which had been hurried forward to Barce. Under command of Lt. Parish, the detachment managed despite the difficulties to supply the Bn. In the absence of Major Fawcett, sick, the main body of the Coy moved forward under command of Capt. Whitlock. Warning was given that the front was crumbling and from Mersa Matruh westwards the unit was warned that an attack from the advancing German spearheads must be anticipated. At Sollum, orders were given to proceed to Tobruk. The position was extremely obscure, and the unit was ordered to wait until 107 Regt RHA could act as escort. This caused a delay of one day before in the late evening the Coy. ascended the steep hill to Capuzzo and moved on to Tobruk.

'At 0200 hrs on the 10th April 1941 the Coy. passed within the Tobruk perimeter, which was thinly held by units of 9 Australian Div., and was established by the main Tobruk-Bardia road. The welcome was in the form of a dive-bomb attack, which caused casualties. Throughout the day, Capt Whitlock made enquiries for the HQ of 7 Support Group but not until late that night was it confirmed that the location was at El Adem. Early on 11 April, with Capt Loch (Workshops Officer), Capt Whitlock set off with a defence truck for El Adem. This was the last party permitted to leave down the El Adem Road. Not until December 1941 was the result of the foray ascertained. Then Capt M.B. Phillips found the remains of the car and nearby their two graves. Both officers had been killed almost as soon as they had left the Tobruk perimeter.

'When Capt Whitlock failed to return, Capt E.D. Riddell assumed command of the Coy. With the cutting of the Tobruk–Bardia road, Tobruk was in a state of siege. The Coy was given the task of Ammunition Coy to 9 Australian Div and formed three APs (ammunition points) between the docks and the perimeter. These points often worked continuously throughout the 24 hrs and supplied almost all the Amn. for the whole defence. The whole area was subjected to air attack and shelling and several casualties were sustained.

'Lt. Parish had entered Tobruk from the West with 1 KRRC at the same time as the main body of the Coy had entered from the east. Under authority of DDST Tobfort, a detachment of 58 Coy was posted in. The Coy was then officered as follows: OC – Capt E.D. Riddell; 2 i/c Capt. M.B. Phillips. Sec. Comdrs. – Capt Parish, Capt Fox (from 58 Coy), and Lt. Phelps. About 250 other ranks were with the Coy. All ranks were housed in dugouts or miniature strong points, each with rations, water and amn. for at least five days. Together with the other units, 550 was prepared for any emergency and to give a good account.

'In the middle of July, after nearly four months, the news arrived that the Coy was to be evacuated. The unit was divided, the first part with Capts Riddell and Phillips embarked on HMS *Vendetta*, which unfortunately holed itself in the jetty at Tobruk and so disembarkation was at Matruh. 7 Arm'd Div HQ was 30 miles south of Matruh, so with a borrowed 15cwt, Capts Riddell and Phillips made a hurried journey to see Lt-Col Eassie, who promised that the Coy should resume its old role with the 7 Support Group. The second party after landing at Alexandria joined up again with the first party at Tahag.'

Rommel took Benghazi, the scene of a recent British triumph, on 3rd April. Three days later a German motor-cycle unit captured a staff car containing Lt-General Neame, commander of 13 Corps and General O'Connor, the victor of Beda Fomm, and Brigadier John Combe, until recently CO of the 11th Hussars. On the following day, 7th April, the commander of the 2nd Armoured Division and much of his command surrendered at Mechili. On 11th April, the Australian 9th Division withdrew into Tobruk, while the Germans swept past to capture Bardia on the 12th. Sollum and Fort Capuzzo fell on the following day. In two weeks Rommel had swept the British out of Libya, and of all their recent conquests, only the beleaguered fortress of Tobruk remained.

When Rommel struck in Tripolitania, 7th Armoured Division were back in the Delta, enjoying a well-earned rest and re-equipping, but because of the developing threat in Greece, most of the equipment arriving in Egypt was promptly sent on to Athens. Ronald Grey was with the Divisional HQ Squadron at this time:

'After Beda Fomm we ended up at El Agheila and from there we handed over to elements of a recently landed division, I think it was the 2nd Armoured Div, and we made our way back to Cairo, where we celebrated Christmas with our Christmas dinner on 1st March, St David's Day, 1941. It was at this time when Rommel and his Afrika Korps made their appearance in the desert and we were hurriedly re-equipped and rushed back to the front. So started the Benghazi Handicap. How many times Benghazi was taken, lost and retaken by either side over the next two years, was almost beyond count.'

As the situation in the West became ever more serious, various units of 7th Armoured were sent hurrying back into 'the Blue'. Among the first to go on 29th March was the 1st Bn. The King's Royal Rifle Corps (KRRC), followed on 5th April by three squadrons of the 11th Hussars, who had now replaced their vintage Rolls-Royce and Morris armoured cars with the new Marmon Harrington.

The 11th Hussars found the Marmon-Harrington's armour too thin and the Vickers MMG an inadequate armament, but they improved this with a Boyes anti-tank rifle and a Bren before moving out to El Adem, where Straffer Gott ordered them to deploy and patrol on a fifty-mile front from Acroma, south to Bir Hacheim.

The 11th Hussars remained in contact with the Germans until Tobruk was surrounded and then withdrew in good order to the frontier wire.

'These were hard days,' recalls the 11th Hussar Journal. 'Crews had no time for washing or shaving and had little to eat. They were on the go twenty-four hours a day, trying to delay the enemy advance, dealing quick blows at the head or flanks of his columns and then away again. On one occasion, three Me110s attacked an 11th Troop and destroyed three cars and the losses continued steadily, usually from air attack throughout the long hours of summer daylight – an interminable summer.' There were, however, two bright spots. In July 1941 orders were issued that all RAC units should adopt the black tank beret, but HM The King ordered that the 11th Hussars were to continue to wear their original rust-coloured beret with its red Cherry picker band. Later that month, the Regiment was ordered to train The Royals in desert reconnaissance and then pass on the art to the 4th South African Armoured Car Regiment, 'A fine lot of fellows, who soon adapted themselves to this peculiar type of warfare.' The South Africans relieved the Hussars in the middle of August 1941.

On 14th April 1941, Brigadier 'Straffer' Gott took command of the forward element of 7th Armoured at Sollum, with the title of O.C. Mobile Force. R. Haslam was with the Royal Signals at this time:

'Gott was our commander and I recall that he was highly respected by all ranks. In fact he was known by the Riflemen as "Gentleman Gott". I have memories of him returning from leave in Cairo and presenting every man in his HQ with a bar of Cadbury's chocolate. I also recall him stopping a Rifleman from digging an officer's slit-trench and making the officer do it himself.

'I also recall an incident during the Tobruk siege, which is as clear now as it was then. I was with a formation known as 'Little Sister' Jock column and consisting of a company of motorized infantry (Rifle Brigade or KRRCs) and a troop of 25-pdr guns (3 RHA or Australians) plus a detachment of Signals, REs etc. We were between the enemy who were investing Tobruk and the Egyptian border. Every evening at dusk we moved back on a compass bearing for about five miles and there leaguered up until dawn, when we returned to our previous positions.

'One evening in leaguer, my last message before going off duty and getting my head down, was from the 11th Hussars, to the effect that they could hear enemy tracked vehicles on the move. Believe me, when I lay down with my head on my rolled-up greatcoat, beside the track wheel, I could feel the vibration of the tracks, a very weird feeling indeed.

'In the morning we were attacked by a column of enemy, who chased us for about 60 miles. I can remember my truck getting one wheel stuck down a slit-trench, but three men with the incentive of German airbursts, managed to lift the wheel out of the hole. As dusk fell a "line abreast" of armoured cars appeared, the 4th South African Armoured Car Regiment. As we went through them, I experienced a terrific feeling of relief. It was like coming home. Within days we were back in our original positions.'

Elements of the Support Group and the 2nd Bn Rifle Brigade joined this mobile force on 30th April. Fortunately, even Rommel had to stop some time to bring up supplies. During the last two weeks of April, Rommel was engaged with investing Tobruk and bringing forward the newly arrived 15th Panzer Division to reinforce the triumphant 5th Light Division and their Italian allies, and this pause gave the British time to re-group after their precipitate retreat all the way across Cyrenaica. The British were now back below the Halfaya Pass, which was held by the Germans, but they still held positions on the escarpment to the east, from where they could hit back and stall any further German advances into Egypt.

General Wavell therefore decided to counter-attack the enemy positions at Sollum and around Fort Capuzzo in an attempt to push Rommel back from the frontier and relieve Tobruk. This attack, codenamed 'Brevity', went in on 14th May. The British front line forces, under Brigadier Straffer Gott, consisted of the Support Group of 7th Armoured, the 11th Hussars and the motorized 22nd Guards Brigade, together with some artillery, plus the 2nd Royal Tanks from the 7th Armoured Brigade, now equipped with reconditioned A9 and A10 Cruiser tanks and the 4th RTR equipped with heavily armoured Matildas. The 22 Guards Brigade and the 4th Tanks opened the offensive with an assault on the Halfaya Pass. Here they achieved complete surprise but were then held up by the Italian gunners who, as always, fought well and knocked out seven Matildas before being overrun. This fight alerted the Germans at Fort Capuzzo, who greeted the advancing tanks of A Squadron, 4 RTR, with a hail of shellfire. Although the fort fell, it was quickly recaptured. Gott's forces continued to press forward during the night, but with more German tanks coming forward and the opposition steadily increasing, he decided to pull back and defend the Halfaya Pass above Sollum, which was held by a squadron of the 4th Tanks in Matildas, and 3rd Bn. the Coldstream Guards. This force held the Halfaya Pass for two weeks until, on the 27th May, Rommel sent three battle groups to push it away; the Coldstreams falling back with the loss of 100 men. The 'Brevity' offensive failed in both relieving Tobruk and in destroying significant amounts of enemy equipment. In fact, thanks to their superior skills in tank recovery, the Germans were able to recover most of their own tanks and capture many British tanks which had been knocked out or had run out of fuel and been abandoned by their crews. With the British once again across the frontier wire, Rommel proceeded to fortify the Libyan frontier with thick belts of mines, covered by the formidable 88mm gun. This done, he sat down to wait for the next British assault.

On 12th May 1941, a convoy codenamed 'Tiger', docked in Alexandria, bringing with it 135 Matildas, 82 of the new 2-pdr-gunned Mark VI Crusader cruiser tanks and 21 light tanks, a total of 238 machines. The Crusader was a fast, good-looking tank, with a number of serious defects. It weighed nineteen tons, carried a crew of five, and mounted a 2-pounder gun and two 7.92mm Besa machine guns. It had frontal armour 40mm thick, and a top speed of 26mph. The problems were that the Crusader was under-gunned and unreliable, with a water-pump that caused continual trouble, a serious defect in the desert where water was always in short supply. All these Crusaders went to equip the 6RTR. The light tanks and Crusaders were destined for 7th Armoured, while the Matildas went to the 4th Armoured Brigade, where they would support the 4th Indian Division, which was now back in the Western Desert after various triumphs against the Italians in East Africa. With this force, Wavell prepared to mount his next offensive, 'Operation Battleaxe', which had, as its stated aim, 'The destruction of Rommel's forces and to achieve a decisive victory in North Africa.' If all else failed, this attack might at least relieve Tobruk, and these instructions were passed on to the new commander of 13 Corps, Lt-General Beresford-Pierse, who had replaced the captured General Neame.

To achieve this aim, the British must capture the old frontier posts at the Halfaya Pass, Fort Capuzzo and Sollum in the first attack. This would be achieved by the 4th Indian Division with the Matilda tanks of the 4th Armoured Brigade in close support. Once they had succeeded in penetrating the enemy line, 7th Armoured would come forward, join with 4th Armoured Brigade and break through to Tobruk. This done, 7th Armoured, now reinforced by the Tobruk garrison, would push on and secure a line along the axis between Derna and Mechili. General Wavell estimated that Rommel had some 13,000 men and 100 tanks close to the wire and another 25,000 with another 200 tanks around Tobruk, eighty miles to the west. He therefore hoped to defeat Rommel's forces on the frontier before reinforcements could arrive from Tobruk. The operation began on the night of 14th-15th June 1941, the British advancing in three columns to Halfaya and the wire.

Wavell had, in fact, over-estimated Rommel's tank strength. The British had some 300 assorted tanks to Rommel's 200, of which only about 100 were the gun-armed Panzer IIIs and IVs. However, Rommel had been given ample time to prepare for this attack, which he had already anticipated, and move forward all his anti-tank forces, including the 88s, against which even the thick armour of the Matilda tanks was to prove totally inadequate.

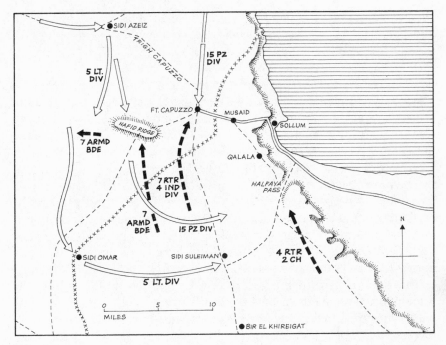

3 **Battleaxe**

The dawn attack by the right-hand column on the Halfaya Pass, made along the top of the escarpment, began badly, when "C" Squadron of the 4th RTR, supporting the 2nd Cameron Highlanders, ran against the entrenched 88mms which were in stone-built sangars, with only their muzzles visible. The "C" Squadron commander, Major Miles, was last heard on the radio reporting, 'They are tearing my tanks apart.' The fight at Halfaya went on until about 1000 hrs when "C" Squadron was down to one Matilda and one light tank, and the Camerons were then forced to withdraw by infantry counter-attacks covered by machine-gun fire, and retreated down the pass with great loss. Other squadrons of the 4th Royal Tanks engaged the enemy along the wire to keep the enemy busy while, further south, advancing along the escarpment, the centre column, led by the 7th Royal Tanks, captured Fort Capuzzo, losing five tanks in the process. Meanwhile, the main force of 7th Armoured Division was preparing to hook round the German southern flank, led by 7th Armoured Brigade, which had been re-equipped with the new Crusaders. To keep these tanks as a surprise, the column was led by the 2nd RTR in A9 and A10 cruisers. The first phase of this advance, to capture the Hafid Ridge, went well, but prior reconnaissance had failed to reveal that the Hafid Ridge was actually *three* ridges. Barney Finnigan of A Squadron 6 RTR, and the 6 RTR Regimental History give a good account of 'Battleaxe'.

'From the 1st to the 12th May, the regiment spent a welcome rest in barracks at Abbassia, and all ranks were given the opportunity of going on leave. Shortly afterwards the Regiment moved to Amirya, a camp some miles from Alexandria, where new tanks were drawn in the shape of the latest Cruiser Mark VI or A15s.

'All ranks were pleased and honoured that the unit was to be the first to be equipped with these latest models. In addition, the Regiment was completely equipped with new B Echelon vehicles, mostly Bedfords. General training continued until, on the 1st June, the Regiment moved to Matruh. Amid familiar surroundings, training and field firing continued uninterrupted, while at the same time a reconnaissance was made of the Habata-Hamra areas.

'On the 14th of June movement orders were received, and from Bir Ramadan the regiment crossed the frontier wire well south of Capuzzo; battle with the Germans was anticipated with enthusiasm; there were many debts to pay.

'The object of the advance was to sweep and attack Hafid Ridge, where the 11th Hussars had reported a large number of German tanks. Supported on the right flank by the 2nd R. Tanks, the regiment went into battle at Hafid Ridge on the 15th of June. Simultaneously, attacks were made upon enemy occupied Halfaya Pass and Fort Capuzzo, which were held by infantry in well prepared positions.

'Acting on the report of the 2nd R. Tanks, which stated that enemy guns had been overrun at Hafid Ridge, B Squadron advanced over the ridge in order to give the support which had been requested. It was then that disaster fell upon this Squadron, for after reports were received of extremely heavy casualties, no more was heard of them. The sole survivors were two tanks which somehow managed to get back. One of them was commanded by an officer and the other by a sergeant. From later accounts, it appears that the Squadron ran into a line of guns concealed behind dummy vehicles. The last that was seen of the Squadron in action was one tank moving towards the west in an endeavour to find cover from the fierce anti-tank fire. It was never seen again.

'True to form, the Germans delivered a counter attack, and C Squadron reported about 35 tanks advancing upon the regiment from the South-east. Although the unit had only 20 tanks left that were fit for action, orders were received to hold this force at all cost. A long-range duel developed, in which the Regiment, with 2-pdrs, was hopelessly out-gunned by the German 75mms, and by nightfall there remained only 15 tanks.

'By dawn on the 16th the unit was able to muster 21 tanks under command of Major R.I. Sciones, and moved off in company with a mobile gun column towards Hafid Ridge, which was reported by the 11th Hussars to be still occupied by the Germans.

'Further orders caused the Regiment to move south to the Sidi Omar area, where actions continued throughout the morning. Two-pounder and Besa fire caused much damage among a large concentration of the enemy, who later withdrew in a north-easterly direction.

'Meanwhile the attack at Halfaya had not been too successful, and although Cappuzzo had been taken at the bayonet point by our infantry, the enemy was obviously reforming for another and stronger counter attack. Reports of tank formations approaching from the north and north-west varied considerably, but the number of enemy tanks was somewhere between 54 and 80. Our own force was no more than 11 tanks fit for action.

'On the evening of the 17th the Germans advanced upon the Regiment and the 2nd R Tanks. Fanning out into two lines, both units were forced to retire, firing as they went. Within 15 minutes the regiment had only five tanks left, and although the 2nd Tanks fought a magnificent rearguard action until nightfall, they were unable to hold the rapid advance of the Germans. With the enemy occupation of Sidi Suleiman the action ended, and the regiment returned to the "Charing Cross" area to be reorganised. Left in the Bir Sofafi-Rabia area were dummy tanks and lorries, which misled the Germans into believing that they were faced by strong British forces.'

During the following weeks, in the Bir Sidi Ali area, the Regiment was brought up to strength with more Crusader tanks, and range firing and divisional exercises were carried out. At this time another eye-witness account of 'Battleaxe' came to light from the observations of Sgt. Hall, who was a tank driver during the 'Battleaxe' operation.

'Advancing across the wire in the early morning, we were full of enthusiasm. More than anything else we wanted to meet German tanks, for up till then we had not met the Panzers with anything like adequate equipment. Our dismay can be easily imagined when we found that the enemy outranged us from the beginning. Firing at maximum elevation with the two pounders our shells fell far short of their targets, while the enemy was able to lie back and hit us with his 75 mms. Because of this we were forced to withdraw several times. A chance encounter with German infantry did give us a good shoot with the Besas, but what we really wanted was to knock out some of the Mark IVs. This opportunity did not occur until the last day of the action, when nearly 80 tanks attacked us at sundown. With only 11 tanks of our own fit for battle, the future did not seem too bright.

'As the German tanks spread out into line formation,' he continues, 'we held our fire for as long as possible. In a semi-hull down position we were able to observe the enemy's movements fairly safely, and through the driving slits I counted over 69 tanks advancing towards us.

'The gunner opened up with the two pounder at a range of 800 yards, and in a matter of minutes I saw him destroy at least five of the enemy. The next moment we were hit. A shell burst beneath the main turret, completely destroying the engine controls, and one of the tracks was severed. No one was hurt, and we received the order to evacuate at once. Unfortunately, the sub-turret gunner was unable to get out at once, as the two-pounder barrel was resting over his escape hatch, and the traverse mechanism had apparently been destroyed. With some difficulty he was assisted to crawl through a small opening into the main turret, from where he was able to get out through the main hatch.

'As the tank was about to catch fire, we ran towards one of the other Cruisers and jumped on the back, where we lay until out of range. Although machine-gun bullets and armour-piercing shells were falling in great numbers, not one of our crew was injured, and we all escaped with our lives.'

The advance of the 2nd RTR had only secured the first ridge at Hafid and Rommel was now hurrying tank and anti-tank gun reinforcements forward from Tobruk. The Crusader tanks of 6 RTR were engaged by Panzer IIIs and IVs, and 17 were quickly knocked out or broke down. The new tanks also displayed an alarming tendency to catch fire when hit. By the end of the first day, 7th Armoured's tank strength had fallen by half. Rommel's forces were still largely intact and now rapidly increasing as 5th Light Division came up from Tobruk.

Stan Cheers was a tank driver in the 6 RTR: 'The 6th Tanks went into action in brand-new tanks, A15s or Crusaders. It is not known to many that they had no training on these tanks, not even simple basics. At the start of these battles we had 51 tanks, and after three days in action we only had six left, and only one tank in the Regiment did not have a hit on it.

'The boys called this action "The June Do". The 6th saw more action and had more casualties than any other unit in the Division, yet no one got an award. It seems that the CO got the boot, the Second in Command got promotion, and when the new CO came, he said, "I cannot sign this list as I was not here at the time." I was interested in this list, as I was told by my SSM, Jock Conie, that my name was on it. He was a real soldier and a gent, liked by all ranks, and unfortunately he was killed later on.'

On the second day of 'Battleaxe' General Creagh decided that the 7th Armoured Division advance should be renewed with another assault on the Hafid ridges by the Matilda tanks of 4th Brigade, which he would recall from assisting the 4th Indian Division. This attack would be supported by artillery, while the Support Group and the 7th Armoured Brigade would stand by to either reinforce the 4th Brigade or smash any attempt by Rommel to hook round behind the 4th Brigade near Sidi Omar. Unfortunately, Rommel attacked first. The 15th Panzer counter-attacked around Capuzzo by night, while the 5th Light made a hook around the British left flank, with the aim of reaching the Halfaya Pass and cutting off both British Divisions from supply or escape down the escarpment.

This move forced General Messervy, commanding 4th Indian Division, to tell General Creagh that he must retain the 4th Armoured Brigade to support his Division at Capuzzo. The dawn attack on the Hafid ridges was called off, but the 7th Armoured Brigade was soon heavily engaged by 5th Light, which came swinging round the left flank of the Division. By nightfall the 7th Armoured Brigade was down to just twenty-five tanks. Two of the Royal Tank Regiments, the 2nd and 6th – and the latter now had only nine of the new Crusaders still in action – had been forced to fight separate engagements all day and were then driven back east of the wire to refuel. Reginald (Sandy) Powell was captured at this time.

'We were involved in Operation Battleaxe on 15th June 1941. There were two wireless operators in our crew and I was the best gunner of the two, which later proved the luckiest position in the tank, as we were hit by an 88 which entered just in front of my feet, injuring the sub turret gunner; he subsequently died from his wounds. The driver was injured but not severely, just bruised. The wireless operator, who might well have been me, was severely wounded with shrapnel in his back. Also the Tank Commander was severely wounded in the back. As for myself, I did not even have a scratch, but the tank was on fire and I had to get out fast and help my mates with the aid of the driver. The only way was through the top. When I opened up and looked down, I was looking down the barrel of a German rifle and there was no hope of escape. Shaken, I ignored this and continued helping my mates out of the tank. The sub turret gunner was the first one I looked at but he turned to me and said, "Sorry Sandy, but I feel it is hopeless with me. Go and help the others," which I thought was a very courageous thing to say, but I did make him as comfortable as possible and checked up on the others. Both the wireless operator and the tank commander were in a very bad way, and I am afraid there was very little that I could do about it, except make them as comfortable as possible. I never saw them again, as the Germans got us together at a point in the centre of the area.'

Rommel took the withdrawal of the 2nd and 6th RTR as a sign that the left flank of the British advance was crumbling. That night, the 16th, he concentrated the 5th Light and 15th Panzer on his right flank and struck hard at the exposed left flank of 7th Armoured. This attack went in at 4.30 in the morning. Creagh had by now withdrawn his Divisional HQ to Alam el Fakhri, twenty-five miles east of the wire, well behind his forward units. From there he called up Beresford-Pierse on the radio, suggesting that the Corps Commander should come up and look at the situation. Their talk was intercepted by German listening posts, and Rommel records, 'It sounded suspiciously as if the British Commander no longer felt himself capable of handling the situation.' Thus encouraged, 15th Panzer and 5th Light struck north, cutting through 7th Armoured Div's lines, heading for the crux of the battle at the Halfaya Pass. The advance of these divisions was checked for a while by the depleted Matilda squadrons of the 4th Armoured Brigade, under Brigadier Alec Gatehouse, but the British forces were now in full retreat. By the morning of 17th June, 7th Armoured Division were back at Sofafi, thirty miles east of the wire, from where they had set out three days before and morale was not good. Losses were not large, less than a thousand men killed, wounded and missing, but ninety-one tanks had been lost and nearly eighty percent of the British tanks were out of action by the time the three-day operation ended. The Germans, with superior tanks, lost just twelve. Rommel and his men had out-guessed and out-fought the British, drawing the tanks onto their guns, notably the 88s and then counter-attacking with his Panzers. The British troops felt, with some reason, that their attack had not been well handled; the Germans always managed to appear in overwhelming strength, the new Crusaders were clearly inadequate against the 88s and 75 mm, and Rommel had apparently done whatever he wished to do and run rings around the British commanders. As the Royal Tank Regiment's history bitterly records, 'Battleaxe became a byword for blundering.'

The initial British assault at Halfaya simply provided tanks as targets for the 88s, for although Rommel had only a dozen of these terrible, high-velocity guns, they could shatter even a Matilda at 2,000 yards or more. The Desert soldiers were always wary of the 88s after 'Battle-Axe', and rightly so, but the Germans also had large numbers of the almost equally effective Pak 38, a long-barrelled 50mm anti-tank gun, with excellent sights and a range of 1,000 yards or more. This superiority in the quality and tactical deployment of anti-tank guns was to be a feature of the Afrika Korps throughout the Desert War. In terms of numbers, the British forces, in tanks and infantry, exceeded Rommel's, at least to begin with, and there are no reports here, as there were later, that the British 2pdr (40mm) tank gun was in any way inferior in hitting power to the 50mm mounted in the Panzer III although, as we have heard, it was outranged by the 75mm.

Winston Churchill was disappointed at the failure of Battleaxe, and in particular with the loss of the tanks sent out on the "Tiger" convoy. He was already discontented with General Wavell, as indeed he was to be discontented with many other generals throughout the war. Wavell was a taciturn man, and his temperament did not match that of the ever-optimistic Churchill, who could not see why the Desert Army did not sweep Rommel back from the frontier and out of Africa. Churchill now decided that Wavell must go. Four days later, General Wavell, who had done so well for so long with so little, was relieved of his command and sent to India, being replaced by General Sir Claude Auchinleck. Five months were to pass before the British attacked again.

5

Crusader
The Battle for Sidi Rezegh

JULY–DECEMBER 1941

Those who know how to win battles
are more numerous than those who know
how to make proper use of their victories.

Polybius

Between Operation Battleaxe in June 1941 and the next British assault, 'Operation Crusader', in November of the same year, both sides received considerable reinforcements in men and material, though both experienced great difficulties with supply. Rommel's main lifeline, from Naples to the port of Tripoli, was open to harassment by aircraft and submarines from the island fortress of Malta, while the British had the choice of either forcing convoys up the Mediterranean from Gibraltar under air attack the whole way, or taking the safer but longer haul, round the Cape and up the East Coast of Africa to Suez. On the whole, the British did rather better in this build-up phase. Auchinleck received another three motorized-infantry divisions and another ten armoured regiments before Crusader, reinforcements totalling another 115,000 men, though none of these was desert trained or fit for immediate operations.

The soldiers of the Desert Army had by now evolved their own dress, none of it smart, and some of it enough to give any peacetime RSM a first-class heart attack. The officers tended to sport fly-whisks and moustaches, corduroy trousers and civilian shirts, set off with Paisley silk scarves. Captain Clay, an Old Etonian and an officer in the 2nd

Royal Gloucestershire Hussars, was captured by the Italians in 1941, wearing ' . . . no badges of rank, but a golf jacket, a pink shirt into which was tucked a yellow silk scarf, a pair of green corduroy trousers and an expensive pair of suede boots.'

Much of this was sensible. Battledress soaked up sand which scratched at the neck and wrists and led to desert sores, while tropical kit was simply not warm enough during the desert nights. As a rule, the commanders did not care how the men dressed, provided their equipment functioned and their weapons were clean, and this popular desert attire was eventually recognized, if not by the higher authorities, then tacitly by the Army at large, through a popular series of cartoons featuring 'The Two Types', a pair of languid Army Officers, dressed much like Captain Clay. This cavalier attire did cause raised eyebrows among the new arrivals, but they were usually quick to adopt it.

Apart from fresh troops, new tanks arrived. The 'Valentine', originally designed as an infantry tank, was an improvement on the A10 cruiser, and a useful addition, though still armed only with a 2-pounder gun. The three regiments of Brigadier Alec Gatehouse's 4th Armoured Brigade, 3rd and 5th RTR plus the 8th Hussars, were re-equipped with the fast American 'General Stuart' light tank, popularly known as the 'Honey'. This tank had a good turn of speed – 36mph – and a high velocity 37mm gun, which had greater hitting power than the 2-pdr (40mm) then in general use throughout the British armoured regiments.

The 7th Armoured Brigade still consisted of the 2nd and 6th RTR and was made up to full strength with the addition of the 7th Hussars. This Brigade had some of the new Crusader tanks, but retained a number of A13s and even a few A10s. Another reinforcement for the Desert Army, and one which was to have a long-term effect on 7th Armoured Division, was the 22nd Armoured Brigade, which arrived in October and consisted of the 3rd and 4th County of London Yeomanry (CLY) and the 2nd Royal Gloucestershire Hussars (RGH), all three regiments being equipped with the fast, new Crusader tank.

The 11th Hussars were now equipped with Humber armoured cars and were joined in the Divisional Reconnaissance role by the King's Dragoon Guards and the 4th South African Armoured Car Regiment, which permitted one recce regiment for each brigade. The British also received good numbers of 3.7 inch anti-aircraft guns, a weapon which, if it had been supplied with armour-piercing ammunition, could have proved as devastating an anti-tank weapon as the German 88mm. This role had been suggested for the 3.7 inch by General Timothy Pile, who had been a tank officer before his removal to Head of Anti-Aircraft Command in the United Kingdom.

Rommel received only a number of medium Mark IIIs and the 90th Light Division, which arrived without tanks and very little transport of any kind. Constant pleas for more of the tank-busting 88s raised Rommel's total to just thirty-five by the opening of the 'Crusader' operation, though most of his anti-tank units now had the Pak-50, which was no mean weapon in skilled hands. The battle-hardened 5th Light Division received the newly arrived Mark III Panzers and changed their name to 21st Panzer Division. With that and the arrival of three indifferent Italian divisions, Rommel had to be content, his total forces now peaking at three German and six Italian Divisions. In addition, the British could now put 700 aircraft into the air, compared with the combined German and Italian total of 320. With all the advantages seemingly lying with the British, Winston Churchill was naturally insistent that Auchinleck should attack soon, not least because the Wehrmacht had attacked Russia in June 1941, and were already making great advances.

Auchinleck refused to advance until his troops were ready, and explained patiently and many times that tanks had to be prepared for desert warfare and troops made accustomed to desert conditions before either were of any use in the field; they could not simply march off the ship and into battle.

Auchinleck's autumn offensive, codenamed 'Crusader', had two aims: (1) to trap and destroy the enemy forces in Eastern Cyrenaica, and (2) to occupy Tripolitania and drive the enemy out of Africa. This would also ensure the relief of Tobruk. The forces to do this were the old Western Desert Force, much expanded and re-christened as the soon-to-be-famous Eighth Army, commanded now by Lt. General Sir Alan Cunningham, a brother of that Admiral Cunningham who commanded the Mediterranean Fleet. The Eighth Army consisted of two Corps, the old 13 Corps under Lt-General Godwin Austin, and the new 30 Corps under Lt-General Norrie; 30 Corps contained the 7th Armoured Division, now commanded by 'Straffer' Gott, who had replaced General Creagh after 'Battleaxe'; the 1st South African Division, and the 22 Guards Brigade. A full Order of Battle for 7th Armoured at the start of 'Crusader' is shown on the facing page. The tank strengths of the three armoured brigades at the start of 'Crusader' were: 7th Brigade 129, 4th Brigade 166, 22nd Brigade 158.

The plan for 'Crusader' was for 13 Corps to attack and pin down the enemy along the frontier wire from the Halfaya Pass to Sidi Omar, while

ORDER OF BATTLE
FOR SIDI REZEGH NOVEMBER 1941

4th Armoured Brigade
2nd RHA
8th Hussars
3rd RTR
5th RTR
2nd Scots Guards

7th Armoured Brigade
7th Hussars
2nd RTR
6th RTR

22nd Armoured Brigade
2nd Royal Gloucestershire
  Hussars
3rd County of London Yeomanry
  (Sharpshooters)
4th County of London Yeomanry
  (Sharpshooters)

Support Group
3rd RHA
4th RHA
1st KRRC
2nd Rifle Brigade
60th Field Regiment RA
One battery 51st Field Regiment
  RA

Divisional Troops
102nd RHA
King's Dragoon Guards
11th Hussars
4th South African Armoured Car
  Regiment
1st Light Anti-Aircraft Regiment
  RA
Divisional Signals

Royal Engineers
4th Field Squadron
143rd Field Park Squadron

RASC
No. 5 Company
No. 30 Company
No. 58 Company
No. 65 Company
No. 67 Company
No. 550 Company

RAMC
2nd Light Field Ambulance
13th Light Field Ambulance
15th Light Field Ambulance
7th Light Field Hygiene Section

RAOC
Divisional Workshops
Divisional Ordnance Field Park
  **In each Brigade and Support
  Group:**
  One Light Repair Section
  One Light Recovery Section
  One Ordnance Field Park
Light AA Regiment Workshops

30 Corps, which had the nine armoured regiments of 7th Armoured Division as a cutting edge, would hook around the desert flank and 'seek out and destroy' the German armour before relieving Tobruk. The task of 7th Armoured, in particular, was to advance and capture the airfields at Sidi Rezegh and El Adem, on the escarpment above Tobruk. Once the enemy were fully engaged, the Tobruk garrison would break out and join with Eighth Army to drive Rommel from Tripolitania.

At the start of 'Crusader', the available British tank forces outnumbered the Germans and Italians by a ratio of nine to four. Even if only gun-armed German Panzers are taken into account, the British still had a superiority of four to one. On the other hand, the Germans had Rommel. One of the wry post-Battleaxe jokes going round 8th Army at this time was that Hitler had telephoned Churchill and offered to remove Rommel from his command, provided Churchill left all his generals in place. Rommel was highly thought of on both sides of the wire, and General Auchinleck found it necessary to issue a Special Order to his commanders on the subject of the enemy general.

TO: All Commanders and Chief of Staff

FROM: Headquarters, BTE and MEF

There exists a real danger that our friend Rommel is becoming a kind of magician or bogey-man to our troops, who are talking far too much about him. He is by no means a superman, although he is undoubtedly very energetic and able. Even if he were a superman, it would still be highly undesirable that our men should credit him with supernatural powers.

I wish you to dispel by all possible means the idea that Rommel represents something more than an ordinary German general. The important thing now is to see to it that we do not always talk of Rommel when we mean the enemy in Libya. We must refer to 'the Germans' or 'the Axis powers' or 'the enemy' and not always keep harping on Rommel.

Please ensure that this order is put into immediate effect, and impress upon all Commanders that, from a psychological point of view, it is a matter of the highest importance.

C.J. Auchinleck
General
Comm-in-Chief, MEF

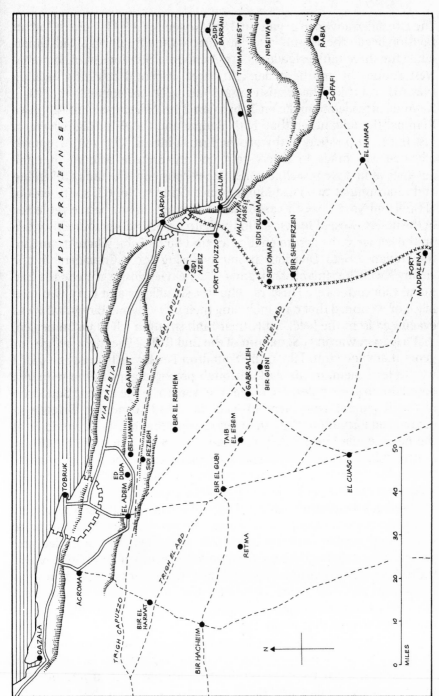

4 **The Crusader Battlefield**

The Crusader advance began on 18th November 1941. Fourth Indian Division began the assault, attacking across the wire north of Sidi Omar, while the three tank brigades of 7th Armoured Divisions hooked north-west round the southern flank in three dispersed columns heading towards Tobruk. The British attack actually pre-empted an attack Rommel intended to make on Tobruk on 23rd November, but this gave Rommel the advantage that 15th Panzer and the 90th Light were in just the right position to thwart the British attack. The 7th Armoured advance was made in heavy rain and by Brigade column, but the advance at first went well, against light opposition, the tanks refuelling and re-arming at two Field Maintenance Centres, No. 63, south-east of El Gubi and No. 65, south-east of Gabr Saleh, which had been established in the desert, west of the wire. On the 19th, the 22nd Armoured Brigade on the left were the first to engage around Bir el Gubi, where it ran into the Italian Ariete Division, promptly losing forty Crusaders to the enemy's well dug-in anti-tank guns. The heaviest losses were to the 2nd Royal Gloucestershire Hussars, who lost six officers and forty-two men killed or wounded that day, including their C.O. Colonel Birley, who was evacuated from the field, while their tank strength fell to just nineteen.

R. Godwin was in H Squadron of the 2nd RGH. 'The night before our general advance into Libya, the Squadron Leader instructed me that I was to lead them, in the dark, through prepared gaps in the wire to a petrol dump some miles into Libya. We were to be the leading Squadron of the Regiment who were to lead the 22nd Armoured Brigade in arrowhead formation. Only then did I realise that our tank would be at the head, while immediately behind were 15cwt trucks with Military Police, full of metal rods some six feet or so in length with metal triangular flags painted red, which they used to mark the route which would become the centre line of the Brigade advance.

'Having duly got through the wire and having completed the necessary distance of the leg, I failed to find the petrol dumps, but they were fortunately located close by in a wadi to my left. We re-fuelled and proceeded on two further legs, to come round south of Bir el Gubi, where the Italian Ariete Division were holding a strongpoint approximately 75 miles from our start point. Here we were, going into action the next day, the 19th, with the feeling that our tanks were invincible and that they were ours until the war ended.

'Little navigation was done again on the same scale, but limited to moving into position in the line usually at night. Later a fair area of desert was gridded using petrol drums with poles set in and given a number, while maps were issued having this grid, so that one could reasonably navigate between these markers. The main navigation was carried out by the regimental Navigator, who remained out of any action but closely plotting the movement of the Regiment, which, once engaged, would quickly become disorientated as these early battles tended to emulate Naval actions with tanks milling around all over the place, raising minor sandstorms.

'Now we were to move into action for the first time at Bir el Gubi. Our Squadron having dealt with some six Italian tanks who were forward of their main positions with a loss of three tanks to ourselves, were quickly regrouped with G Squadron now to lead while we were moved to the left flank.

'We had no experience of battle, neither had our Regular Army leader, who had spent years on theoretical TEWTs, possibly with horses. Sadly, it seems now, we made what amounted to a cavalry charge on these prepared Italian anti-tank positions. In general terms we went in at Regimental strength, and by dark that day were reduced to about Squadron strength ... albeit the Ariete Division never produced any threat again. The main problem had been that we had overrun anti-tank positions who had wanted to surrender, but we were 'green' and without infantry support to take prisoners, the anti-tank gunners re-assumed their positions and went into action again, putting us in a cross-fire situation. We were later strafed by CR42 Italian fighters.

'On advancing the next day, the 20th, towards Sidi Rezegh, a German forward aerodrome, my Crusader tank broke down with a problem which so many of us experienced, that is, the idler sprocket tensioner on the twin fan drive jumped off and dropped into the bottom of the tank engine compartment, causing the fans to stop and the sealed cooling system rapidly overheated, causing a high pitched whistle as the steam escaped through the safety valve. Here then, we find our lovely Crusader tanks with a V 12 Rolls Royce engine and a silly little 2-pdr gun, only effective at a maximum of eight hundred yards, while the enemy was able to knock us out at fifteen hundred yards.

'Having been repaired by Squadron fitters, we set off with two other tanks to rejoin the Regiment at Sidi Rezegh. We were attacked by three Stukas *en route*, who could only record near misses, fortunately for us. This was our first experience of being dive bombed.'

Sgt. Gibson (Tony) Towns was in G Squadron, the 2nd RGH. 'Our first action was on 18th November 1941 at El Gubi, a place more remembered by the Italian Veterans Associations than by us. In fact, they call their main North African Group the El Gubi Association. Our first targets were, in fact, Italian M13 tanks. Our tank survived the day, although a deep groove in the turret marked a near miss.

'The next day, the 20th, we moved to attack Sidi Rezegh airfield and met a group of German Mark IIIs and IVs. We were heavily fired upon and eventually lost a complete track. Before we had decided to bale out, Sgt. Jock Anderson drove up, reversed to us, jumped out and under heavy fire hitched us up to his tank with a towrope and towed us away. For this immensely brave action he was awarded a well-deserved MM. Our driver, Guy Payne, was, of course, unable to steer the tank and we were pulled from side to side on the single towrope. Suddenly, under this uncontrollable motion, we saw, to our horror, that we were swerving towards a slit-trench in which was a South African infantryman. The poor bloke seemed mesmerized, and we were helpless. I can still see the whites of his staring eyes as we lumbered towards him. At the last moment he galvanized himself into action and tried to climb out of the slit trench, but stepped on the rim and fell under our remaining track. The remorseless steel tore off his leg at the knee. We managed to alert Sgt. Anderson and jumped out of the tanks to give first-aid. Someone put a tourniquet on his thigh and we gave him some morphia from the tank kit. Fortunately, among the vehicles swanning about was an ambulance, which took the unfortunate soldier away. I had the unpleasant task of burying his leg.

'Later, when we stopped, we found Guy Payne's shirt soaked with blood. A hit on the tank had sheared off a rivet inside, which had ricocheted and given him a deep flesh wound. He was sent off to the nearest FDS, which, through the ironies of war was immediately overrun and he was captured.

'It was decided to get another tow to the fitters in order to get another track fitted. When we found them, I was left in charge of the tank. Suddenly we were heavily shelled and hordes of vehicles streamed past us. This was the beginning of the famous November Handicap, when Rommel got among the rear echelons. When the shelling was added to by bursts of machine gun bullets, we had no option but to join in. The fitter sergeant ordered us to get on the 15cwt truck, but before doing so, I dropped a grenade down the turret of our lovely first tank. I jumped on the 15cwt, but within a few yards it hit such a bump that it threw me off and nobody noticed. Luckily I was only dazed and, picking myself up, I spotted a tank transporter, which gave me a lift. It was slow but it got us to safety and later I rejoined the Squadron.'

The 7th Armoured Brigade in the centre column swiftly overran the airfield at Sidi Rezegh on 20th November, the 6th RTR capturing and destroying a number of German aircraft. By the time the 7th Brigade moved up to the escarpment overlooking the plain before Tobruk, on which stood the tomb of Sidi Rezegh, the enemy had brought up infantry and anti-tank guns to bar the only track down. Meanwhile, the 4th Armoured Brigade, the right flank column, were advancing to the Trigh Capuzzo, where they were attacked by a German Panzer battle group, Battlegroup Stephan, of 100 tanks and infantry. All three brigades of 7th Armoured were now in action, but all were widely separated when the German counter-attacks came in.

The right flank column, the 4th Armoured Brigade, had been in action almost from the start, and faced the dual task of having to protect the flanks of the centre column (7th Armoured Brigade) and 13 Corps, as it advanced further north. The 8th Hussars were attacked by the German battle group and lost twenty tanks before dark on the 19th, knocking out only three on the German side. This attack was delivered by a German Panzer force, Battlegroup Stephan, hastily formed from a regiment of 21st Panzer when Rommel realized the British were making a major advance. This was only the first of several counter-attacks that were to come in against the scattered Brigades of 7th Armoured. On 20th November, Cambrai Day, the enemy counter-attacked at Sidi Rezegh and the 7th Brigade could barely hang on to the airfield until the Divisional Support Group, commanded by Brigadier Jock Campbell, came up that evening, by which time the great armoured battle of Sidi Rezegh was well under way.

On 21st November, the battle around the airfield at Sidi Rezegh grew in ferocity. The whole weight of 15th Panzer Division fell on the left of 4th Armoured Brigade, driving it south, and by sunset the 4th Brigade was down to just ninety-eight tanks – the Germans had lost a total of seven in the last two days, recovering many damaged or broken-down tanks each night. Seventh Armoured Brigade and the Support Group still held the airfield, but the Germans were mustering quantities of tanks and anti-tank guns to the west of the airfield and preparing to renew the fight. This fight for the airfield and the ridge north of the airfield would decide the outcome of the battle, because whoever held the ridge at Sidi Rezegh controlled the Trigh Capuzzo and dominated the plain before Tobruk. The KRRC and the 6th Field Regiment R.A., with 25-pounders, took up positions just south of the airfield, and were in action for most of the day. At mid-day on the 20th, General Cunningham had instructed the 22nd Armoured Brigade to turn east from El Gubi and help the embattled 4th, which had returned to refuel and re-arm near Gabr Saleh, but this help came too late. Twenty-two Brigade were short of fuel and could not reach the 4th Brigade position, south of Sidi Rezegh, until nightfall on the 20th.

R. Godwin continues: 'Daylight showed innumerable German tanks forming up, and later that day we found ourselves in disarray, almost surrounded with Germans, having broken through the 4th South African Brigade, and in the late afternoon one other tank and ourselves were running the gauntlet in an endeavour to get clear. I lost contact with the other tank, but suddenly in front was an officer with his field cap back to front and waving to slow us down. This we did, and he leapt onto the side of the tank, grabbing hold of the bedding rolls and dragging himself across to the rear of the turret as we rapidly picked up speed, but only to be hit on the offside rear by a shot from an anti-tank gun on the rear of a lorry. The shot, penetrating the radiator, ricocheted off the righthand rockerbox and lifted the engine covers. Fortunately we made it clear of the action before the engine died, finding ourselves in company with a South African armoured car and one other tank. The officer we rescued turned out to be the Second-in-Command of the 4th County of London Yeomanry. The officer in the armoured car was badly wounded in the leg and was nursed through the night with the help of chloroform, which we carried in rather large glass flasks, only protected with cotton wool. It was a bright moonlit night and the enemy commenced spraying the whole area with machine guns, but we were outside their line of fire. Suddenly, we were aware of German tanks coming directly towards us, in line and obviously going into close leaguer. We lay alongside our tank in the foot-wide shadow afforded by the moonlight, and when only about two hundred yards away they suddenly turned right, which was roughly east, and moved out of sight.

'The next day, at first light, we set off eastwards, trying to get information through the wireless and having got an approximate location of our units, we suddenly ran into a South African unit, who had a Medical Officer with them and we were able to get the wounded officer into care. We heard some months later that, although he had lost a leg, he had survived. Having earlier picked up a 3-tonner which turned out to be an officers' ration truck with a South African driver, we transferred from the tank on which we had been riding onto the lorry, and finally rejoined the remnants of the Squadron and found that we were the last crew to be accounted for. Very shortly afterwards, on the 23rd November, vehicles started to run through us at speed, and they were followed by German tanks who had broken through to the echelons who had no protection, and as more and more vehicles joined to outrun the tanks, the whole thing later became known as "The November Handicap". I saw one lorry loaded with ammunition hit a

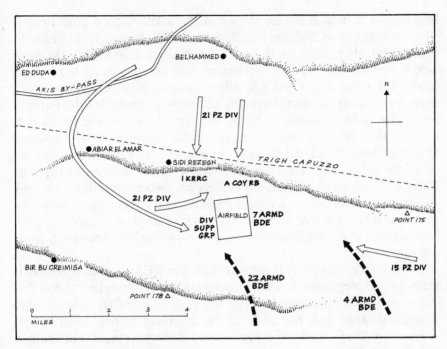

5 The First Day of Sidi Rezegh

slit trench at speed, rise into the air and crash down with a very, very, bent chassis, but still going.'

On the night of 21st/22nd November, Rommel realized Crusader was an all-out attack and decided to delay his assault on Tobruk and drive a wedge between the two British Corps, at their axis around Sidi Rezegh. Therefore, disengaging from the battered 4th and 22nd Armoured Brigades at dawn on the 21st, 15th and 21st Panzer were sent to attack the Support Group and the 7th Armoured Brigade, which still held the airfield at Sidi Rezegh. This force was preparing to assault the German forces on the ridge north of the airfield, when the two Panzer Divisions fell on their rear. A whirling tank and infantry battle then broke out around the airfield and the ridge. The 7th Hussars were overrun and almost wiped out by 21st Panzer, while the anti-tank guns of 15th Panzer eliminated the tanks of the 2nd Royal Tanks who were attempting to defend the soft-skinned transport of the Support Group and the 7th Armoured Brigade. When the KRRC, supported by a company of the 2nd Rifle Brigade and the 6th RTR and artillery attacked the Sidi Rezegh ridge, they suffered severely from machine-gun and anti-tank fire. In this action, Rifleman Beeley of the KRRC won a posthumous Victoria Cross. The 2nd and 6th Royal Tank Regiments took a terrible beating, but they also took the ridge, although the German tanks were able to destroy a great deal of transport and equipment on the airfield before the 22nd Armoured and 4th Armoured Brigades, hurrying up from the south in support, were able to intervene and drive the Panzers away. The KRRC infantry were on the ridge by noon and the British artillery then began to engage enemy traffic along the Trigh Capuzzo. Unfortunately, Lt-Colonel de Salis, of the KRRC, lacked the men to hold all of the ridge, and had to concentrate around the only high point, Point 167, where they hung on as German forces re-occupied the rest of the escarpment. There was fighting all over the Sidi Rezegh area, but the man who appeared to be in the thick of most of it was Brigadier Jock Campbell of the Support Group, whose exploits appear in most accounts.

Frank Black was at Sidi Rezegh with the RHA: 'I was a despatch rider with 3 Regiment RHA, the Regiment being attached to the 7th Armoured Division throughout all the long years of the war. At Sidi Rezegh, so great was the effort of the Regiment in that most hellish week of my life, that after the war ended, J Battery were officially named Sidi Rezegh 'J' Battery. In that particular battle, within twenty-four hours I was a D.R. (in my 8cwt Morris PU); our ambulance was set on fire, so I was then a medic, ferrying casualties to the rear; the same afternoon I was pushed into a fox-hole with the 1st KRRs. The enemy were massing on the airstrip. They dropped a creeping barrage on us but fortunately didn't follow up, thinking we were stronger than we were. So everybody in the Sidi Rezegh battles had to be ready to do anything when called. It was during this action that I stood alongside Jock Campbell, when he earned his VC. In this case he climbed on the large ACV, firing a Verey pistol at a gaggle of Hurricanes which had attacked the wrong side. During this foray we lost our M.O. Campbell was fearless, he actually led some tanks into action in a staff car!'

Hugh Barrow was a Captain, later Major, in the 4th RHA at Sidi Rezegh: 'Eighth Army, newly named and hitherto known as Western Desert Force, launched Operation Crusader at dawn on 18th November 1941. The battles round one of its first objectives, the airfield south-east of the tomb marked as Sidi Rezegh on the maps, continued until 7th December, with little respite for the formations involved. The overall aim of the operation was to enable the beleaguered garrison of Tobruk to break out. This account of what befell my small OP party and our escort on one day, 22nd November, is a sort of vignette to be seen against the backcloth of the whole operation.

'We were the "eyes" of the four guns of D Troop in (Jerboa) Battery RHA, one of the three Batteries of 4th Regiment Royal Horse Artillery. The Regiment was part of 7th Support Group in 7th Armoured Division – the Desert Rats. The Division was in 30 Corps which, with 13 Corps, formed the 8th Army. So, what is written here, two years after the events described, when I was on the voyage home, is a worm's-eye view; it's what happened to the four of us in our Morris 8 cwt truck – the Gunner OP vehicle – as we manoeuvred our way in and out of a considerable mêlée.

'The thrust on Sidi Rezegh by the 7th Armoured Division, working on 8th Army's southern flank, had been made about four days before (18th Nov 1941). The 1st Bn. KRRC had finally secured the landing ground and the escarpment on its north, which dropped down to the Tobruk bypass. In the shifting chances of battle they had, in turn, been dislodged, with heavy casualties, by some 70 enemy tanks thrusting in on their left and rear.

'An enemy attack could be expected from the north, primarily – but as always, like naval warfare, every flank was in fact open to danger. With enough foresight to see beyond the obvious, one could realise that the dangerous flank was any one *but* the north. However, that one had to be watched. Jerboa Battery's guns were in action some three miles south of the escarpment – zero line, due north – giving a range of 6–7,000 yards to the aerodrome. Two years have elapsed, and I am not sure which Battalion was with us forming 'Currie Columns'. (John Currie commanded 4 RHA.) It was probably the 2nd Bn of the Rifle Brigade, as 1 KRRC were no more, and there was a battery of 3 RHA (M, D or J), anti-tank 2-pounders mounted on portees. They, as usual, provided the escorts for the OPs – a section of 2-pounders (2 guns) and probably 2 sections of a motor-platoon (2 x 15 cwt trucks with an NCO and six men), armed with rifles and Bren guns, or perhaps a section of carriers.

'At dawn the two OPs, mine was the left (western) one, moved north to the escarpment, reporting nothing of great import, but a few vehicles moving in the area of the landing ground, sorting out the debris of earlier fighting, and slight, general enemy movement north of our escarpment.

'Jimmy Barton of 7 Bty (they were in our sister column), was within 200 yards of me, the right-hand OP of that column. We had joined 7th Armoured together in June and had much in common – our age, a love of the university, though his was Cambridge, and mutual friends – he was a Rugbeian. The next summer, through almost rash bravery, Jimmy was killed and awarded an MC posthumously.

'Our crews started to prepare breakfast, awaited with eager impatience on those November mornings of great-coats, Balaclava helmets, three pullovers, a scarf or two, gloves, and a thick shirt and vest. If I remember aright, one didn't discard much of that throughout the day. The value of an armoured OP vehicle for gunners had lately been appreciated, and the scale raised to three per Battery. Jerboa had only two before the battle. I had lost the toss with Dudley Smith, the other Troop Commander, and had only a Morris 8 cwt truck, but in a fluctuating battle I was glad of its speed and smallness. Both the Marmon Harringtons had already been hit, one of them beyond repair. These Morris 8s would go anywhere, though with only 2-wheel drive, and had the single fault of a susceptibility to petrol stoppages and autovac trouble. We had lately had hectic moments under long range machine gun fire and inaccurate shelling, when our only method of making our base as an armoured column relentlessly pursued us, had been to drive 400 yards, stop and tinker for temporary repair, proceed with all speed for another quarter of a mile, tinker, proceed, tinker and proceed . . . and so on. On the windscreen frame glinted a small but disquietening scar, I remember, which had not been there twenty-four hours before, and which unsettled me whenever I sat and gazed at it.'

The full weight of the Afrika Korps now concentrated on the 7th Armoured Brigade and the Support Group, to the south of the airfield. Fifty German tanks attacked the 7th Hussars and the other 2nd Rifle Brigade companies, preceded by artillery fire and dive-bombers. Lt. Ward Gunn of the 3rd RHA fought his battery to the last here, maintaining the only gun, with the Battery Commander, Major Pinney, and the Battery NCO, Sergeant Grey, acting as loaders until he was killed. Like Rifleman Beeley, Lt. Ward Gunn was awarded a posthumous Victoria Cross.

By 1600 hrs on the 21st, the 7th Brigade could only muster forty tanks of various kinds and the burden of the battle on the airfield fell on the Support Group, and scattered elements of various regiments and battalions, constantly mustered and remustered by Brigadier Jock Campbell, who led his men back into the attack again and again, standing in his open staff car.

At dawn on 22nd November, the battered Brigades of 7th Armoured Division were deployed as follows: the Support Group were holding the airfield with troops and some tanks of the 6 RTR deployed to the north, east and west. Two miles to the south lay the remaining seventy-nine Crusader tanks of the 22nd Armoured Brigade. The 4th Armoured Brigade lay six miles further to the south-east, near Bir el Reghem. Nothing was left of the 7th Armoured Brigade except twelve tanks of the 2nd Royal Tanks and nine of the 7th Hussars, which were now under the control of Brigadier Campbell's hard fighting Group on the airfield. All these survivors were very short of ammunition and fuel, but as ever, the RASC came through.

Rick Hall was now a sergeant in 10 Company RASC, ferrying ammunition up to the tanks. 'We had a Divisional Forward Ammo Point, feeding the Forward Ammo Point up the front. We kept to the desert to avoid the Messerschmidts which patrolled the tracks and liked nothing better than strafing ammo lorries. Dispersal was the answer – there was no cover – so every lorry stayed 200 yards or more from the others.

'Our day might start with a cup of tea, with sand in it, at about 3 am. Move up to the tanks and replenish, maybe by 4 or 5 am. They'd radio what they wanted, like more 2-pounder ammo, or 75mm later on. The tanks always moved out of leaguer at dawn, after "bombing-up" as they called it. Then a third of Tour column would go back to the FAP. It varied, but that was the routine ... it might be tanks ammo, it might be 25-pounders for the artillery, either way you had two and a half tons of it to unload by hand and as quick as you could, and in the open desert. The enemy had big tanks out there. When we had to pull out I saw tank tracks a foot wide, and then Rommel broke through and all the transport came streaming back, but only the new blokes were worried. The rest of us had seen it all before and we saw it again before it was over. We drove south and then west around the enemy – the desert is a big place, and we soon got over the panic of the November Handicap, as they called it.'

Neville Gillman was now a Squadron Quartermaster with the 4th CLY: 'Our first action was during the Crusader Operation, when the brigade went in at Bir-el-Gubi, south-east of Tobruk. I was still with B echelon, ferrying up petrol in Bedford three-tonners and Chevrolet 4-wheel drive trucks. Our petrol cans were bloody useless and leaked like sieves, and German "Jerry" cans were considered good loot, though we didn't find many. My memories of El Gubi are pretty hazy, it was so chaotic. I knew that 4th CLY put in a cavalry charge in tanks against the Ariete anti-tank guns and had a lot of casualties. Then, some days later, Rommel slammed in his right hook round the south and that caused the so-called November Handicap, a mass rush of all the transport in all directions before the German tanks, mostly to the east. At one time I got within 50 yards of a column before I realised they were Germans. We just kept going and so did they, eyes front and pretending not to see each other. All the transport was mixed up. We used their trucks and they used ours. We used to leaguer every night and finding the leaguer could be difficult. When we were bringing up supplies and knew we were near, we would put up a Verys light – a "toffee apple" – and the tanks would give us a bearing. I remember one night a friend of mine, Teddy Bradbury, had a truck run over a mine and set on fire, and a voice on the wireless said, "Can you see that bright light?" And Teddy replied, plaintively, "I am that bright light."'

During the night of 21st/22nd November, the German forces had also withdrawn some distance to the north-west, to re-organize and replenish with petrol and ammunition, as a preliminary to another thrust against the British next day, but as dawn broke, the Support Group could see a large group of enemy vehicles, including some eighty tanks, mustering 4,000 yards to the north. These were immediately engaged by the 25-pdrs of the 60th Field Regiment, urged on by Brigadier Campbell, who even turned up here to lend a hand with the guns. Events opened with a spirited attack by the twelve remaining 2nd Royal Tanks on this enemy column, an attack led, yet again, by Brigadier Campbell in his staff car, ' ... waving flags and encouraging the tanks on.' The enemy wheeled into line and met this assault with heavy fire and no sooner had the British withdrawn than heavy firing broke out all around the airfield. Enemy tanks had come up from the west and were now engaging the Support Group, while German infantry attacked from the escarpment. This German assault took the Support Group by surprise and it took strenuous efforts to stave off the German advance. At one point in the engagement, Brigadier Campbell was seen, ' ... loading and firing an anti-tank gun at the advancing enemy, with the crew dead or wounded around the gun.' For his gallantry and leadership at Sidi Rezegh, Brigadier Campbell was later awarded the Victoria Cross.

The fight between the Support Group and the tank force from 21st Panzer spread all across the airfield, which was now a litter of burning aircraft, knocked-out tanks, shattered guns and dead or wounded infantry. The smoke and dust of battle concealed events from 22nd Armoured Brigade which, with what remained of 4th Armoured, was now ordered to assist. Their attack came in against a screen of German anti-tank guns, and in spite of Brigadier Campbell's efforts to sort matters out, confusion soon reigned, as lone tanks and troops roamed about in the smoke and dust, seeking to engage the enemy or locate their own units.

It was late afternoon before some order was at last restored. The remnants of the three Armoured Brigades and the Support Group gradually withdrew to another ridge, south of the airfield which 22nd Armoured Brigade had occupied that morning. At about 1700 hrs, two regiments, the 3rd and 5th Royal Tanks, were ordered back to the airfield to assist in the removal of the 25-pdr field guns, which were being threatened by enemy infantry advancing from the edge of the escarpment. The diary of the 5th Royal Tanks states that this effort 'proved futile', for their light tanks were outgunned by the German Panzers, and while they were away from the southern ridge the 4th Brigade endured a further blow when 15th Panzer came up and struck their rear, scattering the 8th Hussars and killing most of the staff of Brigade HQ. After an hour of intense fighting, the 8th Hussars were left with just eight Honeys fit to fight, the Germans capturing no less than 35 by this sudden onslaught. Those remaining were withdrawn into close leaguer, which was then attacked by German tanks and infantry.

While the 7th Armoured Division were hotly engaged at Sidi Rezegh, the other units of 8th Army had not been idle. 70th Division had broken out of the Tobruk perimeter and were advancing on El Duda, though the 2nd Black Watch lost a great many men attacking German positions at the point of the bayonet. Trooper Page was in Tobruk at this time:

'The leading infantry were the 2nd Black Watch, and their Pipers walked ahead of the infantry, playing their pipes. There were heavy losses but we captured a large number of German troops.'

13 Corps had crossed the wire and were pushing west, led by New Zealand infantry and some infantry tanks, and on the night of 22nd/23rd November, the 6th New Zealand Brigade overran the Afrika Korps HQ, capturing most of the staff, though not General Cruwell or his greatly valued Chief-of-Staff Oberst – Leutnant Bayerlin. Nevertheless, this loss of command and communications by the Afrika Korps was of great help to the embattled British forces.

By dawn on 23rd November, 7th Armoured Division was in considerable disarray. 4th Armoured Brigade was scattered, 7th Armoured Brigade was reduced to fifteen tanks, 22nd Armoured could muster just thirty-four Crusaders and the Support Group had been virtually shattered. It was now vital to concentrate these scattered elements before Rommel struck again, for as Rommel later remarked to a captive British officer: 'What difference does it make to me if you have two tanks to my one, if you send them out and let me smash them in detail. You presented me with three brigades in succession.'

General Norrie attempted to reform 30 Corps behind the southern ridge at Sidi Rezegh on 23rd November, screened from the airfield by the 5th South African Brigade and 22nd Armoured Brigade, helped by the 1st South African Brigade which was then coming up. Rommel had other ideas. He sent 21st Panzer to hold the escarpment, while 15th Panzer with the Ariete wheeled away to the south-west and came back from El Gubi into the flank and rear of 30 Corps, producing terrific confusion, and the November Handicap, the hurried flight east of the South African transport and the forward element of the 1st South African Brigade. This left the 5th South African Brigade and the 22nd Armoured Brigade to take the main weight of the German assault. By nightfall the 5th South African Brigade had been annihilated and 22 Armoured Brigade was down to its last, battered, twenty tanks. During the night of the 23rd/24th great efforts were made by both sides to repair and restore tanks left on the battlefield, but when daylight came on the 24th, the victory seemed to lie with Rommel, who proceeded to exploit it.

Most of 30 Corps were now withdrawing rapidly to the east, the retreating British and the advancing Germans all mixed up in glorious disorder ... 'the desert was covered with scores of vehicles all moving east at their best speed,' while Brigadier Campbell and the 11th Hussars roved among the scattered groups and transport convoys attempting to bring troops, squadrons or parts of squadrons back together again.

The Germans, who were enjoying the additional and unusual advantage of good wireless communications, gradually drew out of this mêlée and rallied to the south west, where they attacked and scattered the remaining infantry of the 5th South African Brigade. This brought on another whirlwind engagement when the remaining Crusaders of the 4th County of London Yeomanry and a Squadron of the 2nd RGH swept in to the South Africans' assistance. Twenty-second Armoured Brigade had now been reduced to little more than a composite regiment made up of the remnants of the 3rd and 4th CLY and the 2nd RGH, and they swept in again and again, but by nightfall the 5th South African Brigade had disintegrated, losing over 3000 men and most of its equipment. That night what was left of the three Armoured Brigades leaguered near the airfield at Sidi Rezegh while the Support Group mustered at Gabr Saleh.

If Rommel had returned to the attack on 24th November, the Division might have been wiped out, but Rommel decided that as he had given

30 Corps such a caning, he could now risk slipping past 13 Corps and making a dash for the Egyptian frontier. The first Battle of Sidi Rezegh was over, and 'Rommel's Raid' had begun.

On 25th November, Rommel's leading elements crossed the wire and entered Egypt for the first time, fanning out to north and south, their columns shadowed, as ever, by the 11th Hussars. The one advantage for 7th Armoured in this was that Rommel's advance to the east left them in his rear, with time to recover tanks abandoned at Sidi Rezegh and restore the three Armoured Brigades to some sort of order. Order was slowly being restored to all parts of the battlefield and this stiffening resistance, plus the exhaustion of his men and supplies, forced Rommel to turn about and fight his way back to the west. By some fortunate mischance, Rommel's troops failed to discover either of the two British Field Maintenance Centres, which were crammed with food and petrol and would have given him all he needed. Even so, Rommel's brief appearance in Egypt led to General Sir Alan Cunningham being relieved of his command and he was replaced as head of the 8th Army by General Ritchie.

For the next three days, both sides, while clashing continually, were mainly engaged in equipping and regrouping. One of the noticeable features of the Desert War was the resilience displayed by both sides, an ability to recover from a defeat quickly, helped by the fact that the other side was equally exhausted and equally low on supplies. The 4th Armoured Brigade, for example, though scattered and low in reserves on 23rd November had re-organized and received thirty-six new tanks by the 26th, bringing their tank strength up to seventy-seven. A scouring of the battlefield by tank recovery teams led to the discovery and repair of no less than seventy broken down or lightly damaged tanks, and the strength of 22nd Armoured Brigade rose to a useful fifty.

Rommel then returned from his dash across the frontier and took up the fight again at Sidi Rezegh; the battle was far from over, but since few battles can be so confusing as those around Sidi Rezegh, it might be an idea to look at the state of play on 30th November, two weeks into an operation that still had a month to go. The battle was being fought all over the desert, from Sidi Rezegh to Capuzzo. On 30th November, 4th Armoured Brigade was supporting the New Zealanders and the 1st South African Brigade near Bir Reghem, where they engaged the Ariete and destroyed nineteen tanks. The Support Group were busy around Capuzzo, harassing German transport and infantry.

R. Godwin recalls this time for the 2nd RGH: 'We were involved in many varied actions, mostly nibbling away at enemy flanks until, at the end of December 1941, we were near Agedabia, about one hundred miles south of Benghazi, when we were relieved and transported back for a rest and leave in Cairo. One of the many actions I recall was when we came across a German armoured unit who had been pulled out for a rest and re-fit. We were able for once to get in really close, but again we were heavily outgunned and soon lost the early initiative. The Squadron Leader with others was knocked out. His sergeant driver was killed as was his gunner. Others managed to recover his tank and bring it out of the action. I rejoined as they were hurriedly burying the driver, but we were being harassed, and so the gunner was lifted up onto my tank and we brought him back into close leaguer that night, although we were heavily attacked by Stukas as we made our way eastwards. We buried the gunner in the close leaguer that night. A rough cross was made by someone who surprisingly had some wood among his kit, and so he was left alone in an area of the desert, which I have always felt may never have had a foot over it since. A quick tot of rum, maintenance and a return to Brigade for further instructions.

'Generally speaking, action broke off at dusk and unless there was a moon, it became dark quickly. The nightly routine was then to move into line to form a close leaguer for the night. This may well take an hour and the crews would be smothered in fine sand from the tank immediately in front as it was necessary in the darkness to drive very tightly together. Sand in the hair and clothing, stuck to the daytime sweat with insufficient water to wash properly – we usually shaved in the tea dregs. Quite impossible to wear eye protection with the result that eyelids had to be unstuck each morning from the adhesive formed from the natural secretions of the eyes and the sand. Very often the line would break when, following a halt for whatever reason, a crew may well nod off with total weariness and wake up to find the tank in front had moved on. Usually the tank commander would then jump down and hopefully follow the tracks in the sand, very often to find that they were only yards away. Finally, getting into leaguer was an opportunity for maintenance, and the troop sergeant, which I now was, had to ensure that rations were up from the 'A' echelon (who were generally excellent in arriving wherever we may be), see that petrol and ammunition was topped up and organize the guard, which everyone shared, in order to reduce the length of time on guard duty to a minimum. Usually, by this time, most crews were ready for whatever sleep was possible, which left little time to wander and chat. I recall on one occasion, when the petrol finally arrived it was in fifty gallon drums, and there was only one four-gallon tin in the whole of the Squadron, and it took all night to refuel. Any meal at this time usually consisted of bully-beef and biscuits with salty water, being unable to brew up in the dark.'

On 3rd December the 4th Armoured Brigade supported the 11th Indian Brigade's attack on El Gubi, after which, his men and machines worn out, Rommel began a slow retreat to the west, a retreat that went on until 27th December, by which time the German forces had been moved – one can hardly say driven – from Cyrenaica, and back inside the boundaries of Tripolitania. Seventh Armoured Brigade followed Rommel as he withdrew to the west, the four Armoured Car Regiments of the Division, 12th Lancers, The Royals, the KDGs and the 11th Hussars harassing his columns and shooting up his soft transport, their efforts limited by the shortage of petrol. The Support Group was still in the field, although as the Divisional History recalls, it was now but a shadow of its former self. The 1st KRRC remnants had gone back to Egypt, the 2nd Rifle Brigade had lost fifty percent of its officers, and was forced to amalgamate some companies, and the Artillery Regiments, the 60th Field and the 3rd and 4th RHA had lost many of their officers and men. The 3rd Royal Tanks handed over their remaining vehicles to the 22nd Armoured Brigade, and the Division withdrew from the desert, with the Headquarters entering Cairo in early January 1942. It had been a very close-run thing, but Rommel had been driven away, as far west as Agadabia and the Tobruk garrison was once again linked to the rest of the Army. By constant fighting throughout the 'Crusader' operation, General Auchinleck and the 8th Army could claim a victory on points.

6

Gazala and the Cauldron

JANUARY—JULY 1942

It is not a field or a few acres of ground
we are defending, but a cause, and whether
we defeat the enemy in one battle or by degrees,
the consequences will be the same.

Thomas Paine

Following the 'Crusader' battles, the Germans and Italians withdrew
west as far as Agedabia. Both sides then settled into defensive positions
and there was a certain licking of wounds, though Rommel received
reinforcements on 5th January 1942, which brought the Afrika Korps'
tank strength up to 111 machines. Rommel never enjoyed overall
superiority in manpower or equipment, and 111 tanks was a small
enough force, even in 1942, but given Rommel's aggressive outlook,
this reinforcement was sufficient for his purpose. Thus encouraged,
he counter-attacked the British forces on 21st January. His renewed
offensive took the British by surprise, for General Auchinleck had been
fairly confident that he had done enough in Crusader to make even
Rommel pause, stating in a despatch that it was 'highly unlikely' that
Rommel would attack again in the near future. Auchinleck, too, had
received reinforcements, and the newly arrived British 1st Armoured
Division came up into the Desert to relieve the very tired 7th Armoured
Division, which returned to Cairo.

Back in the Delta, the Support Group of 7th Armoured – which soon
afterwards became the 7th Motor Brigade – held a Memorial Service in
Cairo Cathedral, an event preceded by the the presentation of Brigadier

Jock Campbell's well-earned VC for his inspiring leadership at Sidi Rezegh. Campbell had been promoted General and succeeded Gott as Commander of the 7th Armoured Division when General Gott went to command 13 Corps. Two weeks later, General Campbell was killed in a motor accident in a car driven by Lt Roy Farran of the 3rd Hussars. His death was a bitter blow to 7th Armoured, a great loss to all in 8th Army, and he was succeeded in command of 7th Armoured by General Messervy, formerly of the 4th Indian Division, who had been briefly in command of the newly arrived 1st Armoured. In April, the 11th Hussars were sent east to Mosul and Iraq and were, therefore, not with the Division when Rommel advanced again.

The Italian convoy, which arrived in Tripoli in January, brought Rommel fifty-five tanks, mostly Pz Mark IIIs and IVs. Nineteen of these Panzer IIIs were the (J) Specials mounting a long 55mm gun, with a penetration 50 percent better than the short 55mm. Reconnaissance had revealed that 1st Armoured Division were repeating the old error of dispersing their component units over the desert, so on 21st January 1942, Rommel struck these scattered units with all his force. Two days later his armour took on the three regiments of the 2nd Armoured Brigade, each of which came into action separately and were, as usual, separately defeated, losing over half their tanks. Rommel then burst through the 201st Guards Brigade and reached Msus. On the 28th he took Benghazi, capturing a huge quantity of petrol and ammunition that had been laboriously stockpiled for a proposed British attack – 'Operation Acrobat' – in mid-February. By 4th February Rommel's hustling tactics had levered the British back to Gazala, 150 miles east of Msus. Many British units arrived there in considerable confusion, although Rommel had, in fact, already stopped advancing. Three months later, in May 1942, Rommel advanced to the Gazala line and another major encounter developed there.

In April 1942, the 7th Armoured Division returned from the Delta and, as usual, sent roving 'Jock' columns and the 11th Hussars out on reconnaissance into the emptiness of the No-Man's-Land between the two armies, while General Ritchie, commanding 8th Army, prepared for an advance.

SQMS Neville Gillman of the 4th CLY was in the Support Echelon to one of these "Jock" columns. 'In early 1942 we were working with the Coldstream Guards around Agedabia. When the Germans attacked, we had to move back a hundred miles in a day, over country where you did well to average five miles an hour. I recall making an RV with a supply column of the Guards Brigade, commanded by a Guards RSM, a very formidable figure. We were waiting for our respective units to arrive when another German column appeared and, after a bit, started lobbing shells at us, so I went to see the RSM, who was senior to me, and asked what we should do. His eyes bulged.

'"Do?" he shrieked. "Do? I'll tell you what we are going to do. My orders are to stay here and *that's* what we're going to do." That was the Guards, who held Knightsbridge – splendid chaps.'

Soon after this, Neville Gillman was commissioned from the ranks and in the field, a typically relaxed Desert Army affair. 'Like many others at the time, I was commissioned into my own regiment. I even stayed in the same troop and in the same tank. The Adjutant came over and said, "Your commission's come through Gillman ... come into the mess tent and have a drink." "Yes, Sir," I said, and he said, "You don't call me 'sir' any more, you call me Robert." The men called me "Sir" on parade but we were all on first-name terms and continued to be so.'

H.M. Lassman, a Rhodesian with the 4th RHA, was on a 'Jock' column at this time and records one curious incident: 'We were hidden in a wadi with steep sides, and very narrow. One of the Scout cars had been sent out on a recce but had been spotted, and now we were bottled in. Despite strict rationing, we were out of water by the third day, and the only relief we got was from condensation on our groundsheets. Our tongues were swollen and speech was almost impossible. Orders were written on paper and passed around. The next night, every gun fired three rounds rapid, then we limbered up and drove out and scattered in to the desert. Our Gun-tower and the gun stopped for a brief moment to pick up the TSM, and the driver of the wireless truck which had a hole in the radiator.

'The TSM and I sat on the roof of the tower and a while later we spotted the rocks of a desert well, and directed the driver to it. It took no time at all to pull up half a Jerry can of water, which was rationed out at half a cup per man, and which we drank very slowly. We then filled all our water cans, and suddenly the weight was too much for two men to pull up. Four of us grabbed the rope and heaved and up came the Jerry can with the very dead body of an Arab draped over it. The body was dragged out of the way, and we continued pulling up cans of water until every container was filled. All the water was subsequently drunk – mostly in tea – after we had all met at the rendezvous with only the wireless truck missing. We were very lucky.

'Another time, still behind Rommel's lines, our patrol had ambushed an enemy convoy on the coastal road and we soon had their range and were shelling their trucks. I had just rammed another shell into the breech of the gun, when I heard shouts of warning and swung round. My first thought was that Goliath dressed in a German uniform complete with a rifle and a bayonet was about to carve me up. I jack-knifed away, swinging the rammer at his head as I did so, but the point of his bayonet caught me in the lower abdomen and ripped me up to the navel, which I felt was rather unfriendly of him. However, I had managed to even the score as my rammer had hit him on the helmet with enough force to stop him in his tracks. I sat down in a hurry hugging my stomach.

'One of their foot patrols had been hidden in a nearby nullah and had crept up and nearly overrun us. Our doctor's driver had driven into the nullah when we started firing, and both he and the doctor had been silenced. Fortunately for us, we had some Cherrypickers in support and they managed to take out the enemy patrol. I guess I was very lucky as the bayonet had not penetrated very deeply, and using some medical supplies that we had previously 'liberated', I managed to close up the wound using things that looked like crocodile clips.

'Some two weeks later, on our return to base, I saw the M.O. He removed the clips and said, "Not a very neat job. Keep it bandaged and see me again in a week." I was given seven days light duty.'

This book cannot cover the activities of the Desert Air Force, but there is one story involving 7th Armoured which is well worth retelling, contributed by Mrs P.L. Orgar: 'My father, Frederick Carter, was in India with the Army during the First World War, and called up again in 1939 at the age of 40, going out to the Middle East to join 58 Company RASC, which was part of 7th Armoured, and during that campaign something quite unique happened. My elder brother was a fighter pilot in the Desert Airforce, and in one dogfight he shot down a German aircraft before crash landing himself, and walking back to the British lines. He was picked up and taken into an Army Officer's Mess, where they told him he had stumbled into 7th Armoured, and he said, "My father is serving in this Division," so the Officer sent for my Dad, who was then a Sergeant, and you can imagine their delight meeting each other like that. Dad drove my brother back to his RAF base, and the Mess Manager there gave him a tray of eggs to take back, something that the Desert Army had not seen for quite a while. Dad put the tray on the seat of his vehicle, while saying goodbye, and a few moments later, swung himself into the driving seat and straight onto the eggs. The story of this meeting made front-page news in the national press at the time, and my mother, now 85, still has copies. I also have a photo of them both taken in the desert. My father went right through the war and

BATTLE OF GAZALA
ORDER OF BATTLE APRIL 1942

4th Armoured Brigade
1st RHA
8th Hussars
3rd RTR
5th RTR
1st KRRC

7th Motor Brigade
4th RHA
9th KRRC
2nd Rifle Brigade
9th Rifle Brigade

Divisional Troops
102nd RHA
KDG
15th Light AA Regiment RA
Divisional Signals

Royal Engineers
4th Field Squadron
143rd Field Park Squadron

RASC
No. 5 Company
No. 30 Company
No. 58 Company
No. 67 Company
No. 432 Company
No. 550 Company

RAMC
2nd Light Field Ambulance
7th Light Field Ambulance
14th Light Field Ambulance
15th Light Field Ambulance

RAOC
Divisional Workshops
Divisional Ordnance Field Park
15th Light AA Workshops
In each Brigade – one Workshop

died in 1972, having been through two world wars. My brother was shot down over Ste-Mère-Eglise in March 1944, and although badly burned, he survived the war and now lives in New Zealand.'

Between late January and May, following their withdrawal from the German front at Agedabia, the British had been busy creating the so-called Gazala Line. The Gazala Line was not a 'line' in the 1914–18 Western Front sense of the term. Rather, it was a series of defended 'boxes', running south into the desert from Gazala on the eastern side of the Jebel, each manned by a full brigade and surrounded by thick belts of wire and mines. These boxes were too widely separated to be mutually supporting, but the gaps were patrolled, and hopefully controlled, by roving armoured units. The most important of these boxes was the one to the south at Bir Hacheim, the pivot point for any southern hook round either front. This box was held by 1st Free French Brigade, largely composed of Foreign Legionnaires, and commanded by

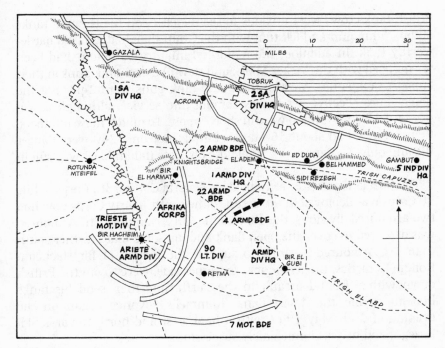

6 Gazala

General Koenig. To their right, but sixteen miles away, lay another box held by the 150th (British) Infantry Brigade, while north again lay the Knightsbridge Box, held by the 201st Guards Brigade, the old 22nd Guards Brigade renumbered to prevent confusion with 22nd Armoured Brigade. Other boxes, manned by British and South African units, continued the Gazala Line north to the sea. Churchill was unhappy that General Auchinleck was proposing a further long delay before assaulting the German line and pressed for an attack that should go in not later than mid-June. However, as had happened before, Rommel struck first.

Rommel was outnumbered in men and tanks, with seven tank regiments (three of them Italian) to the British fourteen. The British now had 700 tanks, some of them the new American Grants, which had thick armour and the 75mm gun, with a further 400 tanks available in reserve or in the Delta. In 7th Armoured, each armoured regiment now had 24 Grants and 20 of the fast, light Honeys. The Grant was a British sponsored version of the American M3 medium tank, the Lee. It weighed $28\frac{1}{2}$ tons, had 57mm of armour on the front of the turret, and mounted two guns, a 37mm in the turret and a 75mm in a sponson on the side of the hull, as well as a .300in Browning machine-gun. The

British tank crews were anxious to see the effect on the German tanks of the 75mm gun and felt that with the Grant they had at last a battle-worthy tank. In addition, the motorized infantry battalions had been re-equipped with the Vicker MMG, and now had anti-tank guns in their Support Companies. Most of these anti-tank guns were 2-pdr but the much more effective 6-pdr was coming into service, although as yet stocks of AP ammunition were in short supply. To match these numbers, Rommel now had about 560 tanks, but of these only 240 were Panzer IIIs and only 38 Panzer IVs, while the obsolete Italian M13 was still in service.

The Gazala Line boxes were held by General Gott's 13th Corps, while 30 Corps was deployed in the desert to the south. Thirty Corps now had two armoured divisions, the 1st and the 7th Armoured. 7th Armoured was deployed to cover the open flank and lay some miles further south than 1st Armoured in order to support the French at Bir Hacheim. Rommel's tactics, the usual ones for either side, were to pin the British down with a frontal assault in the north, and then send his tanks hooking round the desert flank. Rommel's advance began on the evening of 26th May 1942 with a hook east and north towards Sidi Rezegh, and he was immediately successful.

Soon after first light on the 27th May 1942, a huge German tank force was spotted by the 4th South African Car Regiment, moving around the southern flank below Bir Hacheim. Here they were engaged by 'C' Squadron of the 8th Hussars, commanded by Major J.W. (Shan) Hackett.

Shan Hackett: 'I was then commanding 'C' Squadron of the 8th Hussars, in Honeys, working with the 11th Hussars, the KDGs and the South African Armoured Car boys – all very good regiments. We were part of 4th Armoured Brigade and on this night of 26/27th May we did a shoot from a prepared position – Blenheim, I think it was called – and were well prepared to meet Rommel. We stood-to at midnight, and news came that Rommel was making greater speed than expected, so we moved out of leaguer towards Blenheim. The C.O. ordered me to meet the Germans before Blenheim, and as I took my Squadron up a slight rise and reached the top, I saw what looked like the whole bloody German army coming up the slope below. I radio'd back, "Am engaging now," and put up the black battle flag ... well, any tank will shoot at anything resembling a command tank, so everyone fired at me. In minutes my tank was on fire and I was burned, quite badly as it turned out. At the time I just went back to 'B' echelon and got another tank, but after about two days I was taken to a casualty clearing station and eventually back to a Naval Hospital in Alexandria. I was in there for a couple of weeks and then discharged myself and got back to the 8th Hussars. The 8th got badly knocked about during "Cauldron", but C Squadron remained a going concern, as a "Squadron for hire" really. What a state ... we had no C.O., no Adjutant, no Q.M., just fifteen tanks and some 'B' echelon. We formed up with the 3rd RTR into a composite regiment. What else ... ? Messervy was captured early on in the battle, but took off his medals and escaped. Then the remains of the 1st and 7th Armoured Divisions were put together for a counter-attack around Bir Hacheim. Rommel expected it of course; he was no fool, a great adventurer, a great chancer, but we had 70 tanks by now, enough to give him a bloody nose. We called him "Harry" you know. You might be going out on patrol and a sergeant would say, "Watch out Sir, or Harry will get you."

'Well, eventually the Greys came up and we went back to Alamein, where we were put together with the 4th Hussars as a composite regiment, 4th/8th Hussars for Alam Halfa.'

Such was the whirlwind pace of the German advance that at about 8.30am on the morning of the 27th, they overran 7th Armoured Division HQ, scattering the 7th Motor Brigade (the old Support Group), and capturing General Messervy and several of his staff officers. General Messervy quickly removed his badges of rank, and fell in with the Private soldiers, when the Germans mustered their prisoners, and although one German did remark, 'Aren't you a bit old to be an ordinary soldier!' General Messervy remained undetected in enemy hands for twenty-four hours before he was able to make his escape and return to the Division, accompanied by his G1, Lt-Col H.E. Pyman and several other Officers. Meanwhile, part of 7th Motor Brigade withdrew to the Retma Box, fifteen miles east of Bir Hacheim, and the 4th Armoured Brigade fought all day in attempting to stem the onrush of the Panzers, though the 8th Hussars were caught before they could move out and suffered accordingly. By mid-afternoon on the 27th, the Germans had scattered 7th Armoured and were in position to assault the 201st Guards Brigade in the Knightsbridge Box. One report recalls the Germans as 'A black mass of tanks, beginning in the region of the Knightsbridge Box and stretching South, as far as the eye could see'.

Once again, the British had made the mistake of committing their armour piecemeal, although in this case they had little choice in the face of Rommel's fast, though anticipated, advance and the disruption caused by the loss of 7th Armoured Divisional HQ. In his papers, Rommel writes: 'The sacrifice of the 7th Armoured south of Bir Harmat (south of Knightsbridge) served no tactical purpose whatsoever, since it was all the same to the British if they met me there or on the Trigh Capuzzo, where the remainder of their armour (1st Armoured Div) entered the battle ... their aim should have been to bring all their armoured forces into battle at the same time. Their units were fully motorized and able to cross the battlefield at great speed to wherever danger threatened.'

Rommel now pushed his Panzer forces on to the north, moving behind the Gazala Boxes, but British resistance began to stiffen. Unable to maintain his supply route round the south flank, Rommel cleared two paths through the minefield on either side of the 150th Infantry Brigade Box, and very heavy fighting took place in this area, which soon became known as 'The Cauldron'. On 28th May, 4th Armoured Brigade attacked a battle-group of the 90th Light, while the 7th Motor Brigade harried enemy columns near Bir el Gubi. Fifteenth Panzer came to a halt near Knightsbridge, low on ammunition and petrol, and by 29th May the German advance had stopped and Rommel himself had been forced to drive back well west of Gazala to hurry up the supply columns to his forward forces.

Replenished with fuel and ammunition, Rommel's forces awaited the British counter-attack in the open desert, east of the Knightsbridge Box, with the British minefields and the Guards Brigade Box still untaken at their back. This looked a precarious position but the Germans were simply waiting for the British tanks to waste themselves against their dug-in anti-tank gun screen. Fortunately, hampered by a sandstorm, the British attack did not develop, and by the 30th, Rommel had been forced to concentrate his forces in a defensive position near the 150 Brigade Box, ready for the second phase of the battle. The British High Command in Cairo were convinced they now had Rommel 'in the bag', but Rommel again opened the battle with a fierce assault on the 150 Brigade Box, an attack supported by dive-bombing from Stukas. He followed this with fierce attacks on the French at Bir Hacheim, where the now isolated French and Foreign legionnaires put up a magnificent defense. Rommel himself led attacks on their lines and wrote later: 'Never in Africa was I given a stiffer fight than at Bir Hacheim.'

The 150 Brigade Box fell at noon on 1st June, and the fighting now began to open out between the two boxes held by the Free French and the Guards. Units of 7th Armoured were continually engaged during this time between and around these positions. Rommel was now striking out at will from his defensive positions in the Cauldron, while the British were putting in attack after attack, but as General Verney recalls in the Divisional History, 'Very many tanks were lost and the effects on the enemy were less than had been hoped.' When General Ritchie moved to counter-attack on 2nd June, his assault was marked by all the usual errors – it was too slow and too obvious, with uncoordinated units attacking piecemeal and being repulsed in turn, often with heavy losses before the enemy anti-tank gun screens. Rommel's forces waited until the British tanks emerged from the artillery smokescreen and then opened a devastating fire with their anti-tank guns and 88s. By the evening of 6th June, the British tank strength had fallen to 170 machines, and Rommel counter-attacked again, scattering 7th Armoured for the second time in ten days. The day concluded with what the Royal Tanks' history records as 'delays, misunderstood orders, counter-orders and disorder.'

With the British again in some disarray, Rommel sent his Panzers south to attack the stubborn French at Bir Hacheim, where his all-out attacks on 7th and 8th June were somehow resisted. On the 9th, what was left of 4th Armoured Brigade advanced south from Knightsbridge in an attempt to relieve the pressure on Bir Hacheim, but this attack too fell apart under fire from the 88mms. On the evening of 10th June the Germans finally broke into the French defences, and on the next night the gallant remnants of the Free French were withdrawn, though leaving much of their equipment behind. Rommel then turned his attention to the other boxes of the ill-fated Gazala Line. On 12th June, Rommel succeeded in pinning the 2nd and 4th Armoured Brigades between the 21st and 15th Panzer Divisions, and brought on another disastrous day for the British arms, while on the 13th he succeeded in cutting off the Guards Brigade in the Knightsbridge Box. By now, however, even the victorious Germans were very tired, and the Guards were able to withdraw from Knightsbridge, leaving the Gazala battlefield free for the roving squadrons of Rommel's victorious Panzers, watched by the ever vigilant 4th South Africans and the 11th Hussars. This retreat became known as the 'Gazala Gallop'. Then, on 20th June 1942, the advancing Germans captured the fortress of Tobruk, and the British humiliation was complete.

Amid all this clamour and confusion around the Gazala Line and in the 'Cauldron' battles, the various actions of the 7th Armoured Division are somewhat hard to unravel, and are best seen in two parts, the Battle of Gazala, which began with Rommel's advance on 27th May and lasted until the 150 Brigade Box fell on 1st June, and the supporting 'Cauldron' battles, which began on 2nd June and went on until Tobruk finally fell to the German Army on 21st June.

As we have seen, at about 7.30 on the morning of 27th May, 15 Panzer Division struck at the 4th Armoured Brigade near Bir Hacheim and there were heavy losses in men and tanks, especially to the 8th Hussars and the 3rd RTR. By the evening, this last regiment was reduced to just five Grants and eight Honeys. The 4th Brigade's 'B' Echelon was then overrun and most of the petrol and ammunition lost. The Brigade infantry unit, the 1st KRRC, were forced back first to the Retma Box, and then to El Duda. On the same day, the 3rd (Indian) Motor Brigade, which was then under 7th Armoured's command and committed to supplying Bir Hacheim, was also overwhelmed and scattered, reforming in the rear some days later.

The Germans then attacked the Box at Retma, where the garrison – 9th KRRC, 2nd Rifle Brigade, 'C' Bty RHA and a Rhodesian Anti-Tank unit had been ordered to hold out, 'to the last round and the last man.' This they tried to do, but the Panzers came swarming in, accompanied by a heavy artillery bombardment and swiftly overran the 9th KRRC. The rest of the garrison then withdrew east to Bir El Gubi.

Chaos continued throughout 27th May as the Panzers swept forward, hustling the British out of their positions before the defences could be properly organized. Before long retreating tanks and 'soft' transport were streaming past 7th Divisional HQ, and soon afterwards, by 0845 hrs, a number of German armoured cars swept in to the HQ position, capturing General Messervy and some of his staff. The survivors of Divisional HQ had to move several times during the 27th, and this caused a further breakdown in communications and the chain of command. This, in turn, added to the confusion. The whole Division were engaged piecemeal throughout the 27th, over an area of many square miles, from Bir Hacheim to Bir El Gubi and by nightfall were in a state of some disarray.

Fortunately, on the 28th, some order began to emerge. The 7th Brigade began to harry German columns near Bir El Gubi and the 4th Brigade attacked units of 90th Light advancing from the south on El Adem, where the 3rd and 5th RTR did especially good work. On the 29th, Rommel had to pause as his tanks were seriously short of fuel and ammunition. The Germans now began to open lanes through the minefields on either side of the 150 Brigade Box, and were engaged to the north by the Guards and artillery from the Knightsbridge Box. A thick sandstorm then interrupted visibility and reduced radio communications and it was not until evening that the 4th Brigade of 7th Armoured advanced from El Adem to attack the 90th Light again at Bir Harnet.

The 4th Brigade were in action again soon after dawn on the 30th, but were then heavily bombed by the Luftwaffe. The 7th Motor Brigade continued to harry German columns making north for Tobruk, but by the 31st the Divisional tank situation was critical. The 8th Hussars and the 3rd RTR, which had now been in continuous action for five days, were now combined into one regiment but had only 9 Grants and 24 Honeys. The 5th RTR had only 16 Grants and 12 Honeys, while Brigade HQ had 3 of each, a total for the 4th Armoured Brigade of 29 Grants and 39 Honeys. Not all the missing tanks had been destroyed. Scores of tanks now lay out in the desert, lightly damaged, broken down or simply out of fuel. British tank recovery and repair facilities were, as yet, nowhere near as efficient as the Germans, who had repair crews moving about the battlefield all the time, patching up their own tanks and destroying or removing British machines.

Meanwhile, the defenders of the various Gazala boxes were getting low on ammunition. At noon on 1st June, the 150 Brigade Box fell to another German assault, and the first phase – the battle of Gazala – was over. The big question which hangs over this phase is why (in spite of previous experience and adequate preparation, which did include prior warning of Rommel's advance, both from Ultra-transcripts and their own reconnaissance forces) the British were surprised by Rommel's advance.

Lieut. Fletcher, an Officer in the South African Armoured Car Regiment, was out on patrol at dusk on the night of 26th May, the night Rommel moved forward to attack. The dim light of an early moon facilitated his progress and he probed his way well beyond No-man's-land. He was in the neighbourhood of Rotunda Segnal, which the enemy used as a jumping-off point, and where they had enormous supply dumps, when he realized that something more than normal movement was taking place. Soon he spotted two large tank formations, panzers of the 15th and 21st Divisions, moving in a south-easterly direction and he surmised correctly that they were making for a point south of Bir Hacheim.

He signalled back to Headquarters the dramatic message that Axis forces were on the move. By remaining slightly ahead of the advancing tank columns, he 'shadowed' the enemy's every movement and wirelessed up-to-the-minute accounts of their progress back to headquarters.

Fletcher led the two panzer divisions round Bir Hacheim, all the time signalling back every movement. At one stage a dispatch rider often came as close as ten feet to him, but did not suspect anything. After escorting the Germans for several hours, Fletcher's radio became defective. Examination showed that it could be fixed only with a piece of wire which, however, was not available. He searched his car for wire and found a hairpin, which suited his purpose, in a parcel of gifts and comforts for a WAAS, which had accidentally been sent to his regiment. Soon he was able to take up his narrative again.

In spite of the danger in which he found himself with the approaching dawn, Fletcher remained close to the enemy. When daylight broke, Fletcher was spotted by the enemy and soon found himself under shellfire from the tanks.

Major Riddell of 550 Company RASC, supporting 7th Motor Brigade, has an interesting story on this phase of the Gazala battle.

'We knew that something was afoot towards the end of May 1942, for both armies were preparing to attack. Various codewords were decided upon, and as I remember it, there were two important codewords: "Dry Fly" meant that Rommel's attack was imminent, and "Hares" meant that all units were to move into position ready to receive him as he came round the bottom of the Bir Hacheim minefields. Well, the story goes, and it may bear no relation to the truth, but the 4th SA Armoured Car Regiment were observing Rommel closely, and they spotted that the Afrika Korps were on the move, and all through the night of 26th May, every quarter of an hour, they gave the map reference of Rommel's leading forces and the codeword "Dry Fly." These signals were received at Divisional HQ, but as I heard it, there was a new officer on duty who thought the whole thing was just a wireless exercise!

'So, there was 7th Armoured Division, snug in bed, sleeping, not receiving the codewords "Hares" or "Dry Fly", and this certainly applied to me and 550 Company. We were located on a dried-up water hole, a salt-pan. Fortunately, my driver had positioned my bivvy so that the rising sun shone directly on my face. I awoke at the crack of dawn and heard all kinds of noises, unusual to me, which put me on the alert, and I saw the Brigade Field Ambulance driving east across the salt-pan, so we all got ready to move. We got the codewords "Dry Fly" and "Hares" simultaneously, and drove off towards Capuzzo with great alacrity. In fact, as we drove off one end of the salt-pan, the Germans drove on the other end. Fortunately, they were going north to Tobruk, and we were going east to Bir El Gubi.'

Harry Blood was with the RASC when the Germans attacked. 'In early March off we went back "up the Blue" again, in the same old lorries, along the coast road, and up Sollum Pass. The Pass was very steep, rough, and on the seaward side the drop was alarming, so most of us either walked or hung on the running boards, ready to jump! Later, we got to a position, I believe, south of Bir Hacheim, south end of the so-called Gazala Line, the enemy having attacked in January, taken Benghazi and been halted in the Gazala area, having pushed us back a long way.

'On 27th May 1942 the enemy broke through again and though we had been expecting to move, it was a shock when an officer in a jeep came at speed into the camp, waving his arms and shouting something like, "Move, get out ... tanks!" We looked in the direction he had indicated, and could see vehicles coming in our direction. Luckily, much equipment was already loaded, and there was a mad scramble over many tailboards, and we scattered in all directions. Even so, we heard later that the Ordnance lorry had got a shell hole right through its canvas top. The Adv. H.Q. 7 Armoured Division had been unluckier still – some clerks and officers were taken prisoner, including General Messervy, who, I believe, escaped some hours later. I was told that R.S.M. Blissett and Pte Gerry Giltrew did not escape.

'Our trucks just went anywhere, as fast as we could. We broke down after some miles, but were lucky enough to be picked up and towed by an Ambulance lorry, which was also hurrying backwards. We moved back to Gambut, where we managed to join some of the other trucks and then moved forward south of El Adem, but not long after that the general move back started, and we went through the wire once more at Maddalena, and right back to what was to become the southern sector of the Alamein Line.'

J.I. Frapwell of the 2nd Royal Gloucester Hussars also recalls this time: 'By 28th April we were back "up the blue", equipped with Crusaders and one squadron, "F", with Grants. With thicker frontal armour and a 75mm gun we thought they were wonderful, although the Americans had considered them obsolete in 1936. This time we did not spend pounds or even piastres filling our tanks with Eastern delights such as tinned fruit, sweets, extra tea, sugar and cigarettes; Operation "Crusader" had taught us that the tank which we had considered our home, our refuge, was not with us for long. We no longer painted names on the sides. Gone were "Greyhound" and "Gaucho", "Hannibal" and "Horsa", "Fearsome" and "Fearless".

'We were now initiated into the mysteries of "the Box". In theory it was an immovable strong point with the armour kept ready to counter-attack. They did give Rommel some trouble, but with the exception of the Guards Box at Knightsbridge and the French in Bir Hacheim, not enough. As we moved up into position, "F" Squadron were reprimanded by the Divisional Commander for moving their tanks in echelon formation, not in tank formation. However, as the tanks were camouflaged as lorries, they thought they were right and he had to agree.

'On 27th May the Afrika Korps attacked with the classic loop around the South, concentrating their armour on Bir Hacheim. There seemed to be a certain amount of confusion among the Higher Command and conflicting orders were received by the forward troops. At last they agreed that the tanks and troops advancing and firing on us were not our own but the enemy. The Germans must have known about Grants because they singled out "F" Squadron, and in the fierce opening fighting all except one tank were knocked out. The loss of men and materials was devastating but the enemy too, suffered a serious setback.

'The subsequent days and nights in the Cauldron were sheer hell. Those who managed four hours sleep a night were lucky. By the time crews had withdrawn to leaguer, refuelled, reloaded and did some maintenance, it was midnight. Guards had to be mounted and first light was at 4 am, then it was off again to face the Hun for a 16-hour day.

'By 2nd June, we were back to Honeys, although "F" Squadron got some more Grants. It was decided to use the 22nd Armoured Brigade to make a frontal attack with the hope of forcing a tired enemy to retreat. This was a sure way of committing suicide and among our heavy casualties this time was Colonel Birley. He had been badly wounded in the legs and died later from loss of blood. Captain Muir, the Adjutant, was also killed in the same tank. The Colonel, a regular soldier, had been with us since April 1941. He worked hard to train us to his fine soldiering standards. At first he could not understand the Yeomanry attitude but after El Gubi he was converted and realized that amateurs could be as good as professionals. In the months to come he was greatly missed.

'Major Bill Trevor, another regular from the Tank Corps, greatly revered by the other ranks, now took command but fate was to deal us another blow. While at Brigade HQ at Acroma, his car was bombed and he was killed instantly.'

Allan Austin, who joined the 145th (Berks Yeomanry) Field Regt. R.A., a unit of the Territorial Army in April 1939, also recalls this time: 'The regiment was mobilised on Friday, 1st September 1939, the day Germany invaded Poland. We spent ten months in England before embarking at Stranfaer for Larne in Northern Ireland. After eighteen

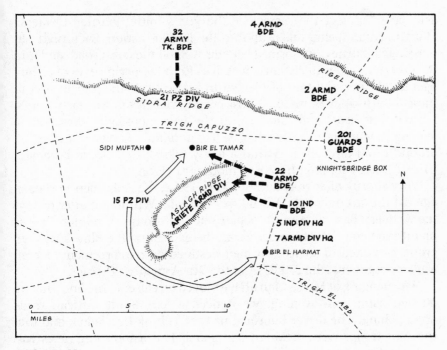

7 The Cauldron

months in Ulster, I was posted to Nottingham in December 1941 to be included in a draft of gunners destined for the Middle East.

'We sailed from Gourock on the Clyde in February 1942, and arrived at Durban in late March. After a brief stay in Durban we boarded the *Ile de France*, a notable French liner, converted to a troopship, and we sailed on 8th April *en route* for Cairo. As we left Durban harbour the famous 'lady in white', standing alone on the pier, sang to us in farewell. This legendary singer had performed in this same way by singing to the troops leaving Durban for the Middle East during the First World War. Her farewell songs were reputed to be a form of blessing to the departing troops and the ship. It was said that no troopship left Durban during both World Wars without her special farewell. This benign and beautiful 'lady in white' passed away some twenty-five years ago, and her death and legendary singing was reported at the time in the national press.

'My stay in Cairo, at the Royal Artillery base of Almaza, was relatively short lived. At this time the 6-pounder anti-tank gun, to replace the weak and ineffective 2-pounder weapon, had arrived from the UK in the Delta Zone. I recall being selected as one of several guard commanders

117

detailed to protect the secrecy of the gun's initial journey to Mersa Matruh, before being taken up into the line for action. Each night, in our staged journey, we formed leaguer well off the coast road, and into the desert, in order to distance ourselves from the prying eyes of enemy agents. My first sighting of the natural desert rat, the jerboa, was in these desert sands at night. Whilst posting sentries in the early hours, I could first hear, and then see, in the pale moonlight, these small, leaping rodents. In fact, they looked like miniature kangaroos, hopping around in all directions. Within a few weeks, I, too, would become a 'Desert Rat' by joining the 7th Armoured Division.

'Very shortly after this, on 26th May 1942, the Axis offensive began against the strongly held Allied line at Gazala. Within a matter of days the Artillery base at Almaza began sending groups of reinforcements up into the line – the term used was "being sent up the Blue". My own group consisted of some 200 men destined as reinforcements for an artillery regiment, the 3rd RHA of the 7th Armoured Division.

'After staging at Mersa Matruh we moved on closer to the line. Having pitched camp one evening, we noticed a lone South African truck approaching. The driver informed us that Tobruk had fallen, and that the Axis troops were making rapid gains. This astonishing news was soon confirmed over our radio, and we quickly broke camp to join the increasing eastbound traffic on the narrow coast road back towards Cairo. It was soon apparent that the bulk of Eighth Army was on this road, and, alas, in full retreat. Damaged tanks, guns, Spitfires and Hurricanes on transporters, armoured cars, military transport of every description was on the move. We joined, too, with our few lorries, running the gauntlet of German air attacks, their planes bombing and strafing almost at will. There was no escape and little defence against these attacks. Some infantrymen resorted to firing their rifles at the low flying enemy fighters with the occasional success. The enemy planes dropped flares during the nights, and this always heralded widespread bombing and machine gunning. Each attack left burning vehicles, and casualties, and added to the general snarl-up of military traffic.

'Somewhere, behind us, what remained of the Eighth Army was engaged in desperate rearguard actions to buy time for the manning of our last line of defence before the gates of Cairo and Alexandria. This last line was at El Alamein. As we retreated at some 30 miles daily, first through Mersa Matruh, then Fuka and El Daba, we finally stopped close to the railway station at El Alamein. Within days we were assigned to our artillery unit supporting the 22nd Armoured Brigade of 7th Armoured Division.'

Gerald Milner was with the RASC: 'We arrived in Egypt in October 1941, and went to a holding depot at Geneifa where we transferred to Heavy Repair Shops for a few weeks to acclimatize, and finally "up the Blue" to join 287 Coy RASC, where the vehicles bore the sign "P" (P ammunition). The Germans were "stonking" – Desert term for steady shelling. This soon turned into a mighty enemy attack to drive a wedge between Tobruk and Bir Hacheim. Tobruk fell; Bir Hachiem held for nearly a fortnight and the great chess game began. The German army knocked us back mile after mile, but always conscious of the thorn in their side at Bir Hacheim. Sandstorms seemed to be getting more frequent, but we were still eluding the forward enemy troops. As my Company had lost most of its equipment during the enemy onslaught, the most urgent things we needed were food and rifles or machine guns. In one mighty sandstorm, we came across a NAAFI which was packing up and clearing out in what one might call "a bit of a hurry". They need not have worried. We helped them by throwing as much as we could into our trucks.

'Then we had a bit more luck. In the clouds of sand we ran smack into one of our own ammo dumps, which, because of the proximity of the German advance column, was to be blown up. The officer in charge, whoever he was, had his hand on the plunger. Our platoon Captain, Mickey Ridgway, ordered the officer with his hand on the plunger to remove himself. With reluctance, and with a little help from an empty revolver, he complied, while we plundered the Bren guns, 303s and as much ammo as we could get in the seconds available to us. We went off, groping our way to the track, and soon a mighty explosion was heard. We had been just in time. Retreating steadily it became obvious that we were following the leading German DR (Despatch Riders). I told Fred Loman, who was for a time my spare driver, what appeared to be the situation. Most of our vehicles had an "observation hole" in the cab roof. Fred stood on a seat and elevated himself through the cab roof, pointing a newly acquired Bren at the rider. After a short burst in front of him, the rider stopped. We took him prisoner. The same fate befell another half dozen before we rejoined our own outfit. I often wonder what the Germans made of a series of motorcycles strewn about the desert.

'By the time we reached our "sticking point" at El Alamein, we had collected a truckload of prisoners. Fred Loman was the sole guard with a .303 rifle. In the sweaty heat, dust had adhered to faces, arms, and in a few cases, to bare chests and legs (shorts, socks and boots were a familiar type of uniform). Fred had the hair shaved from his head and, like the prisoners, looked as though a bag of sand-coloured flour had been thrown over him. I mention this because he was so indistinguishable from the Germans that the receiving officer refused to believe that he was my spare driver. I was reporting to my CO at the time and did not know what was going on. It was with some difficulty that we obtained his release.'

Walter Bilsborough was also with the RASC: 'On the way back to Alamein we hit a Khamsin near the wire. We could only just see the wagon in front. I tailed him for about ten minutes, then he stopped, of course. After waiting some time I got out, then found we had been riding in a complete circle. So an NCO who had a compass set us on our way eastwards. The NAAFI wagon had gone on the road back and the NAAFI stores were at Daba and they were preparing to destroy the dumps. We managed to salvage some stores. Tinned fruit, chocolate etc. We finally arrived at Alamein and were kept busy for a time replenishing the Units who were fighting a rearguard action. I was detailed with the R.E. to lay mines at Alam el Haifa. The R.E. sat on the tailboard, priming the mines then laying them!'

Sergeant Rick Hall was also there, bringing up fuel and ammunition in his truck to the Grants. 'There is an escarpment near Knightsbridge, like the White Cliffs of Dover, and I had an RV with the tanks there. I remember they wouldn't take any dented shell cases. We were hanging about when a German half-track appeared on the coast and took us prisoners ... told us to march west and give ourselves up to the Italians, but after a bit we hid under the escarpment and made our way back at night. They were gentlemen, those Afrika Korps soldiers, they could have machine-gunned us easily. The ammo dumps for the tanks were between the "boxes" and I remember how easy a petrol Grant would brew up ... and the big 75 gun was in a sponson on the side of the turret, too low. We took ammo up to the Guards at Knightsbridge and were shelled from the escarpment as we went in. My corporal was cut in half by a shell fragment on one of these runs. We only had one truck left out of 35 in the Company, so I suppose you could say we were wiped out.'

G.W. Taylor was with the 4th South African Armoured Car Regiment at Gazala: 'After a spell in No. 5 General Hospital, Cairo, I joined Col. Newton King with the 4th S.A. Armoured Cars, and kept up the pressure on dear old Rommel. One morning, we were on a scout around and on surmounting a rise in the good old desert, we saw a Red Cross tent down in the valley. We also saw a German staff car making tracks for the hospital tent and I suggested we machine gun them and capture them if possible. We hesitated, as we did not know what was over the rise, and saw the two occupants of the staff car go into the tent. After a while, as we were on our way down the long slope, they came out, glanced in our direction and scooted like hell to get away. We gave chase, but an 8cwt vehicle is no match for the staff car's speed, so away they went. We returned to the Red Cross tent and were told that Rommel and Schmidt, his *aide-de-camp*, had just left. Getting that lot would have changed the pattern of the war, but the dice falls that way. The sequel is that Schmidt later retired to Durban, and as I was a member of a Pietermaritzburg MOTH Shellhole, we thought it a good idea to have him give us a talk from their side, and I had an opportunity of asking if he remembered the incident. "Too damn well," he said. "What took you so long to come off the rise?"'

John Ireland was tank gunner in the 5RTR and kept an account of his time in a Grant at Gazala: 'It is now May. Considering we started out in late March, there has been little activity on the Regiment's front: I believe a few regiments, including infantry, tanks and artillery, have had minor engagements with the enemy, but they are more forward in the battle area than us. Plenty of air activity all night and day, maybe a build-up to a push. The Regiment is on a 15 minute notice to move up to battle position. I believe the Free French forces and Indian Division went into action last night, so our turn could be soon.

'This is it! Moved up to form a battle line, and German tanks can be seen on the skyline. All guns ready. I take my appropriate position in the tank, the rest of the crew likewise. Tank commander in the turrett, scouring the skyline with binoculars for target to engage. The orders are now coming through the intercom to load the 75 mm gun. Giving the bearing of the target, orders come through – FIRE! (I hear my first shot in anger). From now on it continues all morning – "load, fire, load, fire" with the occasional reply of "Target" – meaning we've hit something, but not too often considering we've been firing all morning.

'Now the German tanks have got their sights on us and shells are bursting around us. Uncomfortable, but we are lucky they are having the same difficulty as us, ranging on target. A sandstorm started and visibility is almost nil, so we halted for a couple of hours. Unfortunately, with manoeuvring the tank round, the clutch is bust; we have to evacuate the tank, leaving a skeleton crew behind (driver and main gunner), hoping the fitters will come along and take the tank away. Later in the day the sandstorm abated and the Regiment moved forward to attack. I and the rest of the crew came out of action and settled in with the spare crews.

'The Regiment fell right into a trap; unknown to our command, the Germans took advantage of the sandstorm and withdrew the tanks, leaving behind a screen of well dug-in anti-tank guns (88mms). The Regiment pushed on in pursuit of the tanks but were met with a hail of fire from the guns and lost almost an entire regiment. The Commanding Officer was killed and lots of tank crews were killed, wounded or taken prisoner. I remember hearing at a later date that one of my best pals who I came out with from England, was wounded and taken prisoner. I guess my first days in action were not pleasant. However, now I know what it's all about.

'Next day we pick up some new tanks and formed up with the remaining tanks, moving forward to have another go at the enemy. This time in with a different crew, I was the main gunner. The skeleton crew, as mentioned previously, who were left behind, were overrun by the Germans, but although immobile, fought with great courage, the driver receiving later the Distinguished Conduct Medal for gallantry, the other member being killed. This setback in the regiment seemed to have a demoralising affect on the men and I, in particular, began to doubt the effectiveness of our tanks. Admittedly, I had only been in action just over a week, but the word '88' coming over the intercom made all the tank crews panic.

'By now we were around the Knightsbridge area and settled down to some give and take with the enemy, and seemed to have our confidence back once more and morale was high after the good reports we had had of the Army's performance in general.

'We had lots of grub and the rum issue made life brighter; although the strain of long hours in battle, days on end, made one wilt a little. From first light around 5 am until 10 pm was a very long day, especially hearing over the intercom the fate of some other crews. In the confines of the tank, life sometimes can be very unpleasant, what with the heat of the day and the smell of cordite fumes, hot, empty shell cases, flies, poor visibilty and hunger. These are just a few of the things we had to contend with, unable to get out because of the shelling and occasional Stuka dive-bomber attacks. We could do something about the targets on the ground, but those Stukas were a dreaded foe.

'We are now in the month of June and have been constantly in action on an average of five days at a time all month. Attacked an Italian column last evening with good results. Down south in the desert the French forces at Bir Hacheim have been overrun and we are trying to relieve the remaining remnants with slight success. After what appeared to be holding action and everything ready for a breakthrough in the enemy defences, the whole front on our side cracked up (don't ask me how or why) but all we could see was a massive German column approaching from the south. Tanks, guns, armoured trucks, vehicles – a marvellous sight if you didn't know what it meant – they were trying to cut the entire army up. The Regiment swung round to meet the threat, but were so out numbered that for the rest of the day all tanks were slowly reversing and engaging on the move backwards. We were holding them back so all our transport could not fall into their hands.

'Casualties on our side were numerous. We have been out-gunned, out-manoeuvred, out-generalled; in other words, led up the garden path. From now on it was a matter of survival and all the army were in full retreat, but the army commanders call it "A Strategic Withdrawal". After handing over remains of the tanks to another tank battalion, all remaining crews were transported on the long haul across the desert, back to the Nile. Passing through the wire frontier boundary into Egypt you had to think to yourself, "What went wrong?" After three and a half months it was back to square one.

'Let me try to analyse the last few months. We had started out as a well-equipped regiment, well trained, good administration, very good officers and NCOs, plenty of experience in tank warfare in the desert. It boiled down to one thing, the enemy had out-gunned us with superior armament and fire power, plus a few very bad decisions by the high command. We must try again. It was just like seeing your favourite football team reaching the final and getting licked 6–0.

'However, although back in Egypt and the enemy pushing down on us with all the might he could throw at us, the army managed to fall back in an orderly retreat. The main defence line was known at a later date as the Alamein Line. To put the icing on the cake, Tobruk fell! It had held out against all odds in the last ten months and was a morale booster for the army. The garrison were all taken prisoner.

'I believe a few top rank generals have been replaced. It could never happen to us. Imagine getting the sack and told to go home, we don't need you.'

After 1st June and the fall of the 150 Brigade Box, Rommel's next move was to mop up the French box at Bir Hacheim and that of the Guards at Knightsbridge. Then, with his position secure, he could advance on Tobruk. On 1st June the 7th Motor Brigade, still operating in columns, were 'shooting up enemy positions and transport columns,' following reconnaissance by the 4th South African Armoured Car Regiment and the Kings Dragoon Guards.

Over the next few days, the centre of the conflict settled in the Cauldron area, which lay south of the Trigh Capuzzo, between Knightsbridge and Bir Hacheim. A sandstorm on 2nd June played havoc with wireless links during a Panzer attack on the 5 RTR and B Battery of the 4th RHA. The guns were overrun by German tanks and Colonel Unaike of the 5th RTR was killed. His regiment was now down to one Grant and two Honeys, leaving 3 RTR as the only effective tank unit of the 4th Armoured Brigade. The Germans also shot up the transport of the South African Armoured Car Regiment, and General Messervy then called the various columns of the 7th Motor Brigade to withdraw from harrying the German columns and to hurry and help the defenders at Bir Hacheim. On 3rd June the 22 Armoured Brigade was again attached to the depleted ranks of 7th Armoured, while Rommel recalled 21st Panzer to help his attack on the French. Fifteenth Panzer also joined in and a whirling tank and anti-tank gun battle took place around the Cauldron on 5th and 6th June. In 22 Armoured Brigade the commander of the 2nd RGH, Colonel Birley, and his Adjutant, Captain H. Muir, were both killed, and the 10th (Indian) Brigade was wiped out. On the 7th, the 4th Brigade, reinforced by the 6th RTR, made another attempt to penetrate the German anti-tank gun screen with the usual disastrous results – tank after tank was shattered by the 88s or blown up by the 50mm PAK-38s anti-tank guns which the Germans had brought forward to the battle. On the evening of the 7th June, the 7th Armoured Division had just fifty-eight Grants and thirty-four Honeys fit for action, all manned by very tired crews.

Between 8th and 11th June, the attacks around Bir Hacheim and the Cauldron area moved to a new height of fury. The Luftwaffe returned to the battle, sending over 100 aircraft to bomb the French and strafe or bomb British tanks in the open desert. Artillery concentrations, followed by tank and infantry attacks, went in continually, but somehow the French held on and somehow 7th Armoured mustered a few more tanks, a company or two of infantry, a battery of guns, to join the battle and aid the defenders of the Bir Hacheim Box. Finally, on the night of 10th/11th June, orders were given for the Box to be evacuated. The French were helped out by the 2nd KRRC, the Rifle Brigade, and by 550 Company RASC who brought in lorries and ambulances to lift out the weary French and their wounded. About 1000 prisoners fell into enemy hands, but some 3000 Free French and Foreign Legionnaires were brought out to fight another day.

Major Duncan Riddell of 550 Company has an account of the Bir Hacheim relief: 'The 4th South African Armoured Car echelon were overrun, and the battle in the Cauldron had gone wrong, and it was obvious that there was going to be some kind of general retreat. Poor General Koenig with the Free French in Bir Hacheim had been attacked and Stuka'd for days, and it was decided that he must be rescued by the 7th Motor Brigade. A number of vehicles, including ambulances were sent to 550 Company to organize this affair. The Field Ambulances had been in the rear-zones and had no experience of the sharp end. Captain Barry Phillips, my second-in-command, volunteered to command this mixed bag of transport, and set off at last light to meet guides who would lead him into Bir Hacheim, with the 60th Rifles on one side and the Rifle Brigade on the other.

'They were shelled on the way in, and had to move one mile south. Captain Phillips caught up the Field Ambulances, which became separated, and got near enough for all in Bir Hacheim, including the wounded, to be evacuated, and next morning they arrived back in the company location, with the Free French soldiers who had had such a gruelling time. The Field Ambulance officer was awarded a decoration, but Barry Phillips, who had led this rescue, received no recognition whatsoever, to my everlasting regret.'

With the fall of Bir Hacheim, the British were unable to sustain the Gazala line, for all the fury of the Panzer Army now fell on the Guards at Knightsbridge, where the 4th Armoured Brigade were now in support. Here they were heavily engaged on 11th June by over 100 Mark III and Mark IV of 21st Panzer with infantry support, which attacked the 4th Brigade from the rear, knocking out over twenty tanks. During this action, General Messervy was again cut off from his HQ and General Lumsden of the 1st Armoured Division took temporary command of both Divisions. The Knightsbridge Box was still intact at nightfall on the 12th, but the Indians at El Adem near Tobruk had already surrendered, and more German units were available to attack the Guards.

On the 13th the Germans attacked the north side of the Knightsbridge Box in great force, overrunning the Scots Guards position before the 4th and 22nd Armoured Brigades could counter-attack. This they did during the afternoon and evening, but at the cost of another twenty-two tanks, and that night, after a most gallant defence, the Knightsbridge Box was evacuated through a corridor kept open by tanks of the 2nd Armoured Brigade. This left two Divisions, the 50th British and the 1st South African, stuck in the 'boxes' to the north of Knightsbridge, cut off by Panzer forces now swarming forward to Tobruk. These Divisions were ordered to break out to the east while Rommel sent 15th and 21st Panzer rolling north to cut them off. The weary units of 7th Armoured battled to stave off the German armour, and most of the 5th Division managed to escape. The 1st South African, withdrawing along the coast road, lost only their rearguard, but 8th Army was now in full retreat towards the El Alamein line.

By the evening of 15th June, the tank strength of the 4th Armoured Brigade, in spite of periodic reinforcements throughout the Gazala and Cauldron battles, stood at just twenty-four Honeys and twelve Grants. These followed the South Africans east, through Tobruk, guided by night through the Tobruk minefields by Major Palmer of the Kings Dragoon Guards. At dawn on the 16th, the 4th Brigade were back at Sidi Rezegh and El Adem, while the KDG armoured crews fanned out on reconnaissance to the south. The 4th Armoured Brigade were sent to attack the Germans, supported by the 20th Indian Infantry Brigade, losing more of their tanks before the German anti-tank gun screen. On the 17th, the depleted 4th Brigade, with the 9th Lancers and some tanks of the 4th CLY under Major Willis, was attacked by a force of over 100 German tanks and forced to withdraw, after 'a terrific slogging match'. The 4th Brigade left the El Adem position and withdrew to the Egyptian frontier, while Rommel went on to capture Tobruk, taking thousands of prisoners and a vast quantity of petrol and other stores.

General Auchinleck still had sufficient forces to stem Rommel's advance, if only they could be re-organized and properly employed. Rommel's recent successes had been due more to his whirlwind tactics and skilfull generalship rather than superior force. It was also obvious that Rommel's practice of leading from the front paid great dividends during fluid tank battles. He could see what was happening on the spot and had the authority to command instant changes in the direction of his forces or the conduct of the battle. This enabled him to concentrate his forces where required, and during any pauses in his advance he sheltered his tanks and vehicles behind an impenetrable anti-tank screen. This, plus the skill and experience of his troops, made all the difference on the day and Rommel knew this at the time. 'What is the use of (the British) having overall superiority,' he wrote, 'if one allows each formation to be smashed piecemeal by an enemy who is able to concentrate superior forces on every occasion at the decisive point.'

Neville Gillman gives the view of a Tank Troop Commander: 'I was still an NCO at the start of the Gazala battles. I was 24 and commanded a troop of four tanks. None of the officers was much older. Arthur Cranley was 26. At Gazala, seen from my point of view anyway, the situation was, to say the least, fluid, not to say a complete shambles. It was supposed to be a set-piece battle, and during Cauldron we had to make a charge into an enemy position – not a recipe for long life, but at least we knew what we were supposed to be doing. My tank had its left track blown off on the way in, so we went swinging off to one side, towards the enemy guns. I told the driver to halt and we jumped out and got behind the tank and then into a hole. Then we were showered with steel and driving wheels as a shell came right through the tank. The rest of the squadron had vanished, so we decided to shove off . . . the tank was eventually rescued. Lots of tanks were eventually brought back, so you were often issued with tanks with holes in them. I can't tell you much about the higher command, as a troop commander you dealt at no higher than Squadron level, but the Germans appeared to be going ahead with a purpose. They called the tune; they acted and we reacted, and you took it for granted that the German stuff was better. After Cauldron we withdrew to the Alamein line, but even if we were, well . . . disillusioned, about our equipment, we were not, repeat NOT demoralized – not at all.'

After Cauldron Rommel's forces were very tired and much reduced. His three German divisions had very few tanks, no more than 44 left in action with 2,500 infantry still on their feet. The two Italian divisions, the Ariete and the Trieste, had about the same number of infantry and just fourteen tanks. Most of Rommel's infantry and support units were now using captured British trucks as their own were worn out. Auchinleck reversed Ritchie's decision to stand and fight at Mersa Matruh, and ordered a mobile withdrawal to the secure line between the Qattara Depression and El Alamein. On the night of 25th June, Auchinleck relieved General Ritchie of his command and took over direct control of 8th Army. Meanwhile, in spite of his depleted state, Rommel kept on coming. On 26th June he launched another attack on the British, and sent more British transport hurrying to the rear, where their sudden arrival spread still more alarm and confusion. Mersa Matruh fell on 27th June and the confusion then became general. The Western Desert was now full of mixed and mingled units, regiments, mixed columns, tanks, lorries, all flowing east – British, New Zealand, South African, French, German, Italian, all intermingled. In some cases the advancing Germans were ahead of the retreating British, but with both sides using each other's transport, it was difficult to tell who was who. Rommel writes of 'a wild melee . . . the RAF bombed their own troops and German units fired on each other.' This retreat came into Desert terminology as the 'Gazala Gallop', and so, gloriously intermingled, the two armies came back together and collided again among the defences of the Alamein Line.

During this time 7th Armoured were frequently in action, though during the early stages after the fall of Mersa Matruh the 4th Armoured and 7th Motor Brigades were under command of Lumsden's 1st Armoured Division and holding the desert flank south of the 2nd New Zealand Division. The KDGs continued to patrol towards Bir el Gubi, falling back slightly as the German advance continued, while the 7th Motor Brigade units, notably the 9th KRRC, operated around Sidi Rezegh before withdrawing to the Alamein line, 'in close company with the Afrika Korps.' All units of 7th Armoured Division were on or behind the Alamein Line by 1st July 1942.

7

Alam Halfa

JUNE—SEPTEMBER 1942

> Oh that the desert were
> my dwelling place.
>
> *Lord Byron*

The fall of Tobruk on 20th June was a crushing blow for British morale, particularly after the town had held out so long, and so successfully the previous year. It also gave a tremendous boost to Rommel's dog-weary Panzer Army and a great haul of booty, including vast supplies of the ever-vital petrol with which to resume their advance. Another commander might have waited in Tobruk, to rest his troops and hold a mild celebration, but not Rommel. He wasted no time in following up the retreating British to the frontier wire and then into Egypt, crossing the frontier on 25th June and arriving that evening at Mersa Matruh, which fell two days later. Auchinleck had decided against making a stand at Mersa Matruh, opting for a gradual withdrawal to the Alamein line which consisted, as at Gazala, of a number of defended boxes, but unlike all other positions on the North African shore, the Alamein Line could not be outflanked to the south, because there it rested on the quagmire of the Qattara Depression. Towards this line swept 'intermingled columns of British, Germans and Italians, all fleeing east.' In the course of this advance the remaining British armour got left behind and mustered at Bir el Tamir, south-west of El Daba. Here they managed to strike at the Italian Littorio Armoured Division, knocking out twenty of its thirty M13 tanks, but this limited success did nothing to stop the German armour reaching Alamein.

Rommel intended to make his main thrust against the Alamein line between the two northern defensive boxes, the northern one held by 1st SA Division, and the next, six miles south, held by the 18th Indian Brigade, then swing north to isolate 13 Corps west of Alamein and cut the coast road. This should bring on the kind of spoiling fight at which Rommel was a master. His attack, which the Tank Corps' History calls 'First Alamein', began on 1st July 1942.

On the first day, without waiting for the Italian Ariete and Trieste divisions, both his leading German divisions, the 90th Light and 15th Panzer, became pinned by the two northern boxes, and the other division of the Afrika Korps, 21st Panzer, got sucked into a battle for the second box at Dier-el-Shein, where the 18th Indian Brigade held out until evening. This put the whole German attack out of joint and then, none too soon, the remaining British armour arrived on the scene from the west.

With Rommel just fifty miles from Alexandria, panic had spread to the General Staff and the citizens back in Cairo. On 2nd July, a gentle rain of ash was falling on the city from the fires lit at GHQ to destroy confidential papers, and the day was referred to by 8th Army in future years as 'Ash Wednesday'. The hoteliers sent every spare sheet to the laundry and looked out their stocks of German flags, while in the bazaar the Egyptian traders prepared for a fresh supply of customers. Meanwhile, preparations were being made both to reinforce the Alamein Line and, if all failed there, retreat across Sinai to Palestine and beyond. Auchinleck, however, stood above all this panic. He mustered his forces, fought to regain control of the situation and prepared to strike back. About this time, General Messervy gave up command of 7th Armoured Division, and Major General J.M.L. Renton took over command and he led the Division in the early fighting around the Alamein Line, and at Alam Halfa.

On 2nd July, the 4th Armoured Brigade became involved on the flank of 15th Panzer, losing a number of tanks to the 88mms, while the main thrust of the Afrika Korps, along the vital Ruweisat Ridge, south of Dier-el-Shein, heading towards the coast road, was hindered by the sudden appearance of fifty tanks of 22nd Armoured Brigade. Rommel's advance had not started until the middle of the afternoon, and at dark his forces halted and went into leaguer.

On 3rd July, concentrating his forces, Rommel tried again, but his total tank force was now down to twenty-six serviceable tanks. Even so, when checked by the 1st Armoured Division, the Afrika Korps knocked out thirty-nine British tanks before coming to a halt. Now surrounded by British forces, his men exhausted and his tank strength virtually gone, Rommel was in real trouble, and Auchinleck at last saw a chance to eliminate his wily opponent once and for all.

Auchinleck's intention was to pin Rommel down with 30 Corps and cut across the rear with 13 Corps. This latter Corps included all that was left of the 7th Armoured Division, the 7th Motor Brigade, and the King's Dragoon Guards and the 4th South African Armoured Car Regiment. The bulk of the armour and all the reserves were sent to 30 Corps. Rommel met 13th Corps with 21st Panzer and neither of the two British Corps was able to press home their attacks. Rommel was able to thin out his forces and although the 15th Panzer Division had been reduced to 200 men and 15 tanks, Rommel disengaged and withdrew without further loss.

Then followed a two-day lull while both sides rested, brought up supplies and frantically tried to repair tanks and bring up reinforcements. The Germans were too exhausted and the British too disorganized to renew the battle, but on 8th July it was Rommel who renewed the attack, sending 50 tanks and 2000 infantry against the British positions. Fighting continued around the Alamein Line for the rest of the month, but there was little shape to it. Field Marshal Michael Carver describes it as, 'a series of sprawling punches, never a knock-out blow.' Each side attacked in turn, only to find that the other had in the interval grown a little stronger. For 7th Armoured, the month of July was a relatively quiet time. The armoured cars were hampered by a good deal of soft sand at the south end of the Line, but the Division was now regrouping and had regained command of both 4th Armoured Brigade (now entitled the 4th Light Armoured Brigade) and the 7th Motor Brigade. The 4th South African Armoured Car Regiment, which had done sterling service, remained under command, but returned to the Delta to refit, while the KDGs came forward and the 11th Hussars returned from Iraq. Seventh Motor Brigade were the most active during this period, with both Rifle battalions in constant contact with the enemy, and on 4th July 1942, Brigadier Lord Garmoyle of the Rifle Brigade was mortally wounded.

The critical situation at Alamein and the continual successes of General Rommel throughout the summer, which had brought him to within sixty miles of Cairo, brought Winston Churchill to Egypt. He found the troops, 'brave but bewildered, but still cheerful, confident and proud of themselves.' He was less happy with General Auchinleck. In his poor opinion of Auchinleck, he might have had some disagreement with General Rommel, who declared later that, 'General Auchinleck ... handled his forces (at First Alamein) with remarkable skill. He did not allow himself to be led on by any of our moves into adopting a second-class solution.' Auchinleck was preparing for a fresh offensive at the end of July, but when Churchill arrived on 4th August, he had already decided that Auchinleck must go. Having reviewed the situation on the spot, he refused to accept Auchinleck's objection to any renewal of the offensive before September. Churchill proposed that the War Cabinet replace Auchinleck, with General Alexander becoming C-in-C Middle East, while the command of 8th Army went to General Straffer Gott, who was then commanding 13 Corps. This was agreed and General Gott was flying back to take up this appointment when his plane was shot down by German fighters. Gott actually survived the crash and escaped from the aircraft, but was killed when he returned to the burning plane to rescue men trapped inside. This was another great blow to the Desert Army, and not least to the men of 7th Armoured, but it brought to the Desert one of the most charismatic generals of the war, a man who was to prove a match for Erwin Rommel, Lt-General Bernard Law Montgomery, the famous 'Monty', who took over command of 8th Army on 13th August. Monty's first move was to import fresh generals from England. Lt-General Sir Oliver Leese took over 30 Corps, and Lt-General Brian Horrocks took over 13 Corps.

Unlike all other positions in North Africa, the Alamein Line could not be outflanked. The northern end rested on the sea, the southern end on the quaking sand and salt flats of the wide Qattara Depression. There were a few tracks across the depression, used from time to time by jeep patrols of the Long Range Desert Group, but these tracks would not support heavy transport or continual use. With his flanks secure, General Montgomery proceeded to thicken his defences, train and revitalize his troops, and ensure a superiority of men, tanks and guns over his German opponent. In this, Montgomery was highly successful. By the time of the Battle of Alamein, or Second Alamein as some accounts call it, in October 1942, Montgomery had over 1,100 tanks, including 210 Grants and almost 270 of the new Shermans. Rommel's Panzerarmee had only 200 tanks, mostly Panzer IIIs, and only 30 of the long 75mm armed Panzer IVs, some with the long 50mm gun, plus less than 300 of the obsolete Italian M13s. Although every British tank crew lived in fear of the 88mms, Rommel had only 24 of these tank-busting weapons, and his 50mm Pak 38s were of less use against the

Sherman, Grant and Valentine tanks which were now starting to arrive. On the other hand the Germans and Italians had Rommel, and he decided to attack before the British position became too strong, striking again in the south, with a thrust towards Alam Halfa at the end of August 1942.

The month of August was spent by 8th Army in re-organization and in reinforcing the Alamein Line. By the middle of the month it had become a true defensive line, with all the box positions held by full divisions and the whole front thickly wired and mined. Into this Alamein Line, ready for the next offensive, came some of the great fighting divisions of the war, and when all had arrived they were deployed as follows: From the North, the tough and experienced 9th Australian Division, then the newly arrived 51st Highland Division, the famous fighting Jocks, who already had a score to settle with General Rommel, dating back to St Valery. Then came the doughty 2nd New Zealand Division, regarded by many as the finest infantry in the desert. 'The British are using New Zealanders, so they must mean business,' wrote Rommel in a despatch. Then came the sorely tried 1st South African Division, then the 4th Indian Division, full of professional, volunteer soldiers from the Indian Empire, then a Greek brigade, and then two British divisions, the 50th, already bloodied in Desert battles, and the newly arrived 44th (Home Counties) Division, which Monty ordered up from the Delta to thicken the Line. This division occupied a ridge, ten miles behind the front line called Alam Halfa. Not all these divisions were in place when Rommel opened the Alam Halfa battle, but the southern end of the Alamein Line was in place, covered with minefields and patrolled by elements of 7th Armoured Division.

South of the vital Ruweisat Ridge, and ready to attack the flank of any force advancing to hook round on Alam Halfa, lay the New Zealanders and the re-equipped 7th Armoured Division, with General Keonig's Free French Brigade.

On taking command, Montgomery took 8th Army by the scruff of the neck and shook it hard. His first decision was to form a real armoured Corps of two divisions, the 1st Armoured and the newly arrived 10th Armoured. There was to be no more 'swanning about in the Blue,' no more columns, no more ad-hoc scattered formations. From now on, like the Afrika Korps, the divisions of 8th Army would fight as divisions. Finding that a commanding officer had not got his officers together for a briefing in months, Monty sacked him on the spot. This caused some talk: 'Here were we, the Desert veterans, and here was this new General, without getting his knees brown, telling us what to do, and getting us up in the morning for P.T.,' recalls Neville Gillman.

Monty has had many critics over the years, but few criticisms are heard from the men who served under him. 'When Monty was in command, at least you knew what was going on ... this is by no means always the case in military affairs,' is just one comment. It would be wrong, and quite unfair, to say that 8th Army was demoralized at the end of the Gazala retreat and after the battles of Mersa Matruh and First Alamein in July, but it is reasonable to say that the troops were a trifle disillusioned, both with the Higher Command and with much of their equipment, but even here, things were improving. The new Crusader tank with a 6-pdr gun was beginning to appear, the American Grant was now in general service at Squadron strength, and 300 Sherman tanks were arriving to equip the tank divisions of 10 Corps. In addition to this, the artillery anti-tank regiments were getting the new 6-pdr anti-tank gun, and the infantry battalions the 2-pdr or, where possible, the 6-pdr. Things were looking up and everyone knew it.

On the Axis side, Rommel had the Afrika Korps, which consisted of 15th and 21st Panzer, plus the 90th Light and brigade of parachute infantry, plus the Italian Army. This consisted of XX Corps, containing the Ariete Armoured Division and the Trieste Motor Division. The Littorio Armoured Division, and three infantry divisions, the Trento, Bologna and Brescia, held the front at Alamein, bolstered by Ramke's parachutists, and the newly arrived Italian parachute division, the Folgore, which had arrived without transport and was virtually immobile.

Rommel had the men and the transport for his thrust at Alam Halfa, but he lacked that vital element, petrol. Repeated requests to, and repeated promises by, the Commando Supremo in Italy failed to produce enough petrol, putting Rommel's entire strategy at risk. In addition, Rommel was ill. He, like many in the desert armies, suffered now from jaundice, complicated by stomach ailments and circulation problems that led to fainting fits. Many of his senior officers were also worn down by two years of constant strain and combat.

Rommel still had only 200 front-line tanks, while the British, at the time of Alam Halfa, had more than 800 and more were arriving daily. However, half Rommel's tanks were now either Panzer IIIs equipped with the long 50mm or Panzer IVs, equipped with the new long barrel 75mm. So, on the night of 30th/31st August, Rommel struck again through the minefields on the southern flank and turned north, intending to roll across the British lines of communication and cut the supply lines feeding the forward boxes. He wrote later that he was relying on 'the slow reaction of the British command, which from experience, we know takes time to reach decisions and put them into effect.'

On this occasion, Rommel's forces found the southern minefields more of an obstacle than they had supposed. While they were held up there, they were subjected to artillery fire from the New Zealanders and the 7th Armoured Division. By dawn on the 31st the Panzer forces had only advanced eight miles behind the minefields to the Alam Halfa Ridge. Here they were held by fire from artillery and tanks of the 22nd Armoured Brigade, and subjected to constant bombing from the Desert Air Force. The leading tanks were engaged by the 22nd Armoured Brigade positioned at the foot of the Alam Halfa ridge, which the enemy did not reach until the evening of 31st August. Twenty-Second Armoured Brigade, now an experienced unit consisting of the battle-hardened 4th CLY, the Scots Greys and the 1st and 5th RTR, which was later attached permanently to 7th Armoured, was then under command of 10th Armoured Division, and commanded by Major General G.P. Roberts.

Before long the Panzer IVs were taking a heavy toll of the Grants and only the precipitate arrival of the Scots Greys stopped the Germans punching a hole through 22 Brigade. The Greys roared down the ridge, urged on by Pip Roberts in typical Cavalry fashion. 'Come on, the Greys. Get your whips out!' By dusk the Greys and the CLY had succeeded in halting the German advance, and the bombing by the RAF continued all night by the light of flares as the German tanks gradually withdrew.

Major Shan Hackett of the 8th Hussars recalls Montgomery and the battle at Alam Halfa. 'The armoured cars were out patrolling the minefields, so we had plenty of notice, and they came back just ahead of the Mk IVs. We then had quite a ding-dong battle. I remember that when it was all over, a Sapper officer drove up in a jeep – a chap in pebble glasses – wanted my map of the minefields to clear the gaps ... I ask you, map, my foot! With Mark IVs ranging on us we didn't have time for marking maps. I told him we had laid about a dozen, and he cleared twelve and blew up on the thirteenth. He was pretty disgruntled about that. I also remember that a lot of us had jaundice and, a day or two later, a staff car drew up and decanted a General, an ADC and a blackboard. The General then proceeded to explain to us how he had won the battle of Alam Halfa, before putting the ADC and the blackboard back into the car and driving off. That was the first time I met General Horrocks.

'I'd already met Monty in Palestine when I was with the Trans-Jordan Frontier Force and he was Divisional General. He sent a memorandum round saying that the training of the mind was of the greatest value, and here was a list of books he wanted all the officers to read. One of them was *Vanity Fair* for God's sake! We had some robust exchanges later ... he was a very vain man, you know. As for the Afrika Korps, we got on very well. After the war, when I commanded 7th Armoured Division in Germany, we made a point of getting to know Frau Rommel and their son Manfred. I greatly admired both of them. We used to play soccer against a team of ex-Afrika Korps veterans – Desert Rats against Desert Foxes.'

Neville Gillman: 'I was a spectator at Alam Halfa. My troop was then in Honeys, detached from 4 CLY and attached to 3 CLY – A Squadron. Major Sandy Cameron of the 4th CLY had a Grant Squadron, twelve tanks, and all of them were brewed up by the Mark IVs. We sat and watched that, and then the Panzers swept past to attack Alam Halfa, where they were thoroughly stonked and bombed by squadrons of Marylands ... there was so much smoke and dust it was hard to see what was happening, but it was our first obvious victory and a tremendous morale booster. At last a plan had actually worked!

'We then went back and did some intensive training for the Alamein battle, by day and night. I went back to the 4th CLY, where I was given the first 6-pdr Crusader tank we had ever seen. It was a bit strange as the gun was so big you had to give up the wireless operator, so reducing the crew to three – driver, gunner, and tank commander, who also operated the wireless. Two days before the battle, a great number of brass-hats, including General Koenig, came to inspect my shiny new tank, and they decided it was much too new and valuable for a chap like me, so I went back to a 2-pdr Crusader, and never got a shot in with my shiny 6-pdr.'

The Desert Air Force played a decisive part in the success of Alam Halfa. Shortage of petrol reduced the German effort on 1st September to a small-scale attack on the Alam Halfa ridge by 15 Panzer, and when Rommel came up to see what was going on, his staff car was bombed six times on the way. 15th Panzer Division put in their attack about 0630 hrs, but by 0830 hrs they too had been driven off. Bombing continued all that day and all the next night, the desert lit again by the incandescant light of parachute flares. With low fuel stocks Rommel started to withdraw on 2nd September, a step-by-step withdrawal, not

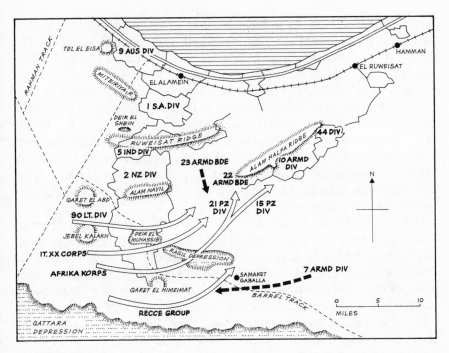

8 Alam Halfa

a rout, but still a welcome if unusual sight to the weary eyes of 8th Army. During the Battle of Alam Halfa, 7th Armoured was ordered to harry the German advance, and the 6-pdr anti-tank guns of the Rifle Brigade did sterling work near Himeimat, knocking out a dozen German tanks during the advance, and the Rifle Brigade then harried the Panzers all the way through the minefields. Allan Austin, then a Bombardier with the Royal Artillery, gives a comprehensive account of this time:

'During the night of 30th/31st August 1942, German and Italian forces moved forward in massive assault, and the battle of Alam Halfa had begun. Twenty-Second Armoured Brigade, and other units of the 7th Armoured Division, defending generally to the south-west of the Alam Halfa ridge, were at the sharp end of the Axis thrust. Artillery units, strategically sited behind the ridge, poured shells continuously into the advancing ranks of enemy armour. Caught in treacherous soft sand, and in the dense minefields, hammered by the Desert Air Force and by our artillery, the attackers had, by 1st September, been repulsed and they quickly fell back to their original start lines.

'Rommel's dream of a victorious march on Alexandria and Cairo was finally shattered here. In fact, the writing was now on the wall for the Afrika Korps. A sandstorm had sprung up unexpectedly at the height of the battle, covering the whole area in a blanket of greyish yellow sand and dust. It was said at the time, but never confirmed, that a light enemy formation had broken through during the battle, and was well on its way to the pyramids at Giza before being mopped up by our forces. This was a short battle, but a crucial one, in the annals of the Desert War. Axis casualties amounted to 3,000 and they lost over 100 aircraft. Our own losses were only marginally less. Major-General Georg von Bismarck, commander of the German 21st Panzer Division was killed at Alam Halfa as he led his division in an attempt to break through the British defensive minefield.

'The Germans and Italians had so stretched their lines of communication that a very serious logistical problem existed for them, even before the Battle of Alam Halfa. They had failed to occupy or neutralise Malta, and this resulted in crippling losses for them, as one supply ship after another, was destroyed in a series of attacks by our Malta based submarines and aircraft. Ironically, a decade or so later, oil was discovered in vast quantities under those very desert sands upon which the Axis tanks ground almost to a halt for lack of fuel.

'Alam Halfa was a Montgomery victory which began to pay huge dividends in the uplift of Army morale – and in the binding together of Army Commander and his officers and men. Things had changed. An air of confidence was everywhere. However, General Montgomery, aiming always at balance before his military moves, decided to bide his time. Time indeed was on his side as the Eighth Army was steadily built up over the next seven weeks. Huge shipments of men, munitions and supplies arrived in the Delta area. Equally important were the visits by General Bernard Montgomery to units throughout the battle areas.

'The Eighth Army commander would arrive at a unit, and call together often 200 or 300 officers and men. He would allow 30 seconds for extinguishing cigarettes, a few more seconds for coughing, then draw the men into a close circle before explaining, in perfectly clear and concise terms, his plan for the forthcoming 8th Army attack, and how the unit being addressed would fit into that plan. At the end of each briefing he seemed to have instilled his own special brand of confidence into every one listening. These talks were always models of clarity, of lucidity and conviction.

'During his inspections of countless units of 8th Army, including our own, General Montgomery would walk through the ranks of officers and men, uttering no words, but looking directly, and squarely, into the eyes of each man paraded. I believe this act, more than any other, was the amalgam which bound commander and men together, and forged indelible, lifelong loyalties. It was an extraordinary exercise in the art of communication.

'The Division continued to be located, during the weeks leading to the final battle, in or around the southern sector. Ragil, Samaket Gaballa and areas to the east of Qatr el Himeimat, and to the north of the Qattara Depression, were all patrolled and defended by the Desert Rats.

'During September and October, the Desert Air Force increased its supremacy and its activity. Flights of Maryland, Boston and Blenheim bombers passed over us every two hours or so, on their way to the enemy positions to the west. These flights were always in formations of eighteen bombers with a dozen, or more, escort fighters. Within minutes of their passing overhead, the thud and crunch of their exploding bombs could be heard, intermingled with the sound, and sight, of the enemy flak. As they flew over us we would sometimes cheer and wave, but always in our thoughts we silently wished them a safe return. Almost always the eighteen would return, roaring overhead, and intact with their fighter escort, on their way back to base. There were occasions, sadly, when the formation returned with the loss of one or two of the planes. We were told that the planes were engaged in systematic carpet bombing of the enemy positions, map square by map square. This must have had a devastating effect on the morale of the Afrika Korps.

'Sleeping on the desert surface, although comfortable enough, could be hazardous. Particularly so when other units' vehicles were being driven through the area at night with restricted lighting. We heard of cases of men being injured in this way. Following day temperatures of well over 100 degrees F. the nights became extremely cold. One's covering blanket would often be quite wet with a kind of desert dew by sunrise, but the powerful sun would quickly remove all traces of dampness from bedding. It was preferable, whenever possible, to bed down in a unit truck or lorry.

'Our maps clearly showed the various well used tracks, and some had rather strange names. I recall particularly the Hat Track, the Bottle Track, the Diamond Track and the Barrel Track. The Barrel Track could guide a traveller across the desert to a point just south of Cairo. We drove along these tracks quite regularly, and so became well acquainted with them. Other tracks, but not used by our unit, were the Sun, Moon, Star, Boat, Boomerang, Springbok and Square Tracks. The Telegraph and Rahman tracks were under the control of the Axis troops, at least until the final breakthrough and pursuit in early November. The tracks which we used were identified by having their symbols displayed on iron staves at intervals of 100 yards or so, and for the entire length of the track. Their constant use, by every form of military transport for so many months, eventually produced some quite bumpy and uncomfortable journeys. Clouds of dust and sand thrown up by the moving vehicles added to the general discomfort. Another good positional guide was a long line of telegraph poles, sited somewhat incongruously, a long way south in the desert, and following a course eastwards from the vicinity of the sinister and brooding peaks of Himeimat. Himeimat, sullen and menacing to the men of 7th Armoured, because for seven long weeks it faced them, sometimes shimmering in the desert heat, and always in the hands of the enemy. An enemy that from Himeimat's twin 600-feet high peaks, could observe and monitor all movement in the flat sea of sand to the east. Enemy armour, guns and infantry had been forced back behind Himeimat following the decisive battle of Alam el Halfa on the 2nd September. Strong German and Italian forces continued to lurk there until the final, savage, assault was made on them on 23rd October 1942.'

After Alam Halfa, and before the Battle of Alamein, there were more changes throughout the Army and to the Division. The 7th Motor Brigade left for 1st Armoured, taking with it the 2nd Bn, The Rifle Brigade and the 4th RHA, which had served in the 7th Armoured Division since Support Group days.

On 7th September it was decided that the 22nd Armoured Brigade should form a permanent part of 7th Armoured Division. It was during this time that General Renton handed over command to a man who became one of the Division's best-loved commanders, General (later Field Marshal) A.F. Harding.

'He had so many fine qualities,' says Field Marshal Lord Carver, who dedicated his own book on the Alamein Battle to Harding, and later wrote Harding's biography. 'He was extremely brave for one thing, so much so that it was dangerous to go on reconnaissance with him. He had a great grasp of the essentials, was very clear-headed, and a first-class leader of men. I learned a great deal from serving with him.' General Harding has left a personal account of his time in command of 7th Armoured, which provides the basis for the next two chapters.

8

Alamein

Now this is not the end. It is not even the beginning
of the end. But it is perhaps the end of the beginning.

Winston S Churchill – Prime Minister
Speech at the Mansion House,
10th November 1942

In the five weeks between Alam Halfa and the opening of the Battle of
Alamein, 8th Army trained relentlessly, by day and night, developed
an elaborate deception plan to conceal the probable point of assault,
and greatly increased its strength in men and tanks. The dispositions
mentioned in the previous chapter were finally completed as more
divisions came into the line, and by the night of the battle, 8th Army's
tank strength rose to 1,350 machines, of which over 1,000 were
with forward units and ready for the assault. The artillery was also
augmented with the field artillery alone able to deploy 832 pieces for
the opening barrage, while the Desert Air Force maintained continuous
raids against Rommel's main supply ports of Tobruk and Benghazi.
Rommel's tank strength was also increasing but slowly at about 20–
25 tanks a day.

Alam Halfa, and the need to train and re-equip, meant that 8th
Army could not attack during the September moon period, which to
Churchill's concern meant delaying any major assault until the next
moon period, and the full moon in October shone on the night of 24th
October. To take full advantage of this, Montgomery opted to attack on
the night of 23rd October, and Churchill was persuaded to accept this,
not least because an attack at the end of October would divert enemy
attention away from the Western Mediterranean, where the Anglo-
American landings – Operation Torch – were due to begin on 8th
November.

Montgomery's plan, which he revealed to the Divisional Commanders on 15th September, was to strike at the Northern end of the Alamein line, where 9th Australian and 51st Highland Divisions of Leese's 30 Corps were to force a gap through which the armoured divisions of 10 Corps could pass. Meanwhile, to divert enemy attention and hold their divisions in the south, Horrocks' 13 Corps, and specifically 7th Armoured Division and the 44th Division would mount an attack, north of Himeimat. Montgomery was well aware that the German and Italian positions on the Alamein line would not be easily overcome. He saw the battle in three phases: a 'break-in' on the first night, 23rd/24th October, a 'crumbling' phase lasting several days or weeks, while the enemy strength was eroded, and then a 'breakthrough'. In the event it took several all-out assaults to achieve the second phase, and 8th Army did not finally break through the German and Italian line until 7th November, two weeks after the start of the battle, one day before the start of Operation Torch.

Meanwhile, the Germans, in full anticipation of this onslaught, were digging in, laying mines, and increasing their tank strength. Many of their senior commanders were exhausted or ill, including Erwin Rommel, now a Field Marshal, who handed over command of the Panzerarmee Africa to General Stumme on 19th September, though declaring that when the British launched a major attack he would return to the command. Among other changes, General Von Thoma took over command of the Afrika Korps, and Von Randow replaced Von Bismark of 21st Panzer, who had been killed at Alam Halfa. Stumme himself was to die of a heart attack on the second day of the Alamein battle. Many other officers, ill with jaundice or amoebic dysentery were home on sick leave, though Rommel himself retired only to Rome, where he harried the Commando Supremo over the ever-vexing matter of supplies, before retreating to rest at a spa in Austria.

For an account of 7th Armoured during this period, we can turn to that of General Harding.

'There is no greater honour or thrill for a soldier than to be given command of a fighting formation. When the formation concerned happens to be an armoured division that has already made a great name for itself, and when the appointment comes at a time when the army is preparing for an offensive, the excitement and elation are all the greater.

'I think it was on 15th September 1942 that I heard the glad news that I was to command 7th Armoured Division – the famous Desert Rats. I was deputy Chief-of-Staff at the time so knew what great events

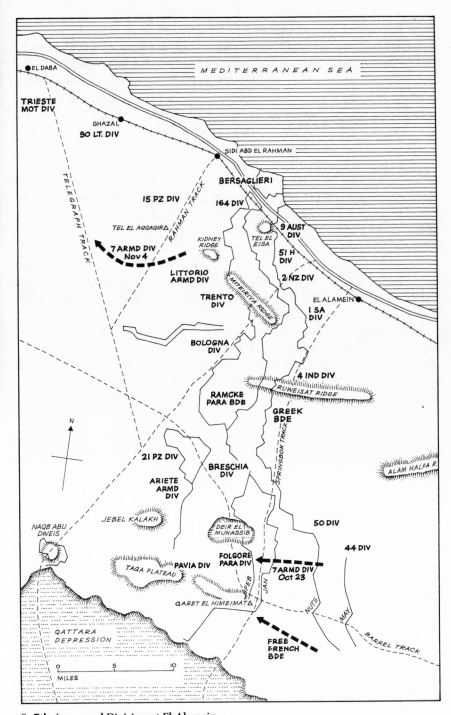

9 7th Armoured Division at El Alamein

were impending, when one evening I was summoned to see the Commander-in-Chief, General Alexander. I had no idea of the reason he wished to see me. It might have been one of a hundred things, so the surprise was all the greater when he told me in his quiet, friendly fashion that he had decided to give me command of 7th Armoured Division, and that I was to report to General Montgomery at 8th Army Headquarters as soon as possible. I shall never forget how thrilled and excited I was.

'General McCreery, the Chief of Staff, was an old friend, and with his help I was able to leave the next day for the Western Desert. After a brief interview with the Army Commander at his Headquarters on the coast, I went on to the headquarters of my new command, which was then holding the left flank of the Army front. There I was welcomed by General Renton, whom I was to relieve, and who most kindly went out of his way to give me all the help he could. I shall always be most deeply grateful to him and to his Staff, who also gave me a warm welcome and could not have served me more efficiently and loyally throughout my four months in command.

'The next few weeks were extremely busy ones. Having served from December 1940 to February 1942 as BGS of Western Desert Force and 13 Corps, I had the advantage of knowing something of the character of the Division and of desert warfare – to put it colloquially, I knew a bit about 'the form'. I also knew that plans were being prepared for a large scale offensive though nothing as yet of the part that 7th Armoured Division would be required to play, nor how much time we would be allowed to prepare for it. Obviously, my first task was to get to know the Division and the front for which I was responsible, and my time was spent visiting units, carrying out reconnaissances, studying intelligence reports and discussing plans with my Commanders and Staffs – getting the 'feel' of units and making myself known to all ranks, getting to know the enemy and the ground. The more I saw of my troops the prouder I became of my new command, and the more confident I was that given the opportunity they would give an excellent account of themselves.

'At this time the Division comprised 22 Armoured Brigade (a normal armoured brigade) commanded by Brigadier (now Major General) G.P.B. Roberts, whom I'd known in various capacities during the previous two years and who, in my opinion, is the most outstanding armoured commander ever produced by the British Army; the 4th Light Armoured Brigade (composed of two armoured car regiments, one light tank regiment, and a motor battalion) commanded by Brigadier Carr who

THIS AXIS
HAS BEEN
LAID FROM

EL ALEMEIN TO BERLIN
VIA:-

AFRICA
TOBRUK
BENGHAZI
TRIPOLI
MARETH
TUNIS

ITALY
SALERNO
NAPLES
VOLTURNO

FRANCE
NORMANDY
THE SEINE
ROUBAIX

BELGIUM
OUDENARDE
GHENT
MALINES

HOLLAND
EINDHOVEN
TILBURG
THE MAAS

GERMANY
THE RHINE
AHAUS
SULINGEN
NIENBURG
SOLTAU
HAMBURG

'The March of the Desert Rats'. This sign was erected on the outskirts of Berlin. (*Courtesy of D. J. Watson*)

11th Hussar armoured cars in the Western Desert. (*Imperial War Museum*)

After the battle – Western Desert, 1941. (*Imperial War Museum*)

...ocked-out tanks and trucks in the Western Desert. (*Imperial War Museum*)

...igadier Jock Campbell, support group of 7th Armoured Division, drives the Divisional Commander,
...ajor General Gott, into Benghazi. (*Imperial War Museum*)

General Grant's tanks in the Western Desert. (*Imperial War Museum*)

Captain E. D. Riddell of 550 Company. (*Courtesy of E. D. Riddell*)

RIGHT Armoured car troopers of the 4th South African Armoured Car Regiment.

LEFT 11th Hussar armoured cars going forward. (*Courtesy of W. J. Diamond*)

RIGHT 4th South African Armoured Car Patrol near Gazala, 1942. (*Courtesy of W. J. Diamond*)

Crusader Tank in the Western Desert. (*Imperial War Museum*)

7th Armoured Division tanks near Villers Bocage. (*Imperial War Museum*)

arrier-borne troops of the Queen's Brigade in Normandy. (*Imperial War Museum*)

roops of the 1/5 Queen's Royal Regiment marching through Ghent.

Victory Parade, Berlin, 1945. 5th R.H.A. Drive Past. (*Courtesy of R. Mallabar*)

General Montgomery inspecting guard of honour from B Company, 9th D.L.I. – 7th Armoured Division. (*Courtesy of Major P. K. Tomkin*)

ALAMEIN

was shortly replaced by Brigadier Roddick. Both brigades had been fully engaged throughout the hard fighting in the preceding Spring and Summer. They had wide battle experience but were short of recent training and still more of new equipment. Many of the vehicles had been "up and back" more than once and were distinctly "ropey". None the less all ranks were in good spirits and full of hope for the future. Their recent success in the battle of Alam Halfa, in which 22 Armoured Brigade had played the leading role, had established complete confidence in the new leadership of Generals Alexander and Montgomery, and in General Horrocks in whose Corps the Division were serving. It had also confirmed the tactical doctrine of employing armour in the mass and in the closest association with artillery, infantry, engineers and the Air Force, which as DMT (Director Military Training) Middle East, I had consistently preached during the previous Spring and Summer. Our steadily rising spirits were based on sound foundations, and were aided by the weather, which in Autumn in the Western desert, is particularly invigorating after the heat of the Summer.

'On the other side of the medal I had three major anxieties: (a) The state of our equipment, which I have already mentioned, and the knowledge that we were not 'on the list' for anything new, so would have to go through the campaign with what we had. This demanded special attention to repair and maintenance before active operations began. (b) The fact that our operational commitment precluded any possibility of comprehensive unit and formation training. Although there was little likelihood of any large scale attack by the enemy after his recent heavy defeat, the possibility could not be entirely excluded, and I had therefore to confine training to what was possible without unduly weakening my front. I was, however, determined that both brigades should have an opportunity, however restricted, to practise their battle tasks, and in spite of all the difficulties that was somehow achieved. (c) My third anxiety was my shortage of infantry, and here I found myself the victim of my own previous plans. I was hoist with my own petard.

'It arose this way ... When General Montgomery arrived in the Middle East, he asked me to submit plans for the organization of a mobile reserve of two armoured divisions and an infantry division. To meet his requirements I had recommended the transfer of 7th Motor Brigade from the 7th to the 1st or 10th Armoured Division. This was done, and in all the circumstances rightly I consider. However, in my new capacity as Commander 7th Armoured Division, I felt compelled to ask General Montgomery for the return of 7th Motor Brigade. My request was

145

politely but most firmly refused, and I must admit that in the circumstances the Army Commander was right. It is an interesting sidelight on the application to war of the saying that "circumstances alter cases". In the event, 7th Motor Brigade played an outstanding part in the battle, and my shortage of infantry was to some extent made good in other ways. However, my experience in this matter brought home to me more closely than ever before the great importance of avoiding, whenever at all possible, changes in the composition of formations.

'These considerations made our immediate tasks clear, namely, training, repair and maintenance and carefully planned patrolling to gain as much information as possible about the enemy without arousing his suspicions of what was afoot.'

This could be difficult, as Corporal J. Percival of the Military Police recalls: 'The 4th Armoured Brigade were lying off the extreme south of the Alamein line, and one afternoon a young German officer was brought into our leaguer. He had been captured in no-man's land between the two armies by the 11th Hussars. There being no provision for prisoners, he was handed over to myself and two other NCOs to guard until the following morning, when he would be sent to the rear and, no doubt, to a POW camp. He spoke excellent English, and after dinner the vehicles drew into the usual three columns and we bedded down on the ground beside the truck, after drawing lots for our guard trucks. I drew the 10pm until 2am spell. We shared our blankets with the prisoner and settled down for the night.

'When my turn came round, the prisoner was apparently sleeping between my two mates by the wheels of our truck, and I was sitting on a petrol can, facing them. It was a dark but starlit night and about 1am the prisoner leapt to his feet and made off across the leaguer. I gave a yell as I made after him, and after the initial burst of speed we settled down to a steady pace with the prisoner a few yards ahead of me. It was instinctive to note the direction of any movement after dark, or indeed in daylight, and I knew we had started in a northerly direction. After a while I realized he was not drawing away from me, and I gradually divested myself of my clothing and my pistol went with my great-coat. Eventually I drew near enough to him to dive for his legs and brought him down. He was completely demoralized and begged me to shoot him. Needless to say I didn't divulge I was unarmed. When we got our wind back, I hauled him to his feet, put an armlock on him and set off in a southerly direction in the hope we could find the leaguer. After a while I heard the "putt-putt" of the engine charging the HQ batteries, and made towards it. Now came the dicey part. I knew the

Brigade would be standing to, but I took a chance and hailed them, and perhaps being the only Northumbrian in the camp, we were recognised and got to safety.'

General Harding again: 'Soon the general plan of campaign was unfolded – the major attack in the North and a holding attack by 7th Armoured Division with the Free French brigade under command in the South, designed to retain the German armour on that flank. At the same time I was given the most explicit instructions by General Montgomery personally; that I must keep my Division in being as an effective fighting formation.

'The divisional plan for carrying out its task is given elsewhere, so I haven't gone into it here. It was easy to discern the strong influence of the Army Commander (who had been an instructor at the Staff College when I was a student in 1928–29) from the care and attention paid to all details of plans and preparations, and particularly to the special arrangements made for security and deception on the one hand, and ensuring that all ranks understood what was required of them and why, on the other. The atmosphere of well-designed objective preparations, lively expectancy and quiet confidence that pervaded the Division, and indeed the whole Army, is the outstanding feature in my recollection of this period. At the same time there was a feeling that we in 7th Armoured Division were to be the Cinderella of the party. Jibes were heard in the Division about the "Corps de chasse" as 10 Corps (1 and 10 Armoured Divisions) with far less desert experience than we had, and the New Zealand Division) who had re-equipped with Sherman tanks and were then training in rear, had come to be called. Also there were rumours that after playing our part in the opening battle we were to be withdrawn to the Delta to refit. I had seen too much of the course of the previous desert campaigns to worry about being left out. The emphatic orders that I had to keep the Division intact as an effective fighting formation left no doubt in my mind that we should have our chance. My only anxiety was how best, when the time came, to hold the balance between that requirement and my immediate task of holding the enemy on my front, which could only be done by a determined attack.'

The role of 7th Armoured Division referred to above, was to contain the 21st Panzer Division in the South during the early days of the battle. If all went well, 7th Armoured were to pass through the two minefields which lay to their front, and then swing North towards Daba. Harding planned to penetrate the minefields north of Himeimat and capture Himeimat Hill and the escarpment to the west. The minefields would be penetrated by 44th Reconnaissance Regiment, which had been trained in mine lifting, while the Free French Brigade, then under command with the Division, would retake Himeimat. This done, the 22nd and 4th Armoured Brigades would pass through the minefields and establish bridgeheads, which would later be occupied by the 44th Home Counties Division. General Harding's problem was to execute these tasks without allowing his Division to be embroiled in any encounter which would reduce its strength below that required of an effective fighting formation ready for future use.

Allan Austin, then a bombardier in the 3rd RHA, gives an account of this time. 'It must be stated that the desert war was fought, by and large, on gentlemanly and humane terms. There was a good deal of evidence of this. The military hospital at Mersa Matruh was full of British, Commonwealth, French, German and Italian wounded in late June 1942, as 8th Army retreated. A hundred or more doctors, nurses and medical staff refused to leave their wounded patients, and stayed on to hand over the hospital intact to the advancing Axis forces. We heard that Field Marshal Rommel insisted on shaking hands with all the medical staff, thanking them for their care of the German and Italian wounded. He apparently asked them to carry on for a few weeks until he was able to replace them with his own medical staff. He would not, he said, allow them to become POWs and he subsequently arranged for their safe conduct to neutral Switzerland.

'We heard, too, of reports that during the earlier fighting in May, around Gazala, a German scout car flying a white flag, drove up to a British casualty station, where some Axis troops were among the wounded. A German medical officer dismounted, and brought in medical equipment and supplies. The German officer accepted the offer of a light meal before driving back to his lines. On another occasion, in late June, as the Germans rolled eastwards towards Mersa Matruh, they shot up a light British column, badly wounding a number of our men. As the Germans approached the burning vehicles, the 8th Army men, although armed, made no attempt to use their weapons, but carried on attending to their wounded. There was no formal truce, as the Germans, led by a young lieutenant, alighted from their vehicles and, moved by the plight of the British party, produced some of their own bandages and helped tend the wounded. Eventually the Germans remounted, and as they did so, the senior British NCO present saluted the German officer who, in turn, returned the salute before moving off to the east.

'Reports of Italian military performance in the desert were, almost always, grossly and unfairly dismissive. Like any other army, the Italians suffered reversals, but it should be remembered that their equipment was not up to the standard of either the British or the German Army. They had few heavy weapons, and their M13 tanks were at a marked disadvantage against the heavily armed British ones. Sandbags were placed round the doors of their tanks to give extra protection. Italians fought with immense courage at El Alamein, and their infantry units were desperately unlucky to have been left stranded without water or transport, deep in the southern sector at the end of the twelve-day battle. When assessing their resistance, and taking into account the massive weight of shot and shell against them, together with heavy and interminable air attacks, it is really a wonder that men were able to resist for so long. The Italian army fought stubbornly at the battles of Mareth and Akarit under General Messe, who had succeeded Rommel as Axis Army Commander. Later, at Enfidaville, as the North African campaign drew to its close, Italians fought with great courage and determination. They were much maligned by reporters, and the media, during the African campaign, and curiously by later generations of writers, and others who, quite simply, have never been in a position to actually verify their stories.

'On driving around in the southern sector, it was not unusual to see wrecked and burnt-out planes of both the Luftwaffe and the Desert Air Force. Very occasionally limited dog-fights took place high above our heads, and with the inevitable casualty. More often, however, it was anti-aircraft fire that caused these wrecks. One day we noticed German Me's flying in from the west at very high speed, and being pursued by South African fighters. The South Africans could not close in on the swifter Me's, and our anti-aircraft fire, intended for the enemy, hit one of the South African planes in error, and tragically brought it down in flames, away to our south-east. We could only watch rather helplessly one afternoon as three or four Italian Caproni bombers flew overhead. We had no defence, and could only take refuge in shallow slit trenches. They flew over us and dropped their bombs half a mile away, on a cluster of vehicles at a military police outpost, leaving a dense pall of black smoke. The Italian Air Force, the Regia Aeronautica, was not seen a great deal over our sector, and there was a marked diminution too, in Luftwaffe activity after the battle of Alam Halfa.

'The main barrage at El Alamein began at 2140 hours on 23rd October 1942. The relative quiet of that moonlit night was torn apart as a thundering, crushing barrage of shells from over 1000 guns rained down on the enemy positions. This was the first major artillery barrage of the war, and certainly the first since the massive artillery bom-

ALAMEIN
ORDER OF BATTLE OCTOBER 1942

4th Light Armoured Brigade
3rd RHA
Royal Scots Greys
4th Hussars and one squadron
  8th Hussars
2nd Derbyshire Yeomanry
1st KRRC

22nd Armoured Brigade
1st RTR
5th RTR
4th CLY
4th Field Regiment RA
97th Field Regiment RA
1st Rifle Brigade

131st (Queens) Brigade
1st/5th Queens Royal Regiment
1st/6th Queens Royal Regiment
1st/7th Queens Royal Regiment
53rd Field Regiment RA
Two batteries 57th Anti-Tank
  Regiment RA
11th Field Company RE

Divisional Troops
11th Hussars
15th Light AA Regiment RA
65th Anti-Tank Regiment RA
Divisional Signals

Royal Engineers
4th Field Squadron
21st Field Squadron
143rd Field Park Squadron

RASC
No. 5 Company
No. 10 Company
No. 58 Company
No. 67 Company
No. 287 Company
No. 432 Company
No. 507 Company

RAMC
2nd Light Field Ambulance
7th Light Field Ambulance
14th Light Field Ambulance
15th Light Field Ambulance

RAOC
Divisional Ordnance Field Park
15th Light AA Workshop
In each brigade – one Ordnance
  Field Park and one Workshop

NB: *Note from now on the inclusion of a full infantry brigade operating as a brigade in 7th Armoured.*

bardments of the Western Front during the First World War.

'The German commander of the 164th Light Africa Division, General Lungershausen, described the opening of the barrage as being like the mighty roar of a thunder clap. It was, he said, as though a giant had banged his fist down on a table. As ever, though, the enemy reaction was almost immediate, and their shelling took an early and heavy toll of our attacking infantry. The sky over the whole of the 40-mile front shimmered, like sheet lightning, with the flashes of the firing guns, and of the exploding shells.

'The 7th Armoured Division was in position on 23rd October between Deir el Munassib and Qatr el Himeimat. The objectives marked out for the division were Jebel Kalakh and the Taqa Plateau, west of the Himeimat heights. The Division ran into immense problems attempting to penetrate the enemy defensive minefields to the north-west of Himeimat which remained firmly in German hands. On 25th October General Feldmarschall Rommel returned to direct the operations of the German and Italian armies. At this time there was a gradual shift in the weight of the battle, in that forces were moved from the south to the northern sector. The heavyweights in Rommel's southern army, the 21st Panzer Division and the Italian Ariete Armoured Division, together with much of the enemy artillery, moved quickly north, and activity in our sector lessened noticeably.'

General Harding's account continues: 'Throughout the period of planning and preparations I was immensely helped by the Corps Commander, General Horrocks, and his staff. My own staff and commanders were also a tower of strength. Lieutenant-Colonels Carver and Turner (GSO I and AA & QMG) call for special mention. At last the great day came, and at dusk the Division began its move through our own minefields, across no-man's-land and the attack began.'

Lance-Sergeant Waddington was one of the gunners firing the barrage at Alamein in support of the 131st Infantry, the famous Queens Brigade: 'The Battle of Alamein began at 9.30 pm on 23rd October and I can recall the frightening experience of the terrible noise that seemed to be all around you. I was in charge of B Gun – 25 pounders, and I remember, after about an hour of firing, the Bombardier from C Gun came running over to me to say his sergeant (always thought to be a real tough guy) had gone raving mad and was shouting all sorts of things and seemed to be going off his head. He was taken away and I had to show the bombardier how to read the firing lift – we had to elevate the gun after so many rounds so that it was always in front of the advancing infantry. We had very few casualties. I lost a pal, Signaller

Les Whittaker from Swinton, Manchester, who was killed laying lines.

'Memories I recall about the Germans and Italians were that the Italians were very poor soldiers compared with the Germans. Their equipment was far inferior. The Germans had an 88mm gun from which you only heard the whistle of the shell after it exploded. Apart from the Sherman tanks which we had, I would say that most of the German equipment was much better than ours. To obtain a German jerry-can was everyone's aim.'

General Harding again: 'My recollection is of a snake-like procession of a mass of tanks and guns and other vehicles in an atmosphere of smoke and dust and noise, all vividly illuminated at one point by a blazing carrier. My anxiety was the danger of confusion or loss of direction, but though there were many delays and mistakes the first part of the night's operations went more or less according to plan, though more slowly than we had hoped. The first of the enemy mine-fields (January) was successfully breached by 44 Reconnaissance Regiment (which in the absence of infantry had been specially organised and trained for this task), and the Sappers. The leading armoured regiments of both brigades passed through and established strong bridgeheads west of the minefield. About this time too, the Free French Brigade reported that they had secured a footing on the Eastern part of their objective, the hill feature of Himeimat, which overlooked the rest of the divisional front and which I had no wish to find still in enemy hands when daylight came.

'So far, so good, but though an attempt was made to breach the next minefield (February), the casualties suffered by 44 Reconnaissance Regiment combined with the small amount of darkness left, deprived us of success. It would have proved extremely costly to continue the effort in daylight, especially as by then the French had been driven back by a German counter-attack with (according to first reports) alarming losses. It was therefore decided to maintain our position and to renew the attack on the night of 24/25th October. For that purpose 131 Infantry Brigade, the Queens Brigade, of 44 Division was placed under my command.

'We were naturally disappointed but by no means cast down as a result of our first night's fighting. A number of prisoners had been taken, our own casualties had not been heavy, and French losses proved far less than first reported. Though our armour in the bridgehead came in for a good deal of enemy artillery fire during the day, little damage was done. Plans were completed for the attack by 131 Brigade and I looked forward hopefully to the next night's operation.

'In their attack in the early part of the night of 24/25th October, 131 Infantry Brigade quickly secured a bridgehead west of the second enemy minefield (February). Then our troubles began. The infantry were pinned to their ground by enemy fire, and efforts to clear lanes through the minefields for the armour proved slow and costly. At last two gaps were reported clear and 4 CLY and 1 RTR moved forward to pass through them. Both regiments lost tanks, especially 4 CLY, though whether from mines or enemy anti-tank guns was not clear. However, remembering my instructions to keep my division intact, I could not risk further losses. As daylight was then approaching, I decided to maintain the infantry bridgehead west of "February", but to make no further attempt to pass armour through that night. Next day the attack was called off, and I was warned that my division would be relieved by 44 Division and withdrawn into reserve on the night of 25th/26th October.'

Neville Gillman, now a lieutenant, recalls this advance through the minefields on 23/24th October. 'As I told you, we had had a period of very intensive training for the Alamein attack, rehearsing our role by day and night. The day before the battle, incidentally, a Mobile Dental Unit turned up in the Squadron position, so we all had our teeth checked! At about 9pm on the 23rd, the bombardment started, quite tremendous and very heartening; the sky was lit with flashes from our end of the line far to the north ... what a din. We already had Monty's Order of the Day. I kept mine for years until one of my sons managed to lose it, and so it was all very exciting and inspiring. The very ground was shaking under the shellfire.

'C Squadron of the 4th CLY was the first tank squadron through the minefield, led by a 2nd Lt. Hubert Smith, who lived to tell the tale and later came to my wedding (he now lives in Australia). The old charging and cavalry tactics were not used here. The Sappers – God bless them – went ahead with the infantry of the Queens Brigade to clear the mines and make a bridgehead in the moonlight, and the leading companies were decimated. We followed a line of lamps across the "January" minefield into the gap between that one and the "February" field, where we stayed all next day, the 24th, sitting inside our tanks being shelled fairly frequently.

'On the next night we had orders to push on through the "February" field ... it's a bit dim after that. We followed what was left of the Queens, and there was no element of surprise now. When we got through the gap everything opened up on us from the flank and front; my searchlight and periscope were shot off, inches from my head, as we went through

153

the gap. As I recall, we were through by about 1 am on the 25th. There were lots of mines and a ring of anti-tank guns awaiting us and one by one my squadron went off the air. In the end there was nothing moving, and suddenly the Colonel came on the air and said, "Any tank which is still a runner pull out and come back". We had been lying doggo between two knocked-out tanks, but we started up and I said, "Driver reverse," and as we started to move, everything opened up on us. That is when the shell came in that ended my career with the 7th Armoured Division.

'The shell, an 88mm I think, came in one side and blew the other side of the turret wide open, killing all the crew except the driver and myself. Being small, I was not sitting in the commander's seat, but squatting on it, and that is what saved me. I felt a blow on my leg and fell onto the bottom of the fighting compartment, and all the ammo was on fire, so I hauled myself out over the gun, out of the turret – I don't know how – and rolled off onto the sand. My leg was broken in two places, but the driver, Corporal Kennedy, hauled me away into a slit trench, dumped me in it and went off to find help. I sat there alone in the dark, feeling a bit isolated. I was taken back to an Aid Post, but the leg got gas-gangrene and eventually it had to come off.'

Derrick Watson gives an account of the infantry fighting with the 1/5th Queen's at Alamein: 'I left England in February 1942 on the liner *Windsor Castle*, along with 15,000 other troops in a convoy which was considered too fast for submarines, so did not need a naval escort. It is ironic that the liner was sunk by a Japanese submarine off the Cape on the way back.

'The 1/5 Battalion of the Queen's Royal Regiment was a Territorial Battalion with some service in France prior to Dunkirk – a firmly knit family almost – when it was thrown into battle in Egypt almost as soon as it disembarked. They were still feeling the loss of so many of their friends at Menassib. (Two Companies, 300 men were lost.) It was some time before Ted and I could feel ourselves members of the Queen's brotherhood. I felt this in the first job I was given, which was to rescue the personal effects from the "big packs" of some 100 of the "missing" men for return to their next of kin in the UK. We were then part of the 44th London Division and were briefed in the inimitable Montgomery style to stage a major diversion in the south. I don't know if it diverted the enemy, but it certainly didn't divert us.

'After a sketchy briefing, I found myself heading an enormous convoy of the entire battalion to an assembly area along an unmarked track, with only a scribbled sketch map and a useless grid reference. After only a few hundred yards, I found myself at a complete loss. I halted the convoy and walked back down the line of vehicles until I found Captain Grant MC. In answer to my frantic plea, he took my place at the head of the column and we reached the assembly area, better late than never. Some 20 years after this, I was told that by getting "lost", I nearly lost the Battle of Alamein. In the Assembly area I was re-united with Ted Sarginson at the NAAFI Van, which had appeared from nowhere to give comforts to us at this critical hour – God bless them.

'At last light on the evening of 23rd October we set out to cross February minefield about 1000 yards wide. To this day I don't know whether they were German or English mines. We hoped and believed they were German Teller mines, which were always buried beneath the sand and required the weight of a vehicle to set them off. As it happens, the mines were the least of our worries. We were to advance behind a creeping barrage of 800 guns – real First World War stuff. There were a number of casualties in Ted Sarginson's platoon on my right, owing to one gun firing short. Subsequently it was rumoured that the gun had been taken out of Cairo museum to "make up the numbers".

'We were led from the front by Lt-Col Lance East, a gallant Regular officer, who walked with the aid of a stick because of a First World War wound. The stick appeared to be his only offensive weapon. We suffered casualties from booby traps attached to the barbed wire, and I can still remember the shriek from Private Mansell as he was blown to pieces by one of them. Cpl Taffy Jones, a garrulous Celt, was heard by several to state he could "murder fish and chips at that moment," but then he was never seen or heard again. Each platoon had wire cutters, so there was congestion getting through the gaps cut in the wire and then frantic attempts to catch up with the others once through.

'Major Cooper, leading the way on a compass bearing had out-distanced Col. East and the rest of us until he was hit by machine-gun fire from the flank. We had reached our objective, having cleared the minefield and were in close contact with the enemy. There was a period of confusion in the darkness, while we vainly attempted to regroup and advance further. Then I found myself sharing a slit trench with Sgt. "Sniffy" Parkin, in response to a shouted command to "dig-in", which was extremely difficult owing to the nature of the terrain. The sergeant had, in effect, constructed a sangar, a wall built up, as you could not get down into the earth more than 2 to 3 ft, and then only with difficulty. Fortunately we were in a slight dip, so we were safe from direct observation by the enemy machine-guns, which continued to fire on the battalion during the day. Lt. Hayes, just near me, occupied himself during the day by mapping the positions of three of these posts (compass bearings, distances etc.) and this sketch map was received with delight by the gunners the next day.

'We occupied our slit trench sangar for the next seventeen hours, and once daylight came it was dangerous to lift your head, and suicide to stand up. We had biscuits and bully and water in our bottles. The Battalion suffered heavy casualties during those 17 hours, particularly from mortar fire. I remember young O'Connell had both legs severed by a mortar bomb and was screaming for help, and then for his mother, before he mercifully died. Major Cooper who had disappeared from sight when hit, called out at intervals during the day, before he, too, fell quiet.

'The only communication was by shouting from one trench to another. An officer runner (Lt. Opperman) was sent back before first light to ask for tanks to come forward in support. In fact, the tanks suffered heavy casualties from German anti-tank guns directed from OPs on Himeimat. Showing great *élan* the Free French had captured this "peak", but in the midst of celebrating their capture, were driven off by a fierce counter-attack. From this peak the enemy's observers had a full view of what was happening and brought down increasingly heavy fire on the bridgehead and the "lanes".

'For some reason the mortar fire ceased in the early afternoon, and then some 20 Italians from the Falgore parachute division surrendered rather sheepishly to Lt. Pat Kingsford, who was in charge of what had been the rear platoon, which had moved up on our right when we had become pinned down. He sent them back in the charge of his runner (Keohane by name). They came under fire from their compatriots and were last seen by us crawling cautiously to the rear.

'As evening approached, Col. East gave the order that we would withdraw at last light, and asked for three volunteers to cover the withdrawal as a rearguard. Those forward of us who were in a position to observe the enemy reported they were gathering in force for an attack. I was nominated by Major Elliott to be in charge of the rearguard, but before I could make any plan there was a sudden rush of feet and the disengagement began. I was the last to disengage, and have no recollection of clearing two barbed wire fences and a thousand yards of minefield. However, I found myself in the midst of our tanks carrying two rifles and "escorted" by some fifteen unarmed Italians anxious to be prisoners.

'Three days later we received the English-language newspapers from Cairo and were relieved to learn that el Alamein had been a great victory, and that they were ringing the church bells in England.'

General Harding continues: 'On the afternoon of 25th October, 4/8 Hussars, who were covering the right flank of the Division, were ordered to advance north-westward in support of operations by 50th Division, on our right. They ran into heavy enemy anti-tank fire and minefields and began to lose tanks faster than I could afford, so the movement was stopped.

'Though I could not escape a feeling of considerable disappointment at the limited successes we had gained, I was told that our attacks had achieved their object of holding enemy armour in the South for the first 48 hours or so of the battle, which cheered me up personally, and there was no evidence of any loss of enthusiasm in the Division.

'Daylight on 25th October found the part of the Division that was deployed between the January and February minefields congested and very exposed. We were subjected to a good deal of long range medium and heavy enemy artillery fire to which we had no effective reply. For me it was a day of considerable anxiety and I longed for nightfall to get my precious tanks back. My CRA, Roy Mews, who was with me at my Tac HQ, was wounded during the day. Fortunately, his wound was slight and he rejoined a week or two later, but later on that evening, my ADC, Harry Cosgrave, was hit and killed by shell-fire as we drove back through the minefields in my jeep. He was a very great loss. On the whole, however, our losses were much less than I had feared, and we were lucky to have a few days respite for repairs and maintenance before we moved to the Northern flank for our next task.

'These first few days fighting were an invaluable experience for me, and I think for the whole Division. They gave us the opportunity of bringing into full working order under battle conditions our system of command and control, our battle movement drill, and team fighting technique without serious losses or damage. All this was to stand us in excellent stead in the following weeks. It provided the opportunity for bringing this brilliant and experienced steeplechaser (7th Armoured Division) back into full training again, and getting him on terms with his new jockey (myself).'

Brigadier C.E.F. Turner kept a scrapbook of his time with 7th Armoured, a fine collection of notes, photographs and letters. Here are some extracts from October 1942, including the first two days of the Alamein Battle:

'4th October: I have spent the last seven years in stuffy offices at big HQs, so I am very pleased to be getting in touch with real soldiering again. The other is necessary too, but not so flashy, *and* I have come to the oldest and crack Armoured Division of the Middle East, the veteran of all the ding-dong battles. I have a Tommy gun in my Ford staff car, and learned how to shoot it yesterday.

'16th October: I went over to a Field Ambulance Unit and saw an operation on a man with a gunshot wound in the stomach. Blood transfusion saved his life. These desert medicos (RAMC) are superb, possibly thanks to Jorrocks (Gen. Horrocks), the son of one, who chivvied them all the time.

'23rd October (to Celia): Our anti-aircraft gunners had good fun the other day, shooting down the enemy a quarter of a mile away. I walked over to congratulate him and found they were from that island where Mummy wouldn't go on holiday, the 15 LAA (Isle of Man). This is my half-birthday, so easy to remember, and, Celia, perhaps your children or grandchildren will be interested in reading this . . . not that I can give you any historic news. Mummy may be anxious but there is nothing to worry about.

'29th October: I have had some strenuous days since the 23rd, but it is easing off now. We don't get mentioned much in the Press, which is a good thing – the foot-slogging infantry do a bit. My own people (the Royal Engineers – the Sappers) have done well. My boss, John Harding, is sad, for his son is far from well and his ADC has been killed.

'I have no letters describing my experiences at Alamein, but I was in charge of Rear HQ at 7th Armoured, with my office in a mechanical contrivance known as an ACV (Armoured Control Vehicle). Harding and Horrocks (Jorrocks) were inspiring leaders. In the GI (Carver's) absence, I had been present in Harding's caravan when General Koenig, the hero of Bir Hacheim, had been briefed for the battle – his brigade, with a Foreign Legion battalion, being under command. Harding had to tell him that his task of attacking the enemy on Himeimat must be "silent", i.e., without artillery support. "It must not be silent for long" was Koenig's taciturn reply. Himeimat overlooked our front and its capture was desirable, and in the event the French reached the top but were driven off.

'A note on the all-important minefields is necessary here. We had some of the newly designed "Scorpion" flail tanks available, but the gaps had to be cleared by the Sappers and then marked by the Military Police – the coppers – the coppers had the hairy job of placing lamps – red and green – along the gaps and controlling the traffic . . . and in the open with no cover at all. The REME had the task of recovering and repairing knocked-out tanks, a task described by John Harding as a battle-winning task. I think I'll get on with the Log!

'*24th October: 0100 hrs approx* – Visited Advance Dressing Station. A dozen cases already there, met by Caption Fulton RAMC.

'*0555 (approx)*: Re-visit ADS – some 60 casualties, many with head wounds – lying out on stretchers awaiting ambulances.

'*0615:* Take bearing on Himeimat on Track 4. A mile short of "January" came on vehicles of 44 Recce Regt, all waiting to go, but vague on situation; suggest they disperse.

'*0730:* Brig. P.P. Roberts of 22 Armoured Brigade going west in his tank. Realise we have not yet got through "February" minefield. A bit of shelling. Troops digging in, taking advantage of low hummock.

'*1030:* Back to ADS. Many more wounded now, some ambulances. Two Rifle Brigade officers, Luke and Turner on stretchers, both anxious to hear if we have taken February.

'*1130:* Making arrangements for spare flail-chains for the Scorpion tanks. Spoke to Capt. Foster RTR, who said only three Scorpions now sound.

'*1200 (approx)*: Hear French on top of Himeimat but driven off. Germans dominating ground between January and February minefields, except for some low ground where our troops are particularly congested.

'*1400:* Temporary breakdown of my armoured car in "Nuts" minefield, so brewed up for lunch – pickles, cheese, tea, slab chocolate. Then to Rear HQ. Slept from 1645 to 1845.'

Log jumps to 25th October.

'*0545:* GI (Mike Carver) on phone to say Queens Brigade now under command 7AD, now through two out of four gaps in February, but that 22 AB are not. I tell him French may have 50% casualties. He tells me large number of Bren-gun carriers crocks on battlefield.

'*0550:* Phone CREME (Commander, REME) and tell him to get to work rescuing BG carriers.

'*0750:* CRE (Commander, Royal Engineers) tells me of heavy losses to Crusader tanks of C of London Yeomanry (22AB) hit by enemy AT gunners – the infamous 88s. CLY claim they went up on mines. Sappers declare two gaps in February were properly cleared??? Gaps made by 21 Field Squadron RE, not Scorpions.

'*0830:* Visited ADS. More casualties, graves of men from Queens and 44 Recce Regt. Two padres, for 4 CLY and RC bury two more.

'*1200:* With Tac HQ 2 AB talking to Pip Roberts and his 2 i/c, Dennis Newton-King – my fag at Wellington – who had, I believe, been commanding the South African Armoured Car Regt. and a fine soldier

... he fell foul of Harding's successor, Erskine, later on. Informed that only 4 Grants and 5 Mk 3 Crusaders left, also low on crews for replacement tanks. Notice generals wearing red hats, not steel helmets. Morale raising?

'Later on the Division was moved north, so we and 1st AD could pursue Rommel after breakthrough.'

General Harding again: 'I cannot remember, nor do the records show, precisely when I was first warned to be prepared to move the Division to the Northern part of the front, nor when it became clear that our future role would be to exploit. In any case, even though 22nd Armoured Brigade had been withdrawn into reserve, 4th Light Armoured Brigade was still committed and we were without infantry except for our motor battalions.

'On the night of 29th/30th October, we were involved in the staging of a dummy attack designed to deceive the enemy as to the future course of operations, though what success, if any, was achieved in that direction we never knew. On 30th October we were busy making arrangements for the move to the North, and the move was actually carried out in daylight the next day, fortunately without any interference by enemy aircraft. Unfortunately for us, we had to leave 4th Light Armoured Brigade behind, though they rejoined us later.

'That same day, the 31st, I was summoned to Army Headquarters where the Army Commander (General Montgomery) told me that he was placing 131 Infantry Brigade, the Queen's Brigade, with sufficient transport to lift all its personnel, under my command, and that 7th Armoured Division was to remain in Army reserve and be ready to exploit the breakthrough he shortly expected to achieve in the northern sector.

'That gave me plenty to do and think about. 131 Infantry Brigade was a brigade of 44th Division. It had fairly recently arrived in the country and had had no experience of mobile operations in the desert or of functioning as a lorried infantry brigade. However, it comprised three battalions of the Queen's Royal Regiment and would, I felt sure, be pleased with its new role and keen to learn. I made a mental reservation to initiate them as gently as circumstances might permit. Meantime, they were busy re-equipping, and all units of the Division took every opportunity for carrying out reconnaissances of the forward routes, and for completing preparations for mobile operations.

'During this interlude we were honoured by a visit by General Alexander, and it was from him on that occasion that I first heard the encouraging news of the plans for a joint British-American invasion of

North Africa. This news, combined with the inspiration and encouragement General Alexander always imparts, raised my own spirits high and I looked forward eagerly to the time to be on the move again. Though they had not the benefit of knowing what was just about to happen in the Western Mediterranean, it was easy to see that all ranks of the Division were right on their toes, and no efforts were spared to make everything ready for mobile operations.

'During my own reconnaissances of the forward areas, I was impressed by the state of apparent confusion that existed and still more by the heavy congestion in the whole area, through which the Division would have to pass in any break-out operations. The forward tracks were clearly marked and well controlled, but they were knee-deep in dust. Movement and shellfire created a thick cloud of smoke and dust, and I foresaw endless opportunities for loss of direction and confusion in the move forward and breakout of the Division when the time came.

'At last, on 3rd November, it seemed certain that the enemy front was about to crack and the Division moved forward to an assembly position where it could take prompt advantage of the break when it came. That night, in 'Operation Supercharge', the infantry launched their final attack and on the morning of 4th November our advance began, with 11th Hussars in the lead, followed by 22nd Armoured Brigade in three armoured regimental columns, with 131 Infantry Brigade bringing up the rear. Our route lay south, through Tel El Aqqaqir, where we were to turn west into the open desert. My orders were to make for Daba to head the enemy off there, though I had my doubts from the start about turning into the coastal road so soon.

'Passing the burnt-out tanks of 8th Armoured Brigade, we ran into a belt of heavy dunes of soft sand, and I spent an anxious hour hoping that the difficult going would not throw our columns into confusion. Fortunately my fears proved groundless and we soon emerged into the open desert south of the coastal belt of sand dunes, which I knew from past experience provided the best going. There were the usual signs of rapid evacuation by the enemy, but no opposition, and we pushed rapidly westward, each column regaining its battle formation as it advanced.

'In the early afternoon we encountered what we subsequently discovered were the remnants of the Italian Ariete Armoured Division moving up from the south. They were promptly engaged by 22nd Armoured Brigade, and in an engagement of a few hours a number of Italian tanks and guns were destroyed and some prisoners captured.

161

'It was with a feeling of great exhilaration and high hope that we continued our advance westwards till nightfall, and resumed it again the next morning.'

9

Alamein to Tripoli

And some there may be who have no memorial;
who are perished, as though they had never
been ... their bodies are buried in peace
but their name liveth for evermore.

Apochrypha 44:7,9,14

Sixteen days after the start of the Battle of Alamein, an Anglo-American army under General Dwight Eisenhower landed on the West Coast of North Africa, around Casablanca, Oran and Algiers. This placed the German and Italian forces between the two jaws of a slowly closing vice. Although it took another six months and much bitter fighting before the final surrender of the Axis forces, after Alamein and 'Torch' the outcome of the war in Africa was never really in doubt from now on.

At the end of 'Supercharge', Montgomery's final push through the German defences at Alamein, an operation involving 1st Armoured Division, the tank-reinforced New Zealand Division, and 7th Armoured, which had been brought north for the purpose, 8th Army still had nearly 600 tanks fit for battle, while Rommel had less than 130. Most of these were Italian M13s. The three armoured divisions of 10 Corps then took up the task of pursuing the enemy as Rommel, abandoning his un-motorized Italian infantry, made frantic efforts to extract his German forces from the British advance and gain enough time and distance to regroup. Montgomery was equally determined not to let go and the pursuit went on, with actions every day, past all the old places and battlefields, through Fuka and Daba and Mersa Matruh. Then heavy rain on 6th November turned the dust of the desert into a quagmire and the pursuit faltered. The wheeled supply vehicles could not get forward in the mud, and the tanks could not continue without regular supplies of petrol. Even so, by 8th November Axis prisoners totalled over 30,000 and the enemy had lost a great deal of their equipment, now including all the Italian tanks and over 1,000 guns. J.W. York of the Queen's Brigade recalls the aftermath of the break-out:

'Our Divisional Commander sent the 22nd Armoured Brigade off at first light on 4th November with a rush, and they pushed on for over 5 miles, meeting little opposition, until in the early afternoon the leading troops came up against the enemy in position with tanks and anti-tank guns just east of Sawani Samalus, about 10 miles south-west of El Aqqaqir. The opposition proved to be the remains of the Italian Armoured Corps, who had formed a new line south of the Afrika Corps. The majority of the tanks turned out to be M13s, in a defensive situation along a low ridge. While the position was being reconnoitred and engaged, we in the Queen's Brigade – having spent the night in our trucks in the minefield area – were just emerging on to the Sidi Rahman track.

'I shall never forget the grim tableau that met our gaze as we finally reached this rough, uneven desert road, and turned left. The sun shone fitfully through vast clouds of dust raised by our vehicles, onto what had been a hard fought field of battle.

'Spread out over the area were many knocked out anti-tank and machine gun positions, with groups of foxholes nearby. Lying in and around these posts were the bodies of German soldiers, veteran Panzer Grenadiers – some in grotesque attitudes, others lying peacefully on the ground. Quite a few were still wearing their white peaked caps, many were torn by shot and shell.

'By a peculiar coincidence, some of these brave and gallant soldiers, who had made their last stand against overwhelming odds, were none other than the men of the 10th Company of the 104th Panzer Grenadier Regiment, who had opposed us so stubbornly during our attack on the minefields in the south, just nine days previously. They had been sent to form a defensive line on the Rahman track, and prevent the breakthrough of our armour.'

Ray Cooper, who served with the HQ of 22nd Armoured Brigade, also remembers this time after the breakthrough: 'It was good to be on the move forward again and although the enemy did not give up easily, he was forced to retreat steadily until on the 6th November the Division encountered tanks near Mersa Matruh, which were found to be the 21st Panzers. As the battle commenced, it began to rain which increased in intensity and continued through the night and into the next morning, by which time the ground had become so soggy, our tanks had to tow

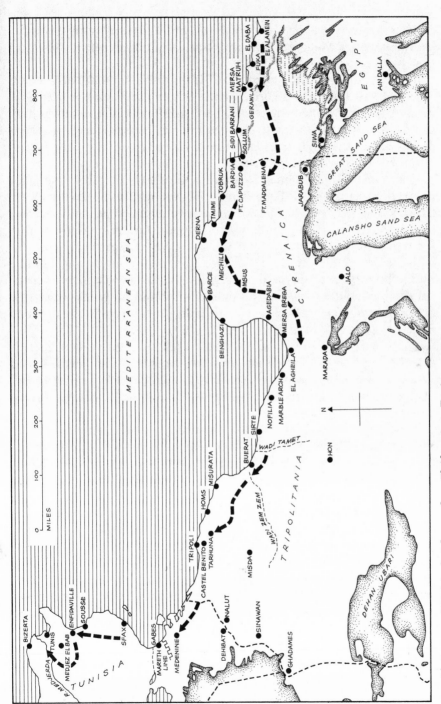

10 The Armoured Division's Advance from El Alamein to Tunis

guns and wheeled vehicles onto drier ground. I remember the day well, as my daughter Maureen Ann was born on 7th November. She was now two years old and I was very homesick.'

By 11th November the enemy had withdrawn through the frontier wire and past Bardia and Fort Capuzzo, where the leading elements of 22nd Armoured Brigade arrived just too late to stop the last train out. Here again, the advance was delayed by lack of petrol, and two days passed before the 11th Hussars entered Tobruk, where the advance – or pursuit – paused for two weeks.

Montgomery had declined to attempt the short cut across the Jebel to cut the road again at Beda Fomm. He was taking no chances with the wily Rommel, who had now resumed command of the Panzerarmee. Eighth Army was now one mighty juggernaut, rolling inexorably forward along the coast road and across the desert, harrying the enemy with the Desert Air Force and probing patrols of armoured cars, fighting now in Division or Corps-sized units, giving Rommel no chance to repeat his spoiling counter-attacks, though the German Luftwaffe were still active, as Sgt. Harry Ellis of the 15th Light Anti-Aircraft (Isle of Man) Regt. RA Coy confirms:

'I saw the war from the viewpoint of a Light Anti-Aircraft gunner in a Troop consisting of 3 guns per Troop at the start of campaigns in the Western Desert to 6 guns per Troop at the landings in France to the end of the war, and occupation of an area close to Hamburg, sorting out POWs and displaced persons.

'When the Regiment joined 7th Armoured before El Alamein, I felt the Division was at home in the desert, despite Rommel's then superiority in arms, such as his Mark III and IV tanks. The 88mm guns also had high muzzle velocity, so we got used to the peculiar noise of their shells. I always had sympathy for our tank crews, because I felt our tanks were inferior in fire power and range of weapons. Between static battles as we chased the Germans and the Italians, we met their rearguards, dug-in very good defensive positions, which we always struggled to overcome.

'I had great admiration for our 11th Hussars and Armoured Cars and other units who roved the desert, often behind the enemy fixed positions. My Troop Commander, Captain Jimmy Kirkpatrick MC, was often called upon to take us on sorties, twice with the Long Range Desert Group, as we were highly mobile with our Bofor guns, dropping into action in less than 30 seconds on occasions, and even firing from the wheels (as we went along) to scare off high flying aircraft, 5000 ft or over.

'Our best efforts were on low flying aircraft, which were usually strafing our guns and any armour in our columns. In the early days we had no protective shields on the Bofors, so we suffered a good many casualties in these engagements. Bombings by groups of 12 to 15 Junker 87s. Stukas were very frequent in the desert campaign. These dive-bombers were diving almost straight down onto our guns with a scream-ing siren effect, to try to unnerve the gunners. I felt some sympathy for the troops around us, who were exposed to this form of bombing, and felt that at least we could hit back at the Stukas. They would start their bombing dive from about 10,000 ft, gaining speed in the dive, but having released their bombs and pulled out, they were slow to pick up speed. This is when we had our hits on most occasions. The German Luftwaffe were roaming the skies almost at will during our push from El Alamein to Tripoli, as we were often too far forward from our fighter bases. We were closing on Castel Benito, an Axis air base, south of Tripoli, making progress with the 4th Light Armoured Brigade (7th Armoured Division), over very rough boulder-strewn ground, when we were attacked by Stukas at ground level, much to our surprise. The going was so rough that our progress was slow, with no way of digging-in as the ground was too rocky, so we endured attack after attack, with the Stukas returning the short distance to Castel Benito to refuel and re-load their bombs.

'My Sergeant, Dougy Counsell, was wounded by a bomb splinter in the spine, so as second-in-command of the gun, I took over command. The ambulances were on the scene with our Battery Commander, Major Sykes-Balls. He promoted me on the spot to full Bombardier (Acting Sgt), so I had control of the gun for the rest of the Stuka raids, which were numerous during that day and the following day. Sgt. Bill Waterson, in command of a Bofors gun within sight of me, was awarded the Military Medal for his conduct during this spell of action.'

Field Marshal Rommel was a great soldier. He did manage to gain some time and distance, and with his supply lines getting shorter and more reinforcements available all the time, he turned on his pursuers at Agheila and again at Buerat. These positions were soon outflanked, and on 23rd January 1943, three months after the first shells fell at El Alamein, the 8th Army at last entered Tripoli. To celebrate this achievement, 8th Army held a Victory Parade, witnessed by Winston Churchill and, among others, by Ray Cooper, who had just rejoined his unit after a spell in the Delta.

'When I returned to Brigade they were in an area of very difficult ground; very stony and making for very slow movement. It was around this time that General Harding, who was standing on the top of a Grant tank observing the enemy, was wounded by a 75mm shell which landed beside the tank. Being wounded by the shell and also in falling from the tank, he was bitterly disappointed when coming so close to Tripoli, then missing the victory.

'Brigadier "Pip" Roberts took over temporary command of 7th Armoured and Tripoli was entered early on the 23rd January, exactly three months from the commencement of the battle of El Alamein, 11th Hussars being the first there. I do not remember exactly when it took place, but there was a Victory Parade with tanks lined side by side on the main street with around fifty pipers of the 51st Highland Division, those marvellous fighting Jocks, leading the parade. The sound of those pipes was absolutely wonderful and certainly moved me greatly.'

A full account of 7th Armoured's role in the breakthrough and after is provided by General Harding: 'I cannot remember whether it was on that day (5th November) or the following morning that the right squadron of 11th Hussars reported Daba clear of the enemy. Whichever it was, the report fortunately reached me in time to order the rest of the Division to continue its advance westward without deviation.'

Among those moving forward was a young lieutenant of the 1/5th Queens Royal Regiment, Derrick James Watson. 'On 1st November 1942, I, Derrick Watson of A Coy, 1/5th Queens Royal Regiment, joined the 7th Armoured Division, together with the rest of 131 (Queens) Brigade as their lorried infantry. After the bloody battles of Deir Munassib and El Alamein, this was a much-needed fillip to morale, particularly the more or less permanent attachment of a platoon of TCVs (troop carrying vehicles). The Division became a pursuit force and did in fact "pursue" all the way to Tunis.

'Our first operation was a left hook across the rocky desert, bumping across the boulders in convoy, scourged by the heat, flies, desert sores and, of course, the enemy, which strangely enough was the least of our worries. Before this operation commenced, however, I suffered the most frightening experience in the campaign, or even in the whole war. I got lost in the desert no more than 50 yards from the Company with whom I had been for about a month. We had "assembled" and put up our bivvy for the night. I had attended Captain Russell Elliott's "O" Group in his bivvy to receive orders for the next day to move off in convoy at first light. Before retiring for the night, I decided I must go for a walk "with a shovel", and because I was still shy about this, I walked at least 50 yards into the night. It was as black as pitch, since darkness comes down swiftly in the desert – there is no twilight. Having done the business and buried the evidence in the interests of hygiene, I realized I did not know which way to turn for the return journey. No more than 50 yards away was the company, some 120 of my brothers-in-arms, sleeping the sleep of exhaustion, but in no direction was there sight or sound of them. In momentary panic I shouted "Help!" once, but did not repeat it. Imagine the humiliation if the whole Company "stood to" because their junior platoon commander was lost 50 yards away. I sat down for about 10 minutes and calmed myself, then worked out a plan. I would pace out 50 paces in the direction I thought the Company was, marking my path with the shovel. If still no sight or sound, I would retrace my steps along the marked path and try the same thing in a different direction. I took the first 50 paces – lo and behold, there was a bivvy with a light in it. I pulled the flap back to see the furious face of Captain Elliott I had left some half-hour previously.

'Then followed two weeks of a hand-to-mouth existence. I had Sgt. "Sniffy" Parker and 22 men in 2 TCVs driven by two splendid RASC drivers. The orders were at all costs "Keep the wheels moving". We twice covered over 100 miles a day. The night of 5th November was spent nose to tail in an uncharted minefield. El Daba landing ground was "captured" by our Rear B Echelon while the Germans were busily preparing to evacuate. It was never recorded which lot was the most surprised!

'On 13th November we reached the outskirts of Tobruk. On the fourth day I was vomiting, shivering and unable to keep anything down, and Freddie King arranged for the M.O. to visit. I showed him my yellow chest and suggested I might have yellow jaundice. After giving the matter some thought, he agreed that might be the case. I was evacuated in a semi-conscious state, my knees covered with desert sores, to the luxury of a hospital in Cairo (sheets!). I spent Christmas 1942 on Lady Lampson's houseboat on the Nile – one week convalescence and then back to Hell on Earth – the Infantry Base Depot at Geneifa on the Sweetwater Canal.'

General Harding again: 'I believe it was on the afternoon of the 6th November that we passed through the New Zealand Division who were engaged with enemy rearguards at Fuka. After some delay, caused by an old minefield, we climbed the Fuka escarpment and shortly after made contact with a strong force of German armour barring our way. This, we discovered afterwards, comprised the remains of 15 and 21 Panzer Divisions.

'That night came the rain; torrential rain. It certainly delayed us and caused us great difficulty, but it seemed to us that there were too many divisions trying to cut off the enemy and competing with each other for fuel and for the limited resources available to transport it forward, and that better results would have been achieved if the pursuit had been conducted by one division (which should, of course, have been ours), and all available transport put at its (our) disposal to keep it (us) going. On the other hand, General Montgomery was determined to avoid the mistake, common to previous campaigns, of outrunning his supplies.'

Rick Hall, now a Sergeant in 67 Company RASC, supporting 22nd Armoured Brigade, recalls this time: 'We had taken eight or nine truckloads of mines up the line on the night of Alamein (and we lay under our trucks during the barrage); it seemed a good idea at the time, but it came on to rain like hell after the breakthrough. You never think of it being wet or cold in the desert, but it was a real swamp. The trucks sank to the floorboards in mud, and the Division was moving fast. We might drive 200 miles a day to supply the forward units, so we went nights without sleep, except for the odd half-hour when we got the chance. We had four-wheel drive Chevrolets, good trucks for the desert.'

General Harding continues: 'No doubt we were as grasping as other formations in our efforts to get petrol and transport, and by 8th November we were well in the lead. Leaving 131 Infantry Brigade on the Fuka escarpment to save petrol, I set off with 22nd Armoured Brigade along the 300 Northing, which I knew to be the best going for the frontier about Maddalena, disregarding suggestions from behind that we were keeping too far South! My idea was to conduct a parallel pursuit across the desert, and not to turn into the road until I was certain I was well ahead of the enemy. The further west we went, the more difficult it became to keep 22nd Armoured Brigade supplied with petrol. Also, our old tanks were feeling the strain and our numbers were steadily dropping through mechanical failure beyond our power to repair.

'On 9th November I was ordered to halt the main body of the Division when I reached Sidi Aziez and to limit any advance beyond that area to reconnaissance by light mobile detachments. Further delays occurred in bringing forward petrol and it was not until 10th November that we reached Capuzzo to find the last elements of the enemy just pulling out. Here an amusing incident occurred when the last German trolley train out of Capuzzo successfully ran the gauntlet of fire from a squadron of 1 RTR tanks. 11th Hussars picked up prisoners from a column of soft skinned vehicles on the Bardia-Tobruk road, but the bulk of the enemy escaped moving fast westward while our tanks had to remain in the Capuzzo-Bardia area, grounded for lack of petrol. We cursed our fate and blamed the rain on the 6th and 7th – perhaps unduly.

'It was exasperating having to wait in the Bardia area while the enemy continued his withdrawal unmolested as far as the land forces were concerned, though the pause was useful for maintenance and repair of vehicles. About this time, 4th Light Armoured Brigade rejoined the Division, and on 13th November our coat-tails were released, and I was ordered to establish the Division west of Tobruk to cover the opening up of that port, and to push forward reconnaissance elements to report on the Derna-Martuba airfields.

'It was good to be on the move again. We found Tobruk unoccupied and by the 14th November the Division was disposed with 4th Light Armoured Brigade west of Tobruk, patrolling into the Jebel, 22nd Armoured Brigade in the El Adem area, and 131 Infantry Brigade in Tobruk, helping to clear the harbour and unload barges.

'Our petrol situation continued to be very difficult and was the determining factor in subsequent operations. By 15th November, with the assurance of some supply by air, we were able to continue the advance. 4th Light Armoured Brigade was given the task of clearing the main road through the Jebel, and I set off with a small headquarters and two armoured car columns across the desert. Each column comprised an armoured car regiment with small artillery and anti-tank detachments under command. The 11th Hussars column leading was directed on to Soluch to cut the coastal road there and then turn northwards to Benghazi to clear that area and join forces with 4th Light Armoured Brigade advancing through the Jebel. The Royals column was directed on to Antelat and Agedabia, where I felt confident the enemy would make a stand of some sort. Plans were also made to allot all remaining "runner" tanks of 22nd Armoured Brigade to one Regiment (1 RTR) and to get that unit, plus the necessary supporting arms, ready to follow the armoured car columns across the desert as soon as the supply position permitted.

'The enemy had taken full advantage of the lull in our pursuit to pull clear. Neither of the armoured car columns encountered any resistance, and by 20th November the 11th Hussars were in Benghazi. The Royals were in touch with the enemy rearguard at Agedabia, the 4th Light Armoured Brigade were steadily opening up the road through the Jebel where their only trouble was delay by demolition and mines.

'With the arrival of 22nd Armoured Brigade, which consisted of only one armoured regiment (1 RTR) we closed with the enemy rearguard at Agedabia. This engagement took the form of a duel between our tanks and artillery, and the enemy's anti-tank guns which were well posted and concealed on an arc astride the road and covering the enemy's right flank. With my limited resources I could not attempt a wide outflanking movement, but we were able to destroy a number of enemy anti-tank guns during the course of the day's fighting. I hoped to pin the enemy down till nightfall and to get a company of motor infantry with anti-tank guns astride the road behind him to cut off his withdrawal. This attempt failed, our infantry were spotted and held off by the enemy who withdrew during the night.

'We followed up at daylight and were much delayed by mines. As expected, we found the enemy holding the Mersa Brega-Suera position in strength. It was obvious that our immediate task was to discover the extent and strength of the enemy's position, which we proceeded to do. By this time we had got out of range of the bulk of our own aircraft, a fact which the German Air Force was quick to appreciate and take advantage of. ME 109s became increasingly active and began taking a steady toll of our vehicles. I had a narrow escape myself when three ME 109s attacked my two armoured cars on the road south of Agedabia, putting both temporarily out of action, and later on the same morning my operator was seriously wounded in an attack by a biggish flight of Stukas on 22nd Armoured Brigade headquarters.'

Driver A. (Ted) Drury of 5 Company RASC remembers the Stukas: 'No doubt you will hear hundreds of stories, some funny, some not so funny. One of the funny ones I can bring to mind was when we were held up before the final push to Tunis. We were stuck at Medenine, between two of our forward airstrips. The enemy dare not come over in the day but they made up in the night – every night. My pal, Taffy Brown, and I got fed up baling out into the slit trench every night, and scouting round we found some deserted buildings. These consisted of a thick stone wall, surmounted by a thick thatch. Lovely – protection and comfort – or so we thought. We moved in with our bedding and prepared for an uninterrupted night for a change. Then things started to move. Thousands of them. The thatch was alive with fleas. Thank heavens there was a bir (well) handy. We spent the next day totally immersing our entire bedding, clothes and other kit under water. From then on we stayed with the bombers. At least they did not bite us.

'One thing that I have tried to find out since the war is where were the last Stuka bombers used? When we had advanced to the Wadi Zem Zem near Nofilia, we had gone too far for our planes to give us fighter cover. The Germans soon found out and used to give us all they had got. For several days, a dozen Stukas came over at daybreak – at one o'clock – and again just before dusk. It was just like the milkman calling, and they did as they pleased until one day they, and we, had a surprise.

They came in on the lunch-time run and suddenly there was a flash of wings far above them and down came the fighters. It was the Kittyhawks of the RAF, mainly piloted by American volunteers. They emptied the sky very quickly, for everyone knows that a Stuka was a dead duck if caught by fighters.

'The point of this story is that we never saw Stukas in action again. Not that we missed them, thank you. I have wondered if this was the last of them, or did the Germans decide that they were obsolete. Even the Old Codgers in the *Daily Mirror* could not find out when they vanished from the arena. I wonder if anybody else knows.

'Another thing that you could delve into is the 7th Armoured's concert party. They were called the *Jerboa Strollers*, and the last time I saw them on stage was after Africa had been cleared and we were resting prior to the invasion of Sicily. I have never seen them mentioned anywhere else. We were at Homs in the Roman amphitheatre. They were very good.

'The comradeship in the 7th was great. All ranks and all regiments were as one. To show you what I mean, a short time ago I pulled into the garage to fill up with petrol. Another vehicle nearby had a 7th Armoured Division sign in the rear window. I said to the driver, "Is that yours." "Yes," he said. With that we had a long chat, finding that we had a mutual friend. He had been in the 11th Hussars and one of his lads, Neil Anderson, was the liaison between his regiment and my company.'

General Harding again: 'At this time, too, we passed from command 10th Corps to 30th Corps. At Alamein we fought in 13th Corps (General Horrocks), from the breakout onwards we were under 10th Corps (General Lumsden), and now we came under 30th Corps (General Leese). Though all three Corps commanders and their staffs were quite different in their ways, we had the most harmonious relationships and the utmost support from all three headquarters. As far as I was aware, there was never any friction. The same applied to our relationships with the RAF, who gave us all possible help and support throughout. Few things can be more damaging in war than bad relationships between commanders and staffs, or between the Services. We were very fortunate in the close harmony that existed all round throughout this campaign, and I personally am most grateful to all who contributed to it.

'At Mersa Brega we had reached the general area that marked the limit of our westward advance in the two previous campaigns, and naturally the thought of what had happened before was in many of our minds. Would Rommel stage another comeback at this critical phase?

Would he stand and fight or withdraw again when pressed or threatened on his southern flank? The Mersa Brega position is inherently strong and well suited to cover a comeback on the lines adopted by Rommel in previous years. Were we strong enough to deal with such a manoeuvre? Were the limited forces available disposed to the best advantage to defeat such a movement? How strong need we ourselves be to resume the offensive? What would be the best plan of attack? How could we best detect the enemy's intention – to attack, to stand and fight, or to withdraw? These and similar questions were in many of our minds at this time – they were certainly in mine.

'With 7th Armoured Division responsible for covering the Army front, my tasks were clear: (a) To keep the enemy under close observation along the whole of his front. (b) To test his strength and intentions. (c) To be ready to follow him up at once if he withdrew. (d) To defeat, or as a minimum hold, any counter-attacks he might launch.

'Progressively my front was strengthened; 4th Light Armoured Brigade came forward and took over the left flank extending our front south to the Pink Hills. 22nd Armoured Brigade was relieved by 8th Armoured Brigade (Brigadier N. Custance) at full strength and equipped with Sherman tanks – up to then the Division had fought with Grants and Crusaders. 153 Infantry Brigade of 51st (Highland) Division was placed under my command. 131 Infantry Brigade, 2nd New Zealand Division, and the rest of 51st Division, began to move forward and any anxiety we may have had about a Rommel comeback faded from our minds. Reconnaissance and vigorous patrolling with armour and infantry to test the enemy's intentions were the order of the day.

'On the 12th December certain enemy activities aroused our suspicions and, sure enough, patrols in the early hours of 13th December confirmed that the enemy was on the move again to the west. According to our previously prepared plan he was followed up at once by 8th Armoured Brigade, with 11th Hussars again in the lead and pressing on fast, in spite of the early morning mist.

'Meantime, 2nd New Zealand Division with 4th Light Armoured Brigade under command had started on a wide outflanking movement by Marada to cut the enemy line of retreat west of Agheila. It may have been reports of this movement that set the enemy moving. Whatever the reason, we all hoped and prayed that the New Zealanders would get round in time.

'On the 14th December we made contact with a strong enemy rearguard south-east of Agheila and a sharp engagement ensued in the course of which we destroyed a number of enemy tanks and captured some prisoners. The enemy withdrew after dark. 8th Armoured Brigade followed up at daybreak but soon ran into the enemy again, strongly posted behind the Agheila marshes.

'An attempt by 8th Armoured Brigade to outflank this position in the south was foiled by the bad marshy going. Enemy artillery and anti-tank fire was heavy and many mines were encountered. The only solution appeared to be a night attack with infantry along the narrow coastal belt of sand dunes, and 131 Infantry Brigade was brought up for that purpose. Before an attack could be launched the enemy withdrew – we hoped into the arms of 2nd New Zealand Division – but once again he eluded our grasp, and when, later, I saw the difficult nature of the country north and north-west of Agheila, intersected as it was by innumerable deep wadis, I was not surprised. The New Zealanders were faced with an impossible task in the time at their disposal.

'Our movement through the Agheila defile in daylight on 16th December was an anxious period. To gain time I decided to move closed up, with vehicles nose to tail, taking a chance on there being no interference by the enemy air force. By this time the RAF had moved forward and re-established superiority over the area of the land battle. None the less I was very relieved when the Division was clear of the defile and able to deploy again on a fighting frontage in the open desert.

'Passing through 2nd New Zealand Division, we picked up 4th Light Armoured Brigade again in the Nofilia area and continued our advance, but once more the supply situation took charge, and though we were able to manoeuvre a small enemy force out of Sirte by threatening his flank and rear with strong armoured car patrols, our advance came to a halt when we made contact again with the enemy main forces hurriedly preparing a defensive position in the Buerat area, with such armour as he still possessed covering his right flank.

'Although the enemy had so far eluded our many attempts to cut off his retreat, we had by this time taken good toll of his tanks, guns and personnel in our numerous engagements with him since Alamein. He had also suffered severely from attacks by the RAF. Provided I could be assured of enough petrol, it seemed to me within the power of the forces at my disposal to force him out of the Buerat position, but the Army commander made it clear that he was determined to wait until he had sufficient troops and supplies to go right through to Tripoli in one movement. So we had to restrain our impatience, and I was given strict orders not to move my armoured or infantry brigades forward.

'Meantime our task was once again to cover the Army front and keep the enemy under close observation, which we did with armoured car patrols. It was a wide front and there were necessarily big gaps between our standing patrols. While touring the front one day with my CRA (Brigadier Mews) in a jeep, we mistook an enemy armoured car patrol for one of our own. Fortunately for us, the enemy hadn't sufficient restraint to hold their fire, and more fortunately still, their first shot, though the range was only about 500 yards, went wide and we were able to dodge behind a hillock and get away in dead ground. I was told later, that the Sergeant commanding the patrol, for which we were looking, had also fired a shot in our direction to attract our attention, and that he was heard muttering to his crew, "There goes the bloody General, getting into trouble as usual," but I can't vouch for the truth of that part of the story. It was certainly a lucky escape.

'As always in such circumstances, as we were placed at this time, we felt some anxiety lest the enemy might try a spoiling attack with his armour, aimed at upsetting our preparations for continuing our advance. I may, on this occasion, have felt more than usually anxious. We were certainly on a wide front and a long way from the support of the rest of the army. Anyway, I had vivid recollections of being chased in my dreams by Rommel on Christmas night after a heavier meal than usual of pork, our first fresh meat for several weeks, washed down by an excellent bottle of wine, a most welcome present from the Corps Commander. General Leese and his administrative staff had taken infinite trouble to ensure that the whole Division had an issue of fresh pork, extra cigarettes and rum with which to celebrate Christmas, all of which were very much appreciated.

'Towards the end of the year, planning began for the advance on Tripoli. 2nd New Zealand Division and 7th Armoured Division were to advance across the desert while 51st Division moved by the coastal route. We were to be on the right of 2nd New Zealand Division and were to advance on the axis Seddada – Beni Ulid – Tarhuna.

'Gradually, as the supply position improved, we were allowed to concentrate forward, and on the morning of 15th January the advance began. We soon made contact with the German armoured divisions, skilfully posted in the broken ground between the Geddahia – Bu Ngem track and the Wadi Zem-Zem. A hard day's fighting followed, in which we destroyed a number of enemy tanks and anti-tank guns and incurred some losses in tanks ourselves. Though we also made a good deal of ground during the day, we were unable to penetrate the enemy's front, nor to outflank his position. Neither could 2nd New Zealand Division on our left. I spent the day with 8th Armoured Brigade, who were inclined to be disappointed with the results achieved, but I felt pretty certain by the evening that the enemy had had a bellyfull and that he would withdraw during the night. I therefore gave orders for particularly active patrolling during the night while the tanks were replenished with fuel and ammunition and the crews given some rest, preparatory to renewing the battle, or following up the enemy at daybreak.

'My guess proved correct, the enemy withdrew in the night and we moved off in pursuit at first driving light. The country proved more broken and difficult than the Libyan desert, but we made reasonable progress and reached the Seddada area that evening, where we had a brief encounter with the enemy rearguard before halting for the night.

'By this time it had become apparent that there wasn't room for two divisions to advance side by side on Tarhuna and Tripoli, so the Army Commander halted the New Zealanders and ordered us to continue the advance alone. I knew from the reports of the Long Range Desert Group that the better going was on the west of the Beni Ulid – Tarhuna track – so I planned to advance with 8th Armoured Brigade on the right, and 4th Light Armoured Brigade on the left, with 131 Infantry Brigade following 8th Armoured Brigade. We avoided the track which the Germans had mined as they withdrew and kept to the open desert. Even so, we were considerably delayed by bad going and had difficulty in finding a way down the escarpment north-east of Beni Ulid, which we had to negotiate to get into the valley leading to Tarhuna.

'Once there we made faster going and in the early morning of 19th January the leading patrols of the 11th Hussars had caught up with the enemy rear parties. I felt we must be hard on his heels and ordered 8th Armoured Brigade to press on with all possible speed with a view to forestalling any enemy attempt to establish a strong front on the escarpment at Tarhuna, astride the road to Tripoli, which would perhaps be the last position suitable for a rearguard action that he could hold south of Tripoli. The fact that 4th Light Armoured Brigade further west was still being delayed by bad going, made it all the more important to exert all possible pressure, and as quickly as possible, on the 8th Armoured Brigade front.

'By this time, 8th Armoured Brigade had cleared the narrow part of the valley and had been able to open out on a fighting frontage. The leading tanks quickly made contact with the enemy and the battle was joined. I had been following 8th Armoured Brigade with my small Tac Headquarters, and went straight forward to a small sandy ridge where Brigadier Custance was conducting the battle from his tank. I had taken special care to ensure that 7th Medium Regiment RA, which had been placed under my command for the advance from Beurat to Tripoli, was well forward and was particularly anxious that it should be brought into action without delay to engage and neutralise the enemy's flank as quickly as possible, to hustle him out of his position and get possession of the road down the Tarhuna escarpment before the enemy could block it effectively with demolitions.

'After discussing these matters with Brigadier Custance while sitting on top of his tank, I was about to return to my own tank to issue the necessary orders, when a salvo of 105mm shells landed on the ridge just in front of us and I received numerous wounds.

'That was the end of the hunt for me, and the most bitter disappointment. For over two years my target had been Tripoli, and it was with great joy that I heard later on that 7th Armoured Division was the first in that port. The crews of the two turretless Honey tanks, that at that time formed my Tac-Headquarters, had 'brewed up' (made tea) in the main square of the town on the day of its capture. How I wished I'd been there with them.

'In command of 7th Armoured Division, the finest body of desert warriors, the most devoted comrades-in-arms, from Alamein to Tarhuna, nearly 1400 miles as the crow flies, in less than three months – what greater honour, what more exhilarating or inspiring experience can any soldier have ever had? In concluding this brief personal account of this great adventure, I would like to pay my tribute to all those who fought through those days with the Division. They never failed or faltered; unmatched in skill and courage they fought as one throughout for duty and in comradeship. May their spirit inspire all those now serving or who ever come to serve in the 7th Armoured Division, and may it never fail.'

Brigadier C.E.F. Turner's account of General Harding's wounding gives some idea of the regard held by the Division for their commander: '21st January 1942: We nearly had a tragedy two days ago and have suffered a severe loss. Our General, John Harding, has stopped one – a shell hit him while sitting on a tank of 8th Armoured Tac-HQ, urging on that "careful", if gallant brigade. It was thought he was a goner, but he has amazing vitality. The surgical teams saved his life but he has lost three fingers and will have a stiff knee for life. He'll soon be back on the job and may I be with him. I was able to sit with him in the ambulance back to the Advance and Main Dressing Stations.

'It was most touching. I helped him dictate a telegram to his wife and took down the names of those who he wants decorated when the names are sent for. I did not have the face to forward my own name for a DSO as he told me to. I was able to say how sorry we all were and how he had inspired us with his leadership. I think he liked that, but all he said, typically was, "Charles, I have only done my duty .... I did want to see it through, but somehow they got me in the end."

'Well, our hero was flown out today, and Pip Roberts reigns, a man most of us know and admire.'

10

Tripoli to Tunis

> How are the mighty fallen in the midst
> of battle ... and the weapons of war
> perished.
>
> *Samuel 1:25,26–7*

After the fall of Tripoli, the 1st Army on the Western flank, under General Anderson, and the 8th Army in the east, under Montgomery, were combined into the 18th Army Group under the command of General Sir Harold Alexander. Eighteenth Army Group then began to squeeze the Germans from either flank, but German reinforcements, including a number of the new Tiger tanks armed with the fearsome 88mm gun had now arrived in Africa. With these the Germans in the west, under Von Arnim, struck at the American 2nd Corps at the Kasserine Pass in Tunisia, inflicting great losses in men and material. Von Arnim then took his Panzers north towards the coast, attempting to repeat this success and cut the First Army off from its supply bases in Tunisia. Meanwhile, 8th Army were held by Rommel on the Mareth Line.

Ray Cooper again: 'Immediately after the Tripoli parade was over, the Army returned to the war. Major General Erskine took over command of the division and Brigadier 'Loony' Hinde of 22nd Brigade in place of "Pip" Roberts, who went to take over 26th Armoured Brigade in 6th Armoured Division.

'Progress was slow, partly due to mines and booby traps. There were rumours of even bodies being booby-trapped. This being so, when we leaguered one evening as it became dusk, and a body was found to be a short distance from where our tank was placed, we dug a trench at the side of the corpse and pulled it in from a distance. After sleeping beside the tank, it was quite eerie when, on waking, we found we had left a hand uncovered. Naturally we quickly rectified this.

'The next place of note that I remember was Medenine where, after a build-up which took some considerable time, a fierce battle was fought covering twenty-four hours, during which time the enemy received a bloody nose.'

The advance of 8th Army, and of 7th Armoured Division had been greatly impeded by mines, and the Divisional History chooses this time to pay a well-deserved tribute to the Sappers, the Royal Engineers, without whom any advance would have been either impossible or very costly. The Divisional Sappers, from the 4th Field Squadron RE, 21st Field Squadron, 143 Field Park Squadron, had developed an uncanny skill in finding and disarming the Teller and 'S' mines sown so thickly in their path, but if skill proved slow, the Sappers were not beyond some raw courage. When the 4th Field Squadron were ordered to clear one of the Medenine minefields as quickly as possible, they lined out across it at six-foot intervals, and 'beat it like a field of roots.'

The Mareth Line, on the Tunisian frontier, had been built by the French between the wars to shield Southern Tunisia from the Italians, and was the most formidable obstacle encountered by the Desert Army since Alamein. Seventh Armoured were involved in the German counter-attack at Medenine, but not in the later battles around the Mareth line, which took place between 18th and 30th March 1943.

Harry Beech, then a Battery Sergeant Major with the 146 Field Regiment RA, went out of the war at this time: 'Having been attached to the Ninth Australian Division before and during Alamein, my "mob", the Hundred and Forty Six Field Regiment, twenty five pounders, ex Thirty Eight Welsh Division, were then put into the Seventh Armoured Division, together with two regiments of Royal Horse Artillery, Third and Fifth, I seem to remember. As for me, I went the length of North Africa with the 146, as far as Tunisia, that was. We left Tripoli a few days after having helped to take it, as the artillery support to a squadron of King's Dragoon Guards armoured cars, with whom we made up an armed reconnaissance unit. This was to chase after the enemy to make sure he was still running. We then waited for the rest of the 8th Army to catch us up at the Mareth Line. Very adventurous, that was!

'I was with my regiment up to the Axis' last gasp (which, with a bit of worse luck would have coincided with mine), at the Mareth Line. On the day that we piled up fifty four (so it was said) of his tanks in the passes, firing down to ranges of a thousand yards, (real 'whites of the eye' stuff), I caught a severe clout from a chunk of German shell, which put me out of the active war pretty effectively, and later became my entry ticket to the ranks of the war pensioners. That was the last time I saw the 7th Armoured Division.'

Lt. Derrick Watson, last seen at the infantry base depot at Geneifa, was trying to get back to his battalion, the 1/5th Queens. 'In February 1943 I was put in charge of thirty men, reinforcements for the Queens, to be conveyed by air from Heliopolis to El Adem. Before departing with relief from Geneifa, I was summoned to the Camp Commandant's office. He was a veteran of the First World War and ran the Camp from his desk, periodically asking the itinerant officers such as myself, to explain why, with 2,000 men on the nominal roll, the Catering Corps were serving, on average, 3,000 breakfasts! He had two important orders for me: "You are to see that the men do *not* have their mugs hanging onto the outside of their haversacks, and they are *not* to throw away their pith helmets."

'On inspecting my new platoon, I recognised those, like me, who had already been up in the blue because they had their mugs hanging on the outside of their haversacks and smiled encouragingly at those with white knees who had recently arrived from England. We had a common bond in a strong desire to get away from Geneifa at all costs. We embussed, and no more than 200 yards from the depot, stopped alongside an enormous pile of pith helmets and added our 30 to the pile. I've often wondered if the pile is still there!

'At the aerodrome we were loaded onto a Dakota (seated on the floor in acute discomfort, having been issued with a brown paper bag instead of a boarding card). My status with my new platoon was increased enormously during the extremely bumpy ride by the fact that I was the only one who did not need to use my bag. On rejoining the Battalion at Enfidaville, I was warmly welcomed by Lt.-Col. W.R. Elsington, who, on the spot, appointed me Battle Patrol Officer, and my new Platoon the Battle Patrol. The Battalion was in a Static Defensive Position (no lorries), and there was to be Aggressive Patrolling to give the Germans no rest. These were the words of the Brigade I.O., who was in charge of the Patrolling, and I hadn't the courage at that time to ask, "What about *our* rest?"

'After a few strolls at night, tentatively probing for the German positions, there came our BIG NIGHT. With Lt. George Cole as my 2 i/c, I was to take my platoon, 30 strong, out about a mile into No Man's Land on a compass bearing, and there establish a firm base. From there, I was to take out a fighting Patrol (2 sections) to a point where Mitch thought the Germans would have a position, and bring back the "odd Bosche". Down and up steep wadis, we reached a strip of golden sands, about 100 yards wide – bright moonlight – deathly silence – 22 of us looked across the sands to the bushes where the Germans were supposed to be. Remembering my training in England in Fighting Patrols and the request for the "odd Bosche", I whispered the orders, "Up on your feet – fix bayonets – at the Double – Follow me!" I just stopped myself saying, "Don't make a noise." They stuck to me like glue till we reached the bushes on the other side, breathless but relieved to find nothing and nobody there. "Unfix your bayonets, we'll go home", I said, or something fatuous like that. We returned to the firm base and now it was George Cole's turn.

'Mitch had said that in the unlikely event of the Fighting Patrol finding nothing, George Cole was to take a Recce Patrol on a divergent bearing to establish the absence of the Germans from a different area. So off George went, eyes down on his compass, escorted by "Foxy" Pavitt, the Company Barber, armed with a Sten Gun. We never saw much of Foxy, but he must have annoyed the Sgt. Major, who had winkled him out for this patrol. We had only just settled down, no more than ten minutes, when there was a lot of firing to our front. The Germans sent up a succession of Verey lights – Spandaus firing tracer on fixed lines – running feet, heralding the return of George and Foxy in full flight. After George had expressed his opinion of Brigade's Intelligence, he explained that he was so intent on the compass, he had stumbled over the prone body of a sleeping German soldier, who had woken up, shrieked out the alarm, and presumably reached for his weapon. Foxy had emptied the Sten magazine into him and the Patrol then withdrew in some haste, but in good order. When asked if there were other Germans there, George replied, with some heat, "I never stopped to find out, but those Spandaus were not being fired by the fairies, that's for sure."

'We got back to our lines at daybreak and I was "debriefed" by the Brigade I.O., who was "disappointed" with the result. Why didn't you bring back the body? You could, at the very least, have removed some form of identification of his unit, so I could have checked my line of battle, etc., etc.

'Before I had a shave and breakfast, I was summoned by the C.O., that great and good man, Col. Errington. "We're on the move, again. We've got our lorries back. You're the I.O. as from now. Go and get some breakfast." This was about 14th April 1943. From then on it was all go for weeks, constantly being shelled by the retreating enemy until we embarked on a route of 140 miles to join the 1st Army. We finally motored into Tunis on 6th May. Flowers, vino and a total of 170,000 prisoners, although we never had charge of more than 7000. As Winston Churchill said in a message to us: "It will be a great honour in the years to come, to be able to say, I marched and fought with the 8th Army."'

Rommel counter-attacked the 8th Army at Medenine on 6th March, but 8th Army had learned a lot about defensive battles in the last few years. The tanks and troops were concentrated in prepared positions, so they let Rommel's tanks come in during dark, then unleashed the fire of their anti-tank guns. Rommel lost over fifty of his scarce and precious tanks, two of them to the 6-pdr gun of Sergeant Andrews of the 7th Queens; others to that of Sergeant Crangles, whose Bren gunner engaged the German tank crews as they bailed out. Rommel, now seriously ill with recurrent attacks of jaundice, handed over command to Von Arnim and flew home to hospital in Germany. He never returned to North Africa, but 7th Armoured were to meet this redoubtable general again in Normandy.

On 17th March, US General Patton led the 2nd U.S. Corps to re-open 1st Army's attack in the mountains of Tunisia. Three days later, 8th Army attacked the Mareth Line. Three days after that, the Mareth Line breached, the Germans withdrew to the Wadi Akerit and the Gabes Gap. Sergeant Bobby Brainwell of the 4th CLY remembers this time:

'The Germans were in a highly fortified position, and we were sup- porting our infantry from 51st Highland Division, who came under tremendous fire. We gave support with our gun while coming under heavy fire ourselves from German guns back in the hills. Then we lost a track and had to sit it out all day, walking back to our own lines after dark. We never moved forward in the dark, but as I recall, the last lap into Tunis was really quite easy. We lost a few tanks but after Gabes the German resistance crumbled quite quickly.'

At first, the men of 8th Army did not fully understand why the men in 1st Army were making such heavy weather of the fighting in Tunisia, but when they reached the Tunisian frontier and saw that the country was very different from the open desert to the east, they began to share and appreciate some of 1st Army's problems. Winston Churchill explained some of these in a letter to Russia's Marshal Stalin.

'Since we entered Tunisia, we have taken some forty thousand pris- oners and killed or wounded some thirty-five thousand German or Italian troops. 1st Army have lost about twenty-three thousand men, 8th Army about ten thousand. Two-thirds of these casualties have been British. The difficulties are compounded by the terrain, which is mountainous, with flat plains surrounded by rugged peaks, every one of which is a fortress, which aids the enemy's defence and slows our attack.'

The German army also received reinforcements, for in April the Hermann Goring Division and the German 9th Division were sent by air to Tunisia. On 6th April, 8th Army stormed and penetrated German positions on the Gabes gap, and began to pursue the enemy north towards Tunis. In the weeks which followed, the 1st and 8th Armies subjected the German and Italian forces to a series of alternate blows from one flank or the other, 1st Army advancing towards Bizerta, 8th Army heading for Enfidaville, the two armies aiming to link up south of Tunis and push the Axis remnants into the sea. Seventh Armoured were transferred from 8th Army to 9th Corps of 1st Army for the assault on the Medjez el Bab, and once this attack had broken through, raced the 6th Armoured Division for the honour of taking Tunis, which fell on 8th May 1943.

The terrain had impeded the advance of 1st Army, but by the time the two armies met outside Tunis, there were few differences between 1st and 8th Armies. Lt. Roy Farran of the 3rd Hussars describes them as follows: 'The 1st Army painted their trucks a dark green, dressed a little more smartly and filled the gutters with drunken soldiers ... the men drank the local wine like beer and suffered in consequence.'

Major Duncan Riddell recalls that when 550 Company RASC were sent to 1st Army, the order came round that the 8th Army men were to smarten up. 'I couldn't start telling the men to polish their brass at this stage in the game, so I said, "Look, while we are with First Army, if you drive with your boots out the window, make sure you have done up your bootlaces."'

Lt-Col B.S. Jones summarises the campaign in Tunisia from the Royal Engineers' viewpoint. 'No big operation could be mounted until the port had been repaired and stocks built up on the ground. Nearly all the histories of this period confine themselves to the celebrations over the triumphant entry, the Victory Parade and Churchill's visit. But for the 7th Armoured Division it was a different story. Comprising the 7th Armoured Brigade, The Queens Lorried Infantry Brigade (131 commanded by Brig Whistler) and supporting units, its task was to push the enemy rearguards back into Tunisia and re-open the road for the subsequent attack on the Mareth Line. The enemy forces were light but their engineers used every device to delay the advance. They cratered the road and railway (especially where they crossed the salt marshes west of Tripoli) and then made them "lousy" with Tellermines and the dreaded jumping "S" (shrapnel) mines. The road verges and likely harbour areas were also mined, nothing of course being visible apart from slight disturbances in the sand. To help with this problem, the 3rd (Cheshire) Field Squadron RE (part of 10th Armoured Division at Alamein) was put under command of the Queens Brigade. The advance became a close struggle between British sappers and German pioneers, each trying to outwit the other. Gradually the casualties mounted up as accidents occurred, nearly all caused by "S" mines.

'The O.C. of the Squadron, (Major C. Tandy) and a troop leader, (Capt. R. Leese) were among those who were killed and buried by the roadside. Every casualty seemed to make the men all the more determined to beat the Germans, and in spite of the difficulties the advance over some five weeks averaged about five miles a day. The Queens Infantry, working with the Sappers, provided the local protection. Once the Division's own Sappers built a timber roadway over the salt marsh, some miles to the south, but the route had to be based on the one good road.

'Early in February a fighting patrol of platoon strength made the first crossing into Tunisia and found the frontier defensive works occupied by Germans. Who would have thought, in 1939, that the Tunisian defences, built by the French as protection against the Italians in Libya, would, in fact, be used by Germans and Italians to defend themselves against a British and Commonwealth army! By the time the 7th Armoured Division had closed up to the Mareth Line, the port of Tripoli was in full operation and the other divisions began to arrive in preparation for the attack on the much-vaunted (and as it happened, over-rated) Mareth Line. The 3rd Field Squadron left the 7th Armoured Division to work directly under the Chief Engineer of the Eighth Army, but before our own attack Rommel launched his, near Medenine, on 6th March, and by chance one of the heaviest attacks was made against the Queens Brigade. They were ready. Their 6-pdr anti-tank guns destroyed so many German tanks that the remainder withdrew. General Montgomery described Medenine as his most successful defensive battle. The Queens Regimental Museum at Clandon, Surrey, shows some photographs of their victorious gun crews after the battle. Medenine was the making of the Queens Brigade as the infantry component of the 7th Armoured Division.'

Soon after this, on 8th April, the Division had their first encounter with a German 'Tiger' tank, one of which was captured intact by the 11th Hussars who, forging ahead as always, entered Sfax on 10th April. On the 11th, 7th Armoured joined 10 Corps where they met Colonel Payne Gallwey, formerly a Squadron Leader of the 11th Hussars, now commanding the Derbyshire Yeomanry. The Division spent the next week harassing the enemy near Enfidaville, and on 30th April, 7th Armoured Division were transferred to 9 Corps of 1st Army, making a journey on tank transports west to El Krib, a distance of some 300 miles, and so came under the command of General Brian Horrocks.

The infantry advance went ahead on 5th May, the Queens Brigade and Sappers moving out with strong artillery support. At 7am on 6th May, a race began between the two Armoured Divisions for the prize of Tunis. This race was won by 'B' Squadron of the 11th Hussars, who entered Tunis on the afternoon of 7th May and met a mixed reception. The French greeted their arrival in the streets with flowers and bottles of wine, the Arabs with indifference, the Germans with grenades and bursts of machine-gun fire. The Hussars were swiftly followed by tanks of the 22nd Armoured Brigade and the Queens infantry, who used their 6-pdr anti-tank guns to great effect, quelling most resistance before the 1st RTR came rumbling through the streets.

Rick Hall remembers Tunis: 'A wonderful place ... 7th Armoured had the freedom of the city for a week, for although other units got in, it was really ours. The French made a fuss of us, free meals and oodles of wine ... they put barrels of wine in our trucks, but the Arabs had laced some of it with octane or anti-freeze, the bastards – one of my blokes died from it.

'Seventh Armoured Division had a great spirit. It was a great experience to serve in that division. I don't know why ... maybe because we'd had so many good hidings before, but once we started out from Alamein nothing could stop us, and nothing did. Even our jerboa shoulder flashes had to have the Desert Rat facing forward.'

All resistance in Tunis had ended by the morning of 8th May, after which the ever-willing German army finally started to collapse. The German forces were now split, some heading for a last stand at Cape Bon, others towards the coast near Bizerta, vainly hoping for an evacuation. Later that day the 7th Armoured Division came up with the retreating enemy again at the Medjerda river, and on 12th May, the last Germans surrendered. Lt. Colonel John Creek remembers the final moments of the Afrika Korps:

'I was Adjutant of the 2nd/7th Queen's – the CO was Col. A.P. Block – when the final surrender of the Axis Forces was taken outside Enfideville. Since that day I have read various reports on that particular surrender and seen one or two variations of it on both British and Italian TV, leading to the conclusion that the writers or the producers involved had not done their homework properly and in consequence gave a description or representation far out of line with what actually happened.

The 2nd/7th Battalion of the Queen's Royal Regiment were still holding the Eighth Army front line from the sea across the only road in that piece of North Africa and to their left, where they joined up with one of the other Queen's Battalions. We, the 2nd/7th, had one company on the right of the road, between the road and the sea, and two companies on our left front, on the left of the road. For two or three days before the actual surrender there had been some coming and going of Italian and German prisoners through our front line, carrying messages, proposals of surrender, from the rear to the Axis command.

'Early on the morning of the day of surrender, 13th May, the 169 Brigade-Major, Major Desmond Gregory, called me on the nine set and said that the Battalion should prepare the site for a surrender ceremony at three o'clock in the afternoon on the road which bisected our front, at a point where our forward companies were dug-in.

'Jokingly – he was a Regular officer and I was not – I asked him how exactly one took a surrender, and he, equally lightheartedly, referred me to my Field Service pocketbook. This bulky pocketbook I looked through from end to end, but found no instructions on how a unit of the British Army should take a surrender. When I called him back on the nine set, he said he had been looking too, and he could not find any pamphlet to help us.

'In the event, we placed men with Bren guns on each side of the road at the very limits of the line as we were holding it, and men with Bren guns on each side of the road thirty or so yards further ahead into No-Man's-Land. Between these two machine gun posts on the roadside, we marked off areas where surrendering troops would deposit both arms and everything else they were carrying. We also set up a blocking point on the road, level with our reserve company and headquarter's company units, to make sure that military "visitors", knowing the war was over for ever in North Africa, would not decide to come up and see what life in the front line was like, and get under our feet whilst we were getting on with the job of receiving surrendering troops, both officers and men, and sending them in an orderly way to the rear.

'The surrender time was fixed for three o'clock; and, all the morning, flights of light and medium bombers pounded the escarpment in front of us, which was a mass of 88mm guns, mortars and retreating troops of every sort who had not been able to get up to Bizerta and away to Sicily.

'Before three o'clock the surrender area was completely empty except for Col. Block and myself, but then the reception party arrived. First the Brigadier, L.O. Lyne, and his Brigade-Major, in a jeep. Immediately after, the Divisional Commander and his acting G1. Both were "newcomers"; Brigadier (acting Major General) "Noisy" Graham had come to the Division only a few days before from the Highland Division when our Divisional Commander, Major General Miles, Grenadier Guards, was severely wounded and flown back to England. His G1, Lt.-Col. Tam Ely, KSLI, had been killed in the same incident. They came in a scout car, quickly followed by the Corps Commander and his Chief of Staff. The last vehicle to arrive was a Sherman tank, which brought up General Freyberg, VC, and a staff officer. General Freyberg was acting Commander of the Eighth Army because General Montgomery had, in these last days of fighting in North Africa, taken a large force round on what some people called the Left Hook, to support the First Army's drive through from the west, while the 8th Army held the line firm at Enfideville.

'In the half-hour before three o'clock the bombers had been over and gone away for the last time and silence had fallen all over the battlefield except for explosions facing us and to our left in the hills, where German units, in defiance of the surrender terms which had been accepted, were spiking their guns.

'By a quarter to three a dark, wide column of troops could be seen coming up the road towards us a mile and a half or so away. At this point, while the reception committee stood about and chatted, and with no one any longer wearing a steel helmet, a gun was fired away to our left along the line of our front at a low trajectory, and a round passed over the reception party's heads.

'As one man, all the distinguished and high-ranking members of the reception committee and their staff aides were on their stomachs and crouching against their vehicles. The shell landed in the sea, and as there was no explosion we concluded it must have been solid shot. No second shot followed, and gingerly the reception party got to their feet again and looked towards the south, from whence the shot had come. Naturally, the queries and comments filtered down rank-wise until the Brigadier came up and asked Colonel Block and me, standing with him, what on earth was going on and what were we doing about it. I quickly got an officer and four or five men going at the double inland, as it were, and later in the afternoon we got the explanation of the single and highly disturbing shot.

'As they had withdrawn, Axis units, knowing that they would never

189

again advance in North Africa, had taken up every marker they could find on minefields they had laid to protect themselves. In this case, a small unit with an 88mm gun in an anti-tank role, posted to fire from south to north across our Divisional front, towards the sea, on seeing their comrades marching in thick rank up the road to surrender, had decided they would like to do the same, but they were unwilling to try a cross-country route to join the surrender on the road because of the minefields. So they put one round of solid shot into their high velocity 88mm gun and fired it into the sea to draw attention to their plight, and thereby had succeeded in giving the reception party a nasty surprise, when they had thought all firing was over for ever, at least in this theatre and campaign.

'Not unexpectedly, some Italians and Germans, seeking to short-cut to the road and join in the surrender, did destroy themselves on their own minefields; and one party stumbled onto a field of S mines sufficiently near our C Company front line to cause casualties among that Company's troops, now out of their slit trenches and in the open, watching the surrender from a distance. The Company Commander, Captain Mike Charlton, was one of the casualties. He survived, but never fought again, and the wounds he suffered that day affected him for the rest of his life.

'By evening the total of men surrendering was around 38,000, of whom 28,000 were Italians and 10,000 Germans. The act of surrender was made to the acting Eighth Army Commander by General Messe, commanding Italian troops still in North Africa, and by General Von Arnim, in command of German troops in the Axis Force.

'One has heard odd stories about the surrender; for instance that when the occasional German or Italian did kill himself by walking onto one of his own minefields when he was trying to get into the surrender march, a high-ranking officer was reported as saying, "Good. Drive as many as you can onto the minefields." As far as I was concerned, or anyone else in the reception party with whom I then or later spoke, there is no evidence whatever that the surrendering officers and men of the Axis Forces were treated with anything but kindness and complete lack of animosity or vindictiveness. Rather, men limping with wounds or in any other sort of distress, were gently escorted away to field ambulance units for attention.'

Three years of fighting up and down the desert, often defeated and dismayed, but always willing to come on again, had finally brought 8th Army its reward. Two thousand miles and seven months on from Alamein, the Afrika Korps had finally been destroyed ... the war in

North Africa was over. The Division now made ready to fight in the very different terrain of Italy and Western Europe.

THE WAR IN
WESTERN EUROPE

1944–1945

Dear Desert Rats!

It is not without emotion that I can express what I feel about the Desert Rats. May your glory ever shine! May your laurels never fade! May the memory of this glorious pilgrimage of war which you have made from Alamein via the Baltic to Berlin never die! It is a march unsurpassed through all the story of war, so far as my reading of history leads me to believe.

May the fathers long tell the children about this tale. May you all feel that in following your great ancestors you have done something which has done good to the whole world, which raised the honour of your country and which every man has a right to be proud of. . . .

Winston S. Churchill
Address to the 7th Armoured Division
Berlin 1945

11

Italy and England

SEPTEMBER 1943—JUNE 1944

The essence of war is violence,
and moderation in war is imbecility.

Lord Macaulay

After the German surrender in North Africa, 7th Armoured withdrew
to the town of Homs on the North African coast, some fifty miles east
of Tripoli, near the ruins of the Roman city of Leptis Magna. Here the
Division got down to re-equipping; cleaning, painting and servicing
every item of equipment, stripping down engines, wireless sets and
weapons, removing the grit and dust of the Desert War. The 11th
Hussar hitting power was increased by the addition of a Gun Troop to
their armoured car Sabre squadrons, with two 75mm guns mounted
on White scout cars. The next stage of the war clearly involved a
landing somewhere in Occupied Europe, so the Division also rehearsed
embarking and disembarking from landing craft in Homs harbour.

The Divisional Staff also gave considerable thought to future operations, for the free-wheeling days of warfare in the open desert were
over. The Division had already had a taste of operating in close country
in the last weeks through Tunisia, but mainland Europe would be
different again. Narrow walled roads rather than open desert, towns
rather than isolated *birs*, civilians everywhere rather than occasional
bands of roving Arabs. The Division had made its name – a great name –
in the open spaces of North Africa. The confines of Europe were an
entirely different proposition, but it was already certain that there
would be an increasingly important role for the Infantry and the Royal

Engineers. The Infantry battalions were now equipped with the PIAT (Projectile Infantry, Anti-Tank), while American infantry had the 3.5inch rocket launcher and the Germans were soon to employ the formidable *panzerfaust*, a tank-busting, hand-held infantry weapon. Tanks now needed infantry for protection against other infantry, armed with these close-contact anti-tank weapons. For future operations therefore, it was decided that the landing order would be the Queens Brigade, then an Armoured regiment, with artillery and engineers in support, then Divisional HQ, then the rest of the Armoured Brigade, and then the various echelons and support units. A full Order of Battle for the Division before Salerno is on the facing page and will repay study. Given these fresh considerations, the Division managed to stage a few small exercises to test these new infantry-intensive tactics, but there was a great shortage of suitable terrain. Peter Hoggarth, an officer in the 1/7th Queens remembers this time:

'The training phase was spent at Homs. When we arrived, my platoon found a large mound of sand on the beach, which we dug into to make a camouflaged area for our 15 cwt truck. To our surprise we found the remains of a Roman villa with a very fine tessellated floor. I think the design was a large snake. We lived in small tents close to the sea and went for a swim first thing every morning. Lt-Col Gordon was the C.O. and Captain Francis was Adjutant. Shortly after arrival I became Assistant Adjutant.

'We had tents and held sand table exercises. I remember one officer trying, with success, to spot the exact place on the Italian mainland where we would land. There was emphasis on weapon training, but there were no nearby rifle ranges, of course, for practice. Grenade throwing was practised with live grenades. As part of a toughening process there was a long, hard route march, lasting over a couple of days, which almost crippled some of us. There were also small scale tactical training exercises at platoon strength. An L.S.T. arrived at Homs Harbour and we practised climbing up the ropes on its side. The artillery paid us a visit and gave us a demonstration of firing 25 pounders. There was also a firing competition between our anti-tank platoon and some RTR tanks – not at each other, I hasten to add. The nearby ruins of the ancient city of Leptis Magna fascinated me. I obtained some notes on the city and took a party from the battalion on a conducted tour. Entertainment facilities were sparse. The Roman amphitheatre was used for ENSA concerts. I spent a short leave in Tripoli. The C.O. set general knowledge questions for the battalion and prizes were awarded.'

Otherwise, the highlight of 7th Armoured's stay at Homs was a visit

ITALY
ORDER OF BATTLE SEPTEMBER 1943

22nd Armoured Brigade
1st RTR
5th RTR
4th CLY
1st Rifle Brigade

131st (Queens) Brigade
1st/5th Queens Royal Regiment
1st/6th Queens Royal Regiment
1st/7th Queens Royal Regiment
'C' Company, 1st Cheshire
  Regiment

Divisional Troops
11th Hussars
Divisional Signals

Royal Artillery
3rd RHA
5th RHA
15th Light AA Regiment RA
24th Field Regiment RA
65th Anti-Tank Regiment RA
69th Medium Regiment RA
146th Field Regiment RA

Royal Engineers
4th Field Squadron
621st Field Squadron
143rd Field Park Squadron

RASC
No. 5 Company
No. 58 Company
No. 67 Company
No. 287 Company
No. 432 Company
No. 507 Company

RAMC
2nd Light Field Ambulance
131st Field Ambulance
70th Field Hygiene Section
21st Mobile Casualty Clearing
  Station
3rd Field Surgical Unit
7th Field Transfusion Unit
132nd Mobile Dental Unit
135th Mobile Dental Unit

RAOC
Divisional Ordnance Field Park

REME
22nd Armoured Brigade
  Workshops
131st Brigade Workshop
15th Light AA Workshop

from H.M. King George VI, who inspected the whole Division and spent much of his time with his own regiment, the 11th Hussars, of which he was Colonel-in-Chief.

On 10th July 1943 the Allies invaded the island of Sicily, but 7th Armoured were not involved in that operation. Their turn came later on 8th September 1943, when they embarked for the landings at Salerno on the mainland of Italy, close to Naples. As the invasion force sailed they heard the good news that Italy had surrendered, but the Germans inevitably fought on, and from commanding positions around the Bay of Salerno, greeted the invaders with a hail of shellfire and counter-attacks as the Allied divisions clawed their way ashore.

A small party, including Brigadier L.H. Whistler of the Queens Brigade landed with the assault waves on the first day, but the main part of the Division did not begin to go ashore until the evening of 15th September. Disembarkation continued under cover of darkness, for the beach-head was still under shellfire, but by midnight the Queens Brigade, with most of the 5th Royal Tanks, were ashore, and the guns of the 3rd RHA were landed in support before dawn. Seventh Armoured Division were the reserve Division for 10th (British) Corps, commanded by General R.L. McCreery, who had taken command after the previous Corps commander, General Brian Horrocks, had been wounded in an air raid.

The Division first concentrated near the village of Battipaglia, four or five miles inland, an area of recently reclaimed marshland, alive with malarial mosquitoes. No one was sorry to leave when the Division, which now had the 23rd Armoured Brigade under command, was ordered forward on 27th September. The first objective was Scafati on the River Sarno, from where the 23rd Brigade would take the coast road between the sea and the rumbling volcano of Vesuvius, while the rest of 7th Armoured would go north of Vesuvius and head for Capua on the River Volturno. The Sappers, who had done such sterling work among the desert minefields, now found that apart from mines in plenty, they also had to deal with booby-traps and with clearing a way for the tanks and vehicles through village streets choked with rubble.Unable to disperse laterally on this stone-walled countryside, the Division deployed from front to rear and at one time was spread out over fifty-five miles of narrow road. As the Divisional History puts it, had the leading elements of the Division been at Brighton, the rear echelons would still have been in London.

Otherwise all went well, with the Division receiving an ecstatic welcome from the local population, which was some consolation for

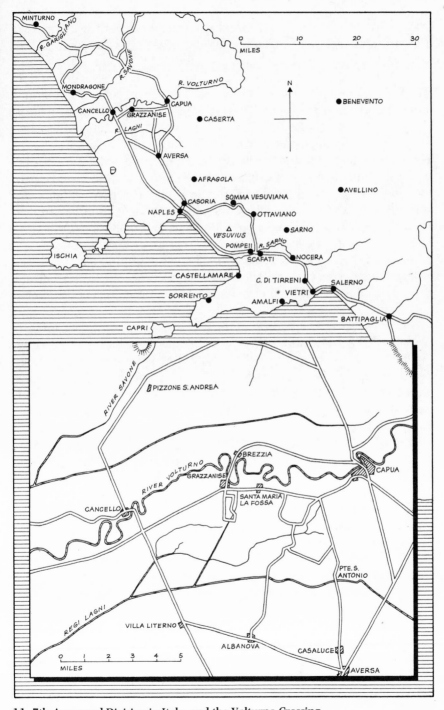

11 7th Armoured Division in Italy, and the Volturno Crossing

fighting in terrain far removed from the open spaces of the desert. The Division, and especially the recce units of the King's Dragoon Guards and the 11th Hussars, clearly felt confined, kept to roads by the stone walls of the fields, and the waterlogged ground, which was, in addition, much cut about by irrigation ditches. The roads soon disintegrated under the weight of the tanks. That rain, about which the Italian Tourist Board is reticent, teemed down relentlessly into the turrets and fighting compartments of the tanks and armoured cars, and the German enemy, as ever, fought tenaciously, strewing the countryside with mines, booby-traps and small parties of German infantry armed with the *panzerfaust*.

'I don't recall much trouble with the *panzerfaust* here – that came later, in Normandy,' says Field Marshal Carver, then commanding the 1st RTR. 'But they did have a quantity of small, mobile anti-tank guns. The Italians don't have low vines like they do in France. In Italy the vines are braced up ten or twelve feet above the ground on high wires. From a turret you can't see down through these, while the German gunners could peer under the vines, deploy their weapons and still have good cover.'

On 1st October, A Squadron of the Kings Dragoon Guards from 23rd Armoured Brigade entered Naples, where George Clark had a strange experience. 'I served in the KDGs in the 7th Armoured Division – Desert Rats – in the Western Desert from 1941 to sometime in 1943. Then near Tripoli, when I transferred to the RAF Regiment. While guarding Naples airport, I got into conversation with a man in uniform looking out to sea in a rather forlorn manner – in a Napoleonic stance. He told me that there were some horses nearby, and being ex-Cavalry, he took me to see them. Some days later I found my old regiment quartered in the local loony bin opposite the airport, and I told Col Lindsay of my meeting with the man, whom I later found was the Chief of Police for Naples. Col Lindsay lost no time in going to HQ to requisition some of the horses and subsequently formed a horse troop, which proved useful in bad weather and rugged terrain.

'I remember Col Lindsay then came to see me and said he was more than grateful for my help. The History then relates how they proved useful for patrols and carrying rations and arms on land impassable even to jeeps. Two hundred and fifty years of horse tradition dies hard.'

North of Naples the country began to open up a little. Twenty-Second Armoured Brigade now took over the lead, with Lt-Colonel Mike Carver's 1 RTR in the van, supported on the left flank by the 4th CLY under Viscount Cranley. Both regiments made good progress but it was still hard country for the roving 11th Hussars. Gone for ever were the days of free manoeuvre in the open desert, of rapid movement from one flank to the other. Now the 11th Hussars and KDGs had to motor steadily along narrow roads where the first contact usually came when the enemy's anti-tank guns opened fire and 'brewed-up' the leading car. Then the tanks and the Queens would come up to probe for the enemy's flanks. This was slow and dangerous work, breaking through roadblock after roadblock, with the occasional stiff fight as well. The 1st Rifle Brigade of 22 Armoured Brigade lost a number of men at Cardito as the Division fought its way forward to the first major obstacle, the Volterno river. Here all the bridges were down and the town of Capua held in strength by the enemy.

An opposed river crossing is no easy task for an Armoured Division. The job of getting across and forming a bridgehead was therefore given to Brigadier Whistler and the Queens. Whistler took the 4th CLY, all the Artillery, and all the Divisional Engineers under command, for the task was a difficult one. The Volturno is a wide, fast-flowing, high-banked river, then swollen by the recent heavy rains. The North bank was strongly defended by a well-entrenched enemy, well supplied with machine guns, with artillery ranged on all the likely crossing points, and well able to engage British units forming up across the river.

The most likely place for a crossing was by the village of Grazzanise, seven miles west of Capua, where a wooden bridge had only been partly demolished. Both ends had gone but the 80ft centre span was still intact. Although the river was 240 ft wide at this point, and about 6ft deep, flowing at around nine miles per hour, and set below banks 15 ft high, this was considered the best place for an assault, though getting tanks across that lot would be a task indeed.

Patrols and swimmers were first sent across the river on two consecutive nights to probe the enemy defences, while the Royal Engineers brought up Bailey bridges to span the gaps in the wooden structure. Even with this reinforcement the bridge was not strong enough for tanks, so bulldozers were brought up to cut and level the banks down to the river, where the tanks must try and find a ford. During these various patrols and reconnaissance missions, the Division was under regular shelling and machine-gun fire. This was answered by the 3rd RHA and a squadron of the CLY.

The actual crossing began on the night of 12th/13th October 1943. The 7th Queens went first, paddling across in assault boats, but many craft were holed by shrapnel or machinegun fire or carried downstream by the swift current, and the first attempt failed to gain a lodgement.

At 0230 in the morning, the Queens tried again, and by dawn had a small bridgehead on the north bank. By mid-day they had 'B' and 'C' companies across and digging in. These men clung on throughout the day and on the next night, as crossing in daylight was suicidal, the 7th Battalion anti-tank guns were ferried across.

The 4th CLY had also found a crossing point just upstream of the wooden bridge, suitable for waterproofed Shermans. A bulldozer then crossed the repaired wooden bridge to level the banks on the far side of the river, and the entire 4th CLY were across by the 17th, only one tank failing to forge across, and even that one was hauled out by the Divisional bulldozer. On the morning of the 16th, the 7th Queens had advanced patrols in Brezzia on the north bank, the 5th Queens were now across and expanding the bridgehead. The 7th Queen's mortar platoon fired more bombs during the Volturno crossing than in the entire African campaign. By 22nd October both the British 10th Corps and the American 6th Corps were across the river and advancing towards the next obstacle, the River Garigliano.

Lieutenant Peter Hoggarth continues: 'The Germans retreated slowly, endeavouring all the time to hold us up in the often close country. Thick vegetation gave opportunities for ambushes. Many mines were laid in the narrow lanes and more than once I saw the remains of humble peasant carts which had been blown up. One night we arrived at a small village to find a cart halfway across the road. The cart appeared to have been abandoned and in the morning we found it had been booby trapped with an "S" mine.

'The Italians welcomed us with enthusiasm and with whatever gifts they had, usually fruit. They were helpful in showing us where mines had been laid, and no doubt provided useful intelligence information. The long, narrow roads, bordered with thick vegetation, were ideal for defensive warfare. I remember, on one occasion, a German S.P. gun knocking out two Sherman tanks accompanying us. A patrol was then sent out from one of the companies to deal with the gun, which was skilfully withdrawn.

'We halted at the Volturno and tested the enemy strength by patrolling. I remember Lt. Ainsworth's patrol wading almost across the river before being forced to withdraw, and Lt. Ashworth's patrol which crossed the river in assault boats. Lt. Ashworth was tragically killed on 10th October.

'At about this time, I again became a platoon commander. We were ordered to advance to the southern bank of the Volturno to simulate a crossing attempt. This was to take some of the heat off 46 Division, which would cross further up the river; I think at Capua. I believe that originally the plan was for our Brigade to cross, but this was changed and we were given a supporting role. Anyway, I was taking my platoon up to the river, when the 25 pounder barrage opened from our artillery. Unfortunately, many shells fell short, killing and wounding a number of 1/7th Queen's personnel. The barrage was instantly stopped on the orders of our C.O. I was wounded slightly. We were able to fire some mortar shells (2 inch) over the river. The same night I was evacuated to Naples in an American Friends' Ambulance, and when I rejoined the battalion, it had reached (I believe) Mondragone. The Friends' Ambulance Service could well merit a favourable mention in any history of this campaign.

'In 1974 I visited the area when on holiday, and noticed a Bailey bridge still in place across the Volturno. The river looked just as sombre as it did all those years ago.'

The 7th Armoured Division now advanced north, clearing mines and repairing the road as they advanced. On the way Colonel Smail of the 11th Hussars was badly injured in a jeep accident and Major Wainmann took command of the regiment. The Division moved to the Agnena river, taking up positions near the coast, from where the 6th Queens, supported by the 5th Royal Tanks, attacked and captured the small port of Mondragone. A week later, on 7th November, the many hopeful rumours that had been circulating among the troops were finally confirmed; 7th Armoured Division was withdrawn from the line, handing over their tanks and vehicles to the 5th Canadian Armoured Division. On 19th November 1943 the advance party of 7th Armoured sailed for home, and their next task, the D-Day landings in Normandy. Sergeant Harry Ellis of the 15th L.A.A. Regiment has an account of this brief Italian campaign.

'Just to jog my memory, I looked up the dates of our Italian campaign – 15th September to 20th December 1943. Having had a rest period and recreation spell, especially swimming at a stretch of lovely beach outside Homs near Tunis, sixty miles away, and after doing well in our swimming competitions, I was sent for by Colonel Henry Kelly and ordered to teach all non-swimmers during morning Physical Training periods. The time after this was spent on training for Combined Operations with a Landing Craft Infantry moored in Homs harbour, waterproofing guns and vehicles for the landings at Salerno followed. General Erskine, the Divisional Commander at this period, gave all Officers and Senior NCOs a briefing on our future role without disclosing our place of landing in Europe. This turned out to be the Bay of Salerno, South of Naples.

'The American 5th Army, under General Mark Clark, had landed on 9th September, and we got the impression that the Americans were struggling to hold the beach-head. General Horrocks, our Corps Commander, had been wounded in an air raid on Bizerta, so Lt-Gen. McCreery took over command of 10th Corps.

'We sailed from Tripoli on Tank Landing Ships or LSTs as they were known. As our regiment were LAAs, we were placed on the top deck with our Bofors-guns ready for action. Meanwhile, over the tannoy aboard ship, came the announcement that Italy had surrendered. The Germans had taken over from the Italians and we knew things would not be easy. Glider bombs and radio controlled bombs were being launched from German aircraft, so as A.A. we could not relax on our calm sailing through the Straits of Messina and up the coast of Italy, with a splendid view of the coastline. Over the tannoy came the news that it would be a dry landing, so we ripped off all the waterproofing materials from our ammo boxes, guns and vehicles.

'As we approached Salerno, we passed by the battleship 'Warspite', which was shelling the hills above the bay with her big guns. I remember thinking that I wouldn't like to be on the receiving end of those! Early on the 16th September 1943, the bow doors of the LST opened and the ramp fell onto dry land. The guns of the 3rd RHA (25 pounders) and some armour were first ashore, with us on the top-deck being last off. The Battery Commander, Major Sykes-Balls, was leading us with his jeep, just off the beach into a wooded area for assembly. There was the usual spasmodic shelling, ours and theirs, so our cook got the brew-up fire going with the can on the fire (desert fashion), when an armour-piercing shell fell near the fire, upsetting Gunner Cardy, the cook and our brew-up equipment. Our gun team was most annoyed that our brew had been delayed, so amid much cursing from the cook, Gunner Fred Cardy, and the rest of the gun team, we managed to salvage our brew-up equipment and start again.

'The Battery Commander turned up to link us up with M Battery 3rd RHA, and we were soon to find out that this was a different terrain from the desert, where we had so much room to manoeuvre. Weather conditions were so much wetter, and added to this was the threat of Malaria, as this coast consisted of reclaimed marshes with mosquitoes galore. The medics issued anti-malaria tablets, face nets and special grease to spread on the skin, which took on a yellow tint. Our Troop Commander, Captain Jimmy Kirkpatrick MC., swore that any gunner whose skin didn't turn yellow was not taking his tablets. Threats of open arrest for any defaulter had some of us worried, my own skin not turning as yellow as most I was under grave suspicion of dumping my tablets, so on some occasions I took some tablets as he watched me.

'The Luftwaffe were strafing us at various times with a greater number of Focker Wolfe 190s. These had cannon and machine guns with a great number of small bombs carried under the wings, which were fused as anti-personnel bombs, exploding before hitting the ground. I had a jammed upper gun stay plunger in one of these raids, which prevented us dropping into action. These American type Bofors guns had soft metal on certain parts which soon showed up in wear and tear, and were not as reliable as our old Mk I Desert Bofors gun. I was astounded on this occasion that we had no casualties from the Fokker Wolfe's 190 anti-personnel bombs.

'The Royal Engineers with Bailey bridges were called into action a great deal, and another type called the Scissors Bridge, on the chassis of a tank which spanned the many gorges, narrow roads and rivers, which were causing a tailback in the advance. I found myself forward with infantry and 6 pounder anti-tank guns. I turned a corner in a small village and came face to face with a Tiger tank. The four 6 pounder anti-tank guns with an officer in charge dropped into action, with my gun just behind. I ordered "Halt Action Tank!" and my crew were dropping our Bofors into action with a box of armour-piercing ammo, when the young officer with the anti-tank guns ordered me to get out of the road. This I did, with my gun crew manhandling our Bofors back round the corner out of the line of fire, leaving it to the better equipped 6-pounder guns. I waited for the guns to open up, but the German Tiger tank's crew came out of a house alongside their tanks with their arms in the air, walking up to the 6-pounders to surrender. We drove past the Tiger tank, which was intact, shortly after. The infantry in their Bren carriers were among us then, and shortly after we ran into German mortar fire, so we pulled into a farmyard area to seek cover, but it was so congested it was difficult to find room to manoeuvre.

'The Divisions' bulldozers were brought up forward, clearing away rubble and filling in craters. Tank crews were finding it hard to pick out the enemy, so the Rifle Brigade carriers and scout cars were in the lead. One carrier ran into the back axle of my gun about this period, bending it and making the Bofors gun untowable. The Troop Commander sent me back to the Divisional workshops run by REME in a pleasant area around Mount Vesuvius, which at that time was starting to erupt. They did quick repairs to the axle of the gun and sent me to rejoin the Regiment who, by this time, were approaching the River Volturno. The Troop Commander, Captain Jimmy Kirkpatrick, decided to get my gun across on a raft, with ropes each side of the river bank, so that we had to pull the gun-towing vehicle across and the Bofors gun. This was hard work for the gun crew, but we made it and went to join some Sherman tanks which had forded the river earlier. I talked to the crews who were preparing for a German counter-attack, which I'm glad to say did not develop, just spasmodic shelling. Supplies were sent across on a raft – rations, mail, petrol and ammo, and after a few days and several successful crossings by the Corps, the pressure eased as we moved forward again to the River Garigliano.

'In early November, word got round that we were going home. We handed all our guns and vehicles over to the 5th Canadian Armoured Division and made for the Sorrento Peninsular to await a convoy to take us home to Blighty. My Bombardier, Bill Hitchen, was to lead volunteers to supply front line troops engaged in the Battle of Mount Cassino. There were some trips to the Isle of Capri, but physical training and small arms practice kept us fit. Then we sailed home to Glasgow, arriving in early January 1944, then I travelled by train to Diss in Norfolk for leave, during which I got married.'

Ray Cooper of 22nd Armoured Brigade remembers his return home: 'We entered the Clyde on the 7th January. Boarding the train, we travelled through the night unaware of our destination. Then, on awaking, we found we were in Norfolk. As far as our HQ was concerned, we left Brandon station, travelled to Swaffham, turned off along a country lane to a camp comprising decaying Nissen huts under pine trees. Not the most welcome of sites or sights, but at least it was England and naturally we were all looking forward to leave.

'I still remember the journey home, the penultimate station being Billing, where the engine packed up, and it took two hours to produce another. Eventually, taking a taxi from the station, I arrived to be met by my wife Brenda, and 3-year-old Maureen Ann who had been only months old when I left. After eyeing me for a few minutes she exclaimed: "Look Mummy, he has boots, legs and a bottom!" This observation was because before bedtime each night, she had been taken to say "Goodnight" to a head-and-shoulders photograph of me.'

After a small amount of home leave and a great number of weddings, the bulk of the Division concentrated in Norfolk. The battalions of the Queens Brigade were at Kings Lynn, where they were joined by the Heavy Support Company of the Royal Northumberland Fusiliers, with 4-inch mortars. Among Divisional reinforcements were their old comrades of the 8th Hussars, and among many visitors were General

Sir Bernard Montgomery, and the overall Commander of the Allied Expeditionary Force, General Dwight Eisenhower.

The Division had returned to the UK entirely bereft of all but their personal weapons, so the first priority was re-equipment. The Armoured Regiments received the new Cromwell tank, but to tackle the growing threat of the 88mm gunned Tiger tank, the Armoured Regiments were eventually equipped on the basis of three Cromwells and one 'Firefly' tank per troop. This Firefly was a Sherman tank mounting a 17-pdr gun, which, it was hoped, could match the 'Tiger' for range and penetrate the thickest armour. Most of the Cromwells mounted 75mm guns, but some had the 6-pdr. Seventh Armoured was the only armoured division equipped with Cromwells; all the other divisions, British, American, Canadian and French had Shermans. The Cromwell was a good, fast, reliable tank, and did not brew up with the ease of a Sherman, but it was under-gunned and under-armed compared with the German Tiger and Panther tanks. Some troops also had Crusader tanks, equipped for an anti-aircraft roll.

R. Godwin remembers this time: 'Coming from the Middle East in late December 1943 into a typical Nissan camp in Norfolk near Brandon was bitterly cold, but after disembarkation, leave (and marriage) we were all kept extremely busy. A new tank, the Cromwell, had to be familiarised with plus being sent to Keswick on a tank waterproofing course, which included a test drive into the lake in swimming trunks in January. This didn't improve the circulation.

'Being considered as a "Crusader" man from my time with the RGH, I suddenly found myself appointed as Troop Sergeant to a troop of six Crusader tanks which had their turrets modified and fitted with twin Orlikon anti-aircraft guns all as for the Navy. So I was sent away again for a week to the Gunnery School at Lulworth, which included a test fire across Lulworth Cove. From there we moved directly back to the Lake District and Egremont for a week on aircraft recognition and practice firing at a drogue from the sea-front at Nethertown. One day we received a message from the pilot of the towing aircraft, which I suspect was routine in order to relieve the monotony. "For Christ's sake, tell those people down there we are pulling the target not pushing it." We went back to camp through the snow to start instructing my crews.'

During this time in England the Division were also visited by their old Commander, General Percy Hobart, who had since raised and trained the 11th Armoured Division. This was now commanded by another 7th Armoured Division Officer, Major General G.P.B (Pip) Roberts. Hobart had just completed the training of the 79th Armoured

Division, the so-called 'Funnies'. This unit never fought as a division, for it was composed of specialist armour to breach the Atlantic Wall and overcome strongpoints. It contained flail tanks to beat a path across minefields, petard tanks to destroy concrete blockhouses, flame-throwing tanks (Crabs), to burn out snipers and machine gun posts, fascine tanks to cross ditches and shell-craters, bridge-building tanks to cross gaps. Hobart had also raised and trained large forces of D-D (Duplex Drive) swimming tanks which could cross rivers or be launched far offshore and swim in to the beach under their own power. After D-Day much of this specialized armour found its way to the more conventional armoured divisions, and was often used to support the advance of 7th Armoured Division. The Division also received another visit from H.M. the King, as Harry Ellis recalls:

'Leave over, we returned to Diss to re-equip with new Bofors guns and vehicles. A gunnery course was held at the old Butlins Holiday Camp at Clacton-on-Sea. H.M. King George and the Queen inspected all the Gunner Regiments at Sandringham, where we formed a hollow square. The 7th Armoured Division were very experienced fighting men and we felt we had been selected to take part in the coming invasion in Europe because of our experiences in battle.'

While the rest of the Division went to Norfolk, the 11th Hussars spent the five months of their stay in England in the leafy surroundings of Ashridge Park in the Chilterns. Here, both Lt-Colonel Smail and the Second-in-Command Major Wainman got married, as did a remarkable number of the Regiment's soldiers. Colonel Smail then handed over command of his regiment to Major Bill Wainmann, leaving to take command of the Royal Gloucestershire Hussars.

The next posting cut even more deeply, for General Montgomery had decreed that all the armoured car recce regiments should be taken from the Divisions and placed under the Corps Commander, which switched the 11th from the 7th Armoured Division to the command of General Bucknall's 30 Corps. In practice this had very little effect, for the 11th kept close to 7th Armoured during the early days in Normandy and returned to Divisional command in August.

In May, just a month before D-Day, the new equipment finally arrived, mainly consisting of American Staghound armoured cars as Squadron and RHQ vehicles, and Hunter scout cars for the Troops. The men found the Staghound far too large and cumbersome, with its crew of five and its 37mm gun, and used the handier Humber car whenever possible.

The Division moved from Norfolk to assembly areas close to their embarkation ports early in May 1944; 22 Armoured Brigade went to

Ipswich, the rest of the Division to Tilbury Docks, east of London. The final briefing from the Divisional Commander, General Erskine, was given in a cinema at Brentwood in Essex, and on 4th June the Desert Rats embarked for their new campaign in France. A personal account of the Division at this time comes from Trooper Duce of the 8th Hussars:

'In December 1941, having recently completed my apprenticeship in carpentry and joinery and thereby just started to earn myself some money, I received papers requiring me to report to Colchester M.O.D. medical Centre for Med-Grading.

'Two weeks after the Christmas break, I received papers requiring me to report to 61st Training Regiment RAC Tidworth, and so there I was, still under nineteen, hardly ever left home and family before, on my way to join the Real Stuff. They certainly put us through it – courses, training, drilling, physical training, lectures, cross-country runs – on the go the whole time. All this was after they had given us an initial intelligence test, which we had to pass for the dubious honour of being R.A.C. I certainly became very fit, and in fact still kept up daily runs when on my first home leave. I gradually realized that I was with specially chosen people, some of them very well educated. The authorities obviously intended the R.A.C. to be a Corps elite.

'The Unit was stationed in Yorkshire, equipped with Covenanters and Crusaders, the predominate types at that time. Months went by with general training and manoeuvres, including a visit to Castlemartin Tank Gunnery Range. The Unit suddenly moved down to Warminster and so I was back in the Plains area again. It was while stationed there that I was first introduced to the Cromwell Heavy Cruiser tank and did a driving and maintenance course on this AFV. It didn't take long to realize that here was a vast improvement on the earlier two mentioned. The Cromwell to my mind was the first real advance in design and technique that our people had come up with; the Rolls Royce Merlin converted to tank use and called the Meteor – producing 540 bhp at governed revs coupled to the Merit Brown epicyclic gearbox and Christie suspension system, 75mm max armour plating, 75mm dual-purpose gun, which no other British built tank had been fitted with before, plus secondary armament of two heavy base m/guns. Steering was through the epicyclic gearbox, hydraulically assisted, a unique feature of which was the neutral turn. This enabled the driver to halt opposite an opening or gateway, put gear lever into neutral position, pull back on either steering tiller, rev up the engine and the tank would turn on the spot, one track forward, the other backward ... whichever.

'The Cromwell was also very fast with power to spare. Governors were fitted to keep speed down to 40mph. This was still some speed for a 28-ton tank, and in the breakout from Normandy, even wheeled vehicles were pushed to keep up with them. With regard to tank guns, the Germans always seemed to be one step ahead of us. When we had the two-pounder (which, strange as it may seem, would penetrate 25mm of armour plate at 500 yards) they had the 50mm gun in their MK IIIs and 75mm in Mk IVs. Now we had the 75mm and 17-pounder, the enemy had the 75mm long special and the formidable 88mm in their massive Tigers, the Panthers taking the special 75mm. Good as the Cromwell was, it was no match for any of these enemy tanks in a tank-to-tank situation in gunpower alone, apart from thinner plating, but then neither was the Sherman really. The Cromwell's strong points were its speed and reliability, and once these factors could be taken advantage of, the slow, ponderous enemy would be taken care of in other ways.

'In the middle of 1943, we heard that a new Armoured Division was being formed, the 11th, an elite formation, full of RAC Regiments, but of course as yet untried in battle. Before my posting came through, 7th Armoured had returned, being stationed at West Tofts near the Stanton Battle Range in Norfolk. Instead of a posting to the new division I was posted to 8th Hussars, which had also served in the desert with 7th Armoured. The Division had arrived in the U.K. greatly under strength in personnel, and so received its quota of replacements.

'I joined 8th Hussars around October 1943 as far as I can remember, and the first thing that struck me was the easy-going manner of all personnel, both officers and ORs. Coming from a Home Unit, I had been used to so much Bull. Also, unlike so many other Divisions, 7th Armoured was quite a cosmopolitan assembly of all sorts of national-ities – South African, Jewish, Lithuanian, Latvian and, of course, all the four home countries. I joined 8th Hussars as a mustered Gun-ner/Mechanic, which really meant I had passed Gunnery – Driving Tracker and Driver I/C courses.

'With 8th Hussars I was first assigned to Transport Section of "D" Squadron. This Squadron in itself was unusual because a Tank Regi-ment is normally made up of HQ Squadron plus "A", "B" and "C" Squadrons. Eighth Hussars had the luxury of an extra Squadron. No trouble spotting the difference between the old hands and replacements. For one thing, they were about ten years older, also they were deeply tanned. In addition they all wore the Africa Star Medal Ribbon. Young replacements were treated with complete indifference at first, and during off duty hours they tended to keep to themselves, but all this changed later as we trained and mixed together. In fact, I was glad to be with these people. They seemed to ooze experience. The Regiment had recently been equipped with Cromwells, so I felt confident on that score. Some of them looked old for their years, but that's what war does to you.

'A troop of tanks consists of three vehicles commanded by the Troop Leader (usually a lieutenant), with a sergeant as Second-in-Command and a Full Corporal in command of the third tank. A Tank Commander has an awful lot to think about and certainly is no dud, accomplished in gunnery, driving, wireless ops., map reading, R/T procedure . . . quick decisions. The Troop Leader has all this plus the other two tanks to consider. I found the Troop Leader, 5 Troop, giving a talk on the following day's exercise. "Ah yes!" he said. "The new man – can you drive a Cromwell?" "Yes Sir," I replied. "I've done a Cromwell course." "Very well," he said, everybody weighing me up. "We'll try you out in tomorrow's manoeuvres. You can drive my tank."

'There were a few untanned faces in that hut, including the Troop Leader's, who appeared to be a year or so older than myself. Next morning at the Tank Park I learned that this was a one-day exercise, Reds versus Blues – everyone in place and ready to go – headsets on – driver turn on master switch – intercom alive – driver request to turret – prime pump (fuel) – W/Op reaches through hole in bulkhead and primes the carb. – driver presses starter button – terrific roar at rear as engine with no silencers bursts into life – coil assisted magneto ignition – never fails if batteries are up. It was a terrific feeling to have all this power in my control. Driver advance – creep forward out of the long, neat lines of tanks – halt – neutral – turn to the left – into bottom and away. The day's exercise progressed with the usual stopping, starting, moving to Hull Down, moving into woods, observing, pretence at firing and so on. It finally ended with a charge at the 'enemy lines'. It was potentially dangerous but we had to obey orders.

'Back at camp the Troop Leader spoke to me. "You did all right, but you're inclined to over rev in low gears. This brings the governors into operation. There's a place for you as Co/Driver Hull M/Gunner. Go and see the Corporal." The Corporal was a small, dark, tanned, very serious chap, who never spoke two words when one would do, a Regular Soldier, straight as a die with you, and very cool under fire. Sad to say, he did not survive the war. I very soon settled in with 5 Troop and the crew of "Aly Sloper" in particular.

'Soon after my joining 5 Troop the whole Division took part in a full scale exercise in the Norfolk battle area, lasting two weeks. This was the longest period I had ever had to sleep on *terra firma*, in the little bivvy which is part of tank equipment. Also the longest I had gone without a decent wash. In fact, this exercise brought home to me what it must be like to be in action and living like this all the time. Rough and ready food, and five people trying to sleep in that little bivvy. By now, with but a few exceptions, the desert types had accepted us youngsters and were quite friendly and helpful. They had certainly become pretty resourceful at concocting something to eat and drink. One of their specialities was a 'desert pancake' – army hardtack biscuits ground into a kind of flour, mixed with a little water into a paste, fried with a little margarine over a cut-down petrol tin, and washed down with a mug of so-called tea, thick with Nestlés milk. A sure diet for constipation. Of course, at this stage we were still getting cook's wagon. We did not quite complete the two weeks manoeuvres because "Aly Sloper" developed valve trouble in that marvellous engine. We were towed back to West Tofts camp by "Mac" Recovery truck, and next day were issued with a brand new Cromwell. 8th Hussars being a Cavalry Regiment, all tanks were named after race-horses. This was to be the one we took to Normandy. Though we did not realize it at the time, this last big exercise was intended to be our last intensive workout and a chance to iron out problems. It had certainly done this with our tank.

'In May 1944, intensive preparations were underway throughout the Division for beach landings. The favourite guess as to our destination seemed to be somewhere on the Dutch coast. Lorry drivers were practising wet landings and reversing up simulated landing ramps; tank crews were busy waterproofing certain points in the hull with special packs of mastic; extension ducts were welded over air intakes on engines and at exhaust louvres for obvious reasons. Some tanks had anchor points welded to engine plates to enable small vehicles such as jeeps to be "given a lift" ashore. Invasion was in the air and Southern England seemed packed with units and equipment.

'We had one false alarm at the end of May when we were paraded in Battle Order and marched down to the seafront to our respective vehicles, with the intention of moving off, but after having mounted up and kept hanging about for orders, it was suddenly cancelled. So back we went to our billets. This bears out the reports that D-Day was intended to take place earlier than 6th June but weather conditions were against it. Looking out to sea from our billets we could see these huge rectangular objects, apparently floating yet no shipping of any kind. We didn't know it then, but we were looking at part of a Mulberry Harbour, the artificial harbour which was towed across the Channel and sunk off Arromanches to form a huge breakwater.

'A few days later we left Bognor Regis in long columns of vehicles and turned inland, eventually ending up in a large transit camp in some huge wood with barbed wire around us and Military Police at the entrance. They were making sure we couldn't desert. Two days later we were on our last journey in the U.K. We simply had to follow the tank in front with no idea where we were going. Everywhere, people watched us pass through the villages and hamlets of Southern England – Hampshire, Sussex, Surrey lanes and secondary roads, all absolutely packed with all kinds of vehicles. This was when I first set eyes on the Sherman Mine Flailer, also the Churchill Crocodile Flamer and 9-inch Mortar Thrower. The latter two were very effective against pillboxes.

'We moved through the streets of Gosport in the early hours of 6th June and received orders to kip down on the pavement beside our tanks after hot cocoa. At around six o'clock next morning we were roused and gazed bleary-eyed about to find we were the centre of attention. Townspeople were looking from their bedroom windows, registering amazement at the sight in their streets and obviously amused at the various state of dress of the Troops. After a hurried breakfast of porridge, a special treat of peach slices in syrup was served at the cook's lorry.

'From the nearby houses we heard the BBC news bulletins announcing "Air drops and other activities" on the Normandy Coast. By the end of that day, 6th June, the 7th Armoured were aboard their respective landing craft. We set sail on the evening of 6th June in pitch darkness, with quite rough seas. What a task those "Wavy Navy" lieutenants must have had navigating with all the activity and conditions! After the impressive sights travelling through Southern England the day before, we were to see an equally unforgettable sight early the next morning, 7th June. As we approached the coastline, there were all kinds of ships and small craft at anchor. We literally weaved in and out on our journey to the beaches, thanks to that air superiority again. The landing craft grounded with still some distance to the water's edge, but fortunately it was not too deep. The ramps dropped down and the waterproofing was put to good use as the tanks pushed through quite a head of water.

'Once on the hard-packed, wet, shiny sand, the Beachmaster directed us to the white-taped lanes, which had been swept by the Mineflailer

Shermans. What a Godsend they were, and what high calibre men crewed them.'

The 7th Armoured Division had arrived in Normandy and some very hard fighting lay ahead.

12

The Battle of Normandy

7TH JUNE–31ST AUGUST

> The bravest are surely those
> who know what is before them,
> glory and danger alike, yet
> knowing this, they go to meet it.
>
> *Pericles*

Soon after dawn on D-Day, American troops began to go ashore on UTAH and OMAHA beaches, at the Western end of the Bay of the Seine. Because of the tidal set, British and Canadian troops, supported by tanks of General Hobart's 79th Armoured Division, went ashore on the Normandy beaches half an hour later, at 0730 hrs on the morning of D-Day, 6th June 1944.

A recce party from the 22nd Armoured Brigade were the first men of 7th Armoured to land in Normandy, coming ashore on D-Day with the HQ of the 50th Division and charged with finding an assembly area for their brigade, which began to come ashore at Arromanches on 7th June. All the units of 22 Armoured Brigade were ashore by that evening, but it was not until 12th June that the Queen's Brigade was complete, their arrival having been delayed by the great storm that punished the beaches and the 'Mulberry' harbours. By then, some units of the Division had already seen action. Tanks from 'A' Squadron, 5th Royal Tanks were sent to assist 56th Brigade in the close *bocage* country behind the coast, where one officer, Lt. Garnett, had the unnerving experience of having enemy infantry actually leaping onto his tank from the high banks at the side of the road, not an experience encountered in the

215

desert. He and the wireless operator had to drive them off with revolvers, a small but significant indication of the close, sometimes hand-to-hand *bocage* fighting that was to mark the weeks which followed.

The Calvados country, south of the Bay of the Seine, can be roughly divided into two parts, the open *campagne*, south and south-east of Caen, which is rolling, fairly open country, and the close *bocage*, south and south-west of Bayeux. Modern farming methods introduced since 1945 have greatly changed the bocage, rooting out many thick hedges and levelling high banks to make large open fields, but in 1944 this *bocage* was a maze of small, high-banked fields, thick copses and woods, narrow lanes and steep-sided valleys. Visibility was never more than fifty yards and, as the Armoured Corps' journal briefly remarks, ' . . . everyone who came in contact with it heartily detested it, for fighting in it bore a close resemblance to continuous street fighting.' It was here, as the spearhead of a thrust south, to the west of Caen, that 7th Armoured were first committed to battle in Normandy.

Apart from problems of terrain, the tanks and armoured cars had – as we have seen – to cope with small pockets of roving German infantry, operating at ease in that thick country, many armed with the formidable *'faust patronen'*, or *'panzerfaust'*. This was similar to the American bazooka, and consisted of a hollow charge projectile on a rocket tube. The panzerfaust had a range of about 75 yards, and was extremely effective against tanks in the hands of determined infantry, especially if the tanks were unsupported by infantry of their own. The panzerfaust also had other disadvantages from the tank crew's point of view. It was much more difficult to spot a camouflaged man armed with a panzerfaust than an anti-tank gun and crew, and a panzerfaust strike usually set a tank on fire, unlike the solid A.P. shot from a gun which frequently went right through, or knocked off a track. Finally, crews bailing out of a knocked-out tank at eighty yards range or less, were usually in the middle of the ambush position and subjected to heavy small-arms fire, which greatly reduced their chances of getting out alive.

The invasion forces, British and American, met little tank opposition in the first hours of the landing, since the German Panzer divisions had been kept back from the beaches, where the defences were manned by second-line infantry. This was against Rommel's own wishes. He felt, rightly as it turned out, that Allied air superiority would limit the mobility of German Panzer forces, which should therefore have been kept close to the beaches to mount an immediate counter-attack and throw the invaders back on the first day. In this he was overruled by Hitler, who believed, until some days after the Normandy landings, that

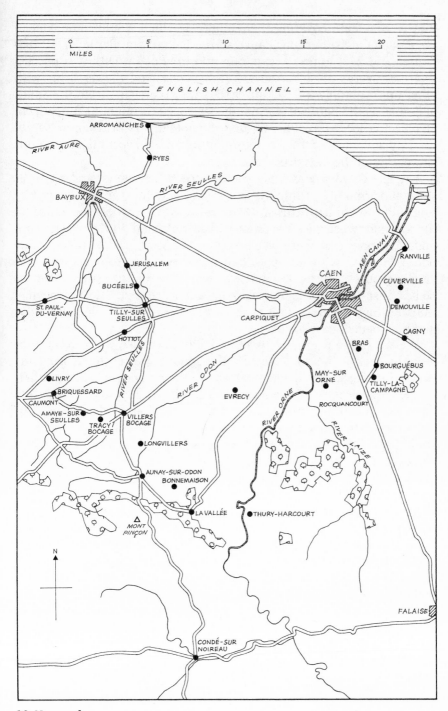

12 Normandy

they were a feint, covering the real attack which would come later in the Pas de Calais. German Panzers from Falaise and Bernay – 12 (SS) Panzer and 21st Panzer – came up into the line on D-Day, supported soon afterwards by 2 Panzer, 17 (SS) Panzer and Panzer Lehr, with other units, notably 2 (SS) Panzer (Das Reich) arriving from the South of France as the Battle of Normandy developed throughout June. Caen, an objective for D-Day, the 6th June, did not fall into British hands until 7th July, and most of the previous month had been spent in continuous battle around the outskirts of the city.

Bertram Vowden was a Sergeant in the 8th Hussars, and gives his story of Normandy. 'I think it is best if I deal with the part played by 8th King's Royal Irish Hussars from D-Day plus 1, when we landed on the Normandy beaches. We crossed in daylight and hit the beach about mid-afternoon, and there was so much to absorb and so much going on. We landed with no opposition and were ashore in about ten to fifteen minutes, but we knew it was war. The sea was supporting the bodies of so many British soldiers on a gentle swell, and I remember thinking that we had had it cushy – those chaps were alive yesterday and had made it easy for us.

'We were given no time to sit and stare, because we were at once brought back to harsh reality by the shouts directed to us from the British Red Caps. They looked straight off the parade ground with their spotless appearance, and made us all think we were back home and being controlled in a huge traffic jam. The Military Police showed us the route off the beach and told us of the importance of the white ribbon bordering each side of our exit road, with the notice: "Mines cleared to verges only. Keep within the white tapes." What a help this was to us. We re-grouped as a Regiment, complete with all our vehicles, in an allotted assembly area, where we carried out our de-waterproofing of all vehicles. We were given our brief for the following day and spent our first night in France in a contented mood. We now realised we were back in the line once more and were the armoured reconnaissance Regiment for the 7th Armoured Division of 30th Corps of British 2nd Army. We had Bedford supply lorries from Canada, and sported with pride the Jerboa (Desert Rat symbol) with the Regimental No. of 45. We had 50th Infantry Division, the Queen's and the County of London Yeomanry, our old desert friends.

'As a recce Regiment we were not too involved in any full confrontations with enemy armour, but the old enemy of 15th and 21st Panzer Divisions (ex-North Africa) were again facing us, as was Rommel. We started our activity on D-Day plus 3, and sustained our

NORMANDY
ORDER OF BATTLE JUNE 1944

22nd Armoured Brigade
1st RTR
5th RTR
4th CLY
5th Royal Inniskilling Dragoon
  Guards

131st (Queens) Brigade
1st/5th Queens Royal Regiment
1st/6th Queens Royal Regiment
1st/7th Queens Royal Regiment
No. 3 Support Company, Royal
  Northumberland Fusiliers

Divisional Troops
8th Hussars
11th Hussars
Divisional Signals

Royal Artillery
3rd RHA
5th RHA
15th Light AA Regiment RA
65th Anti-Tank Regiment RA

Royal Engineers
4th Field Squadron
621st Field Squadron
143rd Field Park Squadron

RASC
No. 58 Company
No. 67 Company
No. 507 Company
No. 133 Company

RAMC
2nd Light Field Ambulance
131st Field Ambulance
29th Field Dressing Station
70th Field Hygiene Section
134th Mobile Dental Unit

RAOC
Divisional Ordance Field Park
22nd Armoured Brigade
  Ordnance Field Park
131st Brigade Ordnance Field
  Park

REME
7th Armoured Troops Workshop
22nd Armoured Brigade
  Workshop
131st Brigade Workshop
15th Light AA Workshop

Royal Armoured Corps
No. 263 Forward Delivery
  Squadron

first casualties, as a result of enemy anti-tank guns which we were destined to meet around almost every corner in the narrow lanes of the bocage country, with sides so steep and dense with hedges it was almost impossible to leave the road and take cover. Added to this, the hedge boundaries were heavily mined.

'With conditions so very different from the desert days, my own feelings were that it was a picnic in comparison with the tank battles in the desert. We enjoyed almost complete control of the air, we seemed to have more ammunition than the Germans and our artillery was the best in the business. As a recce unit, a leading tank could call up by wireless through the Regimental link to Tactical Air Force, and would, in a very short time, see some Typhoon rocket firing planes fly in and destroy the enemy target with 60 lb rockets fired from under the aircraft's wings.'

On the 10th, all the units of the Division then ashore – 22 Armoured Brigade, the 5th RHA and some of the 8th Hussars, plus some Queen's infantry – were ordered to advance on Tilly-sur-Seulles with the 4th CLY in the lead. So far, the invaders had met little Panzer opposition, but the German resistance was stiffening daily. The enemy was first encountered by the hamlet of Jerusalem, five miles south of Bayeux. Here the CLY knocked out a Mk IV tank before advancing a mile further south to Buceels, but the infantry took a number of casualties, some of whom lie buried in the little roadside war grave at Jerusalem. On 12th June the Queen's Brigade came up, accompanied by 1 RTR under Lt.-Col. Mike Carver. On the same day, General Erskine was ordered to advance on the town of Villers-Bocage, where the 4th CLY became involved in a hard battle with elements of two crack German divisions, 2nd Panzer and Panzer Lehr.

The word 'Lehr' means training, but Panzer Lehr was no training formation. This had been the demonstration unit for all the German Panzer forces, and was therefore equipped with the latest tanks and manned by first-class and highly experienced officers and men. The 4th CLY could not have encountered a more formidable combination, though much of the damage was done by two Tiger tank companies of the 501 (SS) Heavy Tank Battalion, commanded by Obersturmfuhrer Michael Wittmann.

Sergeant Bobby Bramwell of the 4th CLY tells the story of his Regiment's first few days in Normandy and the fight at Villers-Bocage: 'As you know, we re-equipped with Cromwells in Norfolk. I still think they were atrocious tanks, fast enough but thin-skinned and somewhat undergunned. My O.C., Lt. Bill Cotton, told H.M. King George VI as much when he came to visit us during training. He took the King inside his tank to show him the form, and all the senior officers hung about anxiously outside, hoping he wouldn't overdo it. Our training in Norfolk largely consisted of cleaning our new tanks and firing and calibrating the guns. We did no tactical training that I can recall. I was commanding a Firefly tank in 3 Troop, a Sherman tank with a 17-pounder gun – very good kit.

'Anyway, we landed on D-Day plus one and advanced to Tilly-sur-Seulles. We met some opposition from German infantry here and there, and then were ordered to take Villers-Bocage and the high ground beyond it to the east. This move began with a long road march, which took all day, to Briquessard, and we leaguered that night at Livry, just north of the Caen road. So far, so good. Next day was the fatal day.

'We were on the move early, by just after first light, moving up on Villers by road. "A" Squadron went first, then Recce Troop with Honeys and Scout cars, then RHQ, and then "B" Squadron, and finally "C". It was a nice day, at least to begin with, though it poured in the afternoon. We met no opposition on the way but "A" Squadron did call up that they were under observation from German armoured cars on the hill east of Villers, so the Germans certainly knew about us. Brigade said the town was clear and although the Colonel wanted to do a recce, Brigadier "Loony" Hinde came up and told him to push on as fast as possible. So "A" Squadron went through the town to the heights beyond; RHQ and Recce stayed in the town centre, and my Squadron "B" stayed just outside to the west, with "C" Squadron between us. It was about 10.00am when we first heard firing from the town, machine guns and the vicious "crack" of an 88mm. That was the first hint that anything was wrong. A Tiger came into the village, I think up the road from Longvillers. First it wiped out the Artillery observer tanks – these were Sherman tanks, with the gun removed to make space for extra radio, but equipped on the outside with a wooden gun barrel – poor devils. Then it got most of Recce Troop. They didn't get the C.O. then because he had gone up to "A" Squadron. The Tiger smashed its way through Villers to the western outskirts on our front, where my colleague, Sergeant Lockwood, also in a Firefly, engaged it with his 17-pdr. He didn't knock it out but he certainly scared it off.

'Meanwhile, other German tanks were attacking "A" Squadron on the hill. They blew up the leading tank, then the one at the back, which pinned the rest of the squadron down, and then rolled down our line knocking out all the rest, killing or capturing a lot of our chaps. It was a shambles. The C.O. went off the air, and we had no contact with

Brigade or the Artillery, but "Ibby" Aird took charge. We were all on the Regimental wireless network, so he could talk to those of us who were still intact.

'My troop – 3 Troop of "B" Squadron – was ordered to try a push round to the south of the town, and perhaps help "A", and so off we went, my tank in the lead in case we met Tigers. Lt. Bill Cotton was in charge. Bill was a short, stocky chap, quite fearless, a great character and a fine leader of men. We found a German concentration of half-tracks on a road before we were stopped by an embankment south of the town. That has long gone but it was a real obstacle back in 1944.

'We then filtered back into the town. Villers was just a large village really, with lots of firing going on, mainly concentrated on a square near the High Street. Villers was bombed flat later, and when I went back in 1985, I could not even find the square, though there is a *Rue des Sharpshooters* on the outskirts, incidentally. My Firefly halted about fifteen yards from the junction of the square with the High Street.

'Soon afterwards three German tanks came down the High Street. I am sure the one in the lead was a Mark IV – some say it was a Tiger, but I fired at it and I know it wasn't. I missed, incidentally. The range was too short to sight the gun properly. Fortunately, a 6-pdr anti-tank gun of the Queen's was brought up and they knocked it out.

'The next tank along certainly *was* a Tiger. I had reversed back a bit and I could see it through the windows of the house on the corner, so we traversed our gun and began to engage it through the windows, first with H.E., which made a terrible mess of the house, and then with A.P. I don't know how many shots we fired, but anyway, we knocked it out.

'I suppose it was now about mid-day. There was fighting, with machine guns and anti-tank fire all over the town, and in the afternoon there were reports that the Queen's were in action with tanks and infantry coming in from the South. The third German tank, another Tiger, then came back round the corner of the square, but I had now sighted the 17-pdr, not with the sights, the range was too short, but by peering down the barrel at a sign on the wall on the far side of the High Street. When the Tiger blocked the sign we fired, and that was that. It was now pouring with rain, and one of these tanks had caught fire. Their crews were either dead or had bolted, but the Germans could have recovered and repaired them, so Bill Cotton got a jerry-can of petrol and some blankets and we went off to destroy them. Because of the rain, Bill put up an umbrella – we must have been mad! There was Bill with his umbrella up, and the blankets, and me with the jerry-can, and we went from tank to tank, soaking a blanket with petrol, tossing it into the turret, then slinging in a match. We learned later that the local Fire Brigade came round and tried to put the fires out, probably for fear the tanks would blow up, but I saw nothing of that. That night we withdrew to Amaye-sur-Seulles, a little west of Villers, and went into leaguer. The Regiment had been mauled. We had lost "A" Squadron and the RHQ, and some of Recce Troop, as well as Colonel Onslow and a number of officers. Soon after this I was commissioned. There was nothing formal about it. "Ibby" Aird took me to see Brigadier Hinde, who asked me a few questions, and that was that – I was an officer.'

Well, not quite. For his gallant actions against the tanks at Villers-Bocage, Sergeant Bobby Bramwell was awarded the Military Medal.

Lt. Derrick Watson was at Villers-Bocage with the 1/5th Queen's. 'The *bocage* is a maze of small fields and numerous orchards, surrounded by high-backed hedges of pollarded trees. We advanced through this country on foot, impeded at first only by snipers and spasmodic shelling. Our first casualties included Lt. Randolph Churchill of "A" Coy, and the C.O's batman, who was wounded doing the C.O's laundry in the comparative safety of Battalion HQ. Also wounded at this stage was Lt. Keith McEwan of "A" Coy while on a forward probing patrol. Spotting a Spandau post, McEwan ordered his platoon to cover him while he moved round to a flank to throw a grenade. Unfortunately, the Germans were aware of these tactics and put a burst through his throwing arm. At this point, Major Elliott called for support, as he was pinned down, so I rode up in a tank to be greeted by three ringing cheers from the men dug-in at the edge of the wood. They were my old platoon.

'The next alarm was from "B" Coy, who reported a Tiger tank in the woods no more than 50 yards from their position. On orders from the C.O. I directed an M4, a self-propelled gun – the only one with enough power to deal with a Tiger – to the area. The M4 stalked the Tiger, and in a very few minutes brewed it up. I subsequently inspected the damage and a very grisly sight it was.

'At this stage, the information came through that our leading Tank Regiment, the 4th City of London Yeomanry, the CLY, had run headlong into Tiger tanks in numbers. They were later identified as belonging to 501st SS Heavy Tank Battalion, five of them commanded by Captain Michael Wittman, who was responsible for one of the most devastating single-handed actions of the war, but that was not known at the time. The last message received from Lt.-Col Lord Cranley, the C.O. of the 4th CLY, was, we were told, "Burn your tanks and get out."

'Meanwhile, our sister battalion, the 7th Queen's, arriving to support the 4th CLY, spent the day in desperate fighting, deployed amongst the houses, to meet a new German armoured and infantry attack on the town of Villers itself. The 7th Queen's had an hair-raising experience in Villers-Bocage. As they made contact with the reserve squadron of the CLY, a Tiger tank suddenly appeared from a side road and proceeded to blow down a corner house in the main square, where the troops were assembled.' (N.B. It is more than probable that the house was actually blown down by fire from Sergeant Bramwell's Firefly.) 'With Piats and anti-tank guns, the Germans were beaten off, with the loss of 9 tanks.

'While the 1/7th Queen's were fighting desperately in Villers-Bocage, the 1/5th Queen's had taken up a battle position to the east of Tracy Bocage, and enemy tanks were seen and heard to be forming up. Almost immediately the forward companies were attacked by two battalions of Panzer Grenadiers. Owing to the terrain it was a close range battle, and I recall a battery of RHA cheek by jowl with Ba.HQ engaging the enemy infantry over open sights with air burst and Bren guns. The forward Coys were in close contact with the enemy, so from Brigade the order came for the reserve "D" Coy to move over to the right flank in support. Major "Boy" Burton, the 2 i/c, ordered me to take my Intelligence Section, reinforced by one of the Cooks and a Storeman (who were both able to find their rifles for the occasion) and occupy the positions vacated by "D" Coy. I was then to report back to him. Moving off to carry this out, we were met by a white-faced straggler from "D" Coy, who said that the roads just vacated by that Coy were occupied by hundreds of Germans and advised us not go go there! Undeterred (or at least not much), we pushed on through thick woods until we came to our slit trenches. The woods were silent, although we could still hear the battle raging in the area we had just left. I was on the horns of a dilemma then – had I to abandon these 6 riflemen without any communication in accordance with the orders given to me, or should I stay with them far from the action? No problem really – leaving George Offiles, (a schoolmaster before the war) in charge, I returned to my post at B.H.Q. As soon as I could contact Col. Wood, I reported all was quiet on the former "D" Coy front, and could I bring the six men back? The C.O. replied somewhat testily, "Good God! Are they still there? Bring them back immediately." I returned to the woods, still perfectly silent, and when approaching the position of my men was immensely relieved to behold George Offiles puffing away happily at his pipe. He reported "All Quiet" and we returned without undue haste to Ba.HQ, where there was a temporary lull.

'The Panzer Grenadiers suffered severe casualties and 8 Mark IV tanks were destroyed. The 1/7 Queen's, on the other hand, lost 8 officers and 120 men at Villers, destroying 9 enemy tanks. There being no infantry reinforcements available, we became an "island" with long lines of communication back to the beachhead. We were withdrawn from Villers-Bocage and its environs to enable heavy bombers of the RAF to bomb the town and Aunay-sur-Odon further south, firstly into a Brigade box and then further back on reverse slopes just north of the shattered village of Livry, in an area which was "bocage" at its worst. There was no real task for the armour. It was a trying period for us, to say the least, as infantry (no longer lorried), living in slit trenches in the rain, suffered a steady drain in casualties from shell and mortar fire, and occasionally from snipers. All the time enclosed in the damp prison of the bocage, the lines of sight bounded by a hedge two hundred yards away. At night there was the constant anxiety of patrolling through close hedges, which were often mined, to pin down or identify an elusive enemy.'

One of the more curious events of the battle at Villers-Bocage concerns the audacious Major Werncke of the Panzer Lehr. 'On 13th June our old friends of the 7th Armoured Division, the *"Wustenratten"*, the Desert Rats, were around Tilly and Villers-Bocage. I was sent from HQ, Panzer Lehr, to recce their advance and see what they were doing. I had left my driver and Scout Car and was moving on foot through the undergrowth, when I heard the rumble of tank engines and, crawling forward, saw a troop of the new Cromwell tanks deployed along a lane, with all the crews up in front with an officer, looking at a map.

'Now all tanks, even British tanks, are more or less the same, so I ran across and climbed into the last Cromwell. The design was like an early Panzer, not our Tigers or Panthers. The engine was running and I shoved it into gear, spun it on the tracks and drove it off to the east. Unfortunately I was unable to see the faces of the English crews as I drove away.

'Pretty soon I was crossing the lines where our Tigers had been in action – there were burning tanks and Bren-gun carriers and dead Tommies. I then saw a German soldier in a ditch, stopped the Cromwell and waved him over. He was reluctant, but he came, and I ordered him into the turret to wave a white rag if any of our own forces appeared. I then drove the Cromwell to our HQ at Chateau Orbois, but I could not manoeuvre it through the gates, so I went over the wire and up the drive. When they saw us coming, all the Staff and guards dived for cover ... before they recognized the uniform of a German corporal in the turret. That was that, but I could not discover how to turn off the engine. In the end, I drove the tank against a big tree, accelerated and stalled the engine ... and we stopped!'

J. L. Cloudsley-Thompson tells his tale of Villers-Bocage: 'The move began at 4.00 pm on 12th June and all went well as far as Livry, when the advance guard bumped into an enemy force and lost one tank; the Motor Company of the Rifle Brigade had to be called up to help clear the village. From a hill further back I watched the tanks of the leading squadron of my regiment, the 4th County of London Yeomanry (Sharpshooters), fan out in a cornfield and saw the tracer of their machine guns firing at the German infantry. The R.B. Colonel walked past and I offered him a grandstand view from my own tank, which he accepted. That night we leaguered several miles further inland than any other of the allied forces.

'Next morning we pushed on at first light, the Recce Troop, "A" Squadron, 4th CLY and "A" Company of the 1st Rifle Brigade leading. The countryside was pleasant and the French peasants greeted us with delight, giving us butter, cider and throwing flowers at our tanks. Meanwhile, local reports suggested that German tanks were stranded in Tracy Bocage through lack of petrol. There was still no opposition however, and we hoped to seize the high ground beyond Villers Bocage before the enemy could forestall us. Just before we entered the town, a German armoured car was spotted down a side road by the commander of the tank in front of mine, but it had vanished before I could get into a position to shoot. Villers Bocage is a fair-sized country town; there was no sign of the enemy so we drove straight along the main street. The Brigadier and the Colonel went forward in their scout cars to join the leading troops and we were ordered to close up as much as possible.

'"A" Squadron had got right through and RHQ, which I was commanding, were just leaving the town when the rear tanks of "A" Squadron burst into flames and the crews baled out. Every RHQ tank began to reverse. (One of the faults of the Cromwell was that its maximum speed in reverse gear was about two miles per hour.) The Brigadier, who had been discussing the situation with the Colonel, ran across the road, jumped into his scout car, and drove back past us, followed by another scout car. Then an armour-piercing shell whizzed between my wireless-operator's head and mine. It passed so close that although I was wearing headphones it made me slightly deaf for 24 hours afterwards. I felt sure there must be a hidden anti-tank gun firing down the road, so I told the driver: "Left-stick" and we backed through a hedge between two houses. Pat, the Adjutant, reversed his tank alongside mine. He was bleeding from the forehead. He told me later that a burst of Spandau machine-gun fire from one of the first floor windows of the houses had just missed his head and chipped fragments of steel from the turret of his tank, some of which had cut him.

'By this time all the tanks immediately in front seemed to be on fire. Through the smoke loomed the gigantic form of a Tiger. It cannot have been more than 35 yards away, yet our 75mm shots just bounced off its massive armour. I fired the 2-inch bomb thrower, but the smoke bomb passed clean over it. The Tiger traversed its big 88mm gun very slightly. Wham! We were hit. I felt a tingling between my legs and wondered if I had been wounded again. A sheet of flame licked over the turret and my mouth was full of grit and burnt paint. "Bale out," I yelled and leaped clear. I saw my crew bale out, then a machine gun fired at me, so I flung myself into the grass. The Tiger rumbled past and Pat's Cromwell followed it down the road. I took off the headphones which were still round my neck and waved to him. Then I heard my name called softly and looked round. There were my crew, hiding under a currant bush. Miraculously they were all safe. My Troop Sergeant in the hull machine gun position had had a lucky escape as he was leaning sideways when the tank was hit. The shot must have gone just over his shoulder, passed between my legs and landed up in the engine. A fragment of metal had cut him behind the ear.

'Jo, the driver, white and shaking, crouched with drawn revolver. He looked like a cornered rat. Machine gun bullets and shells screamed overhead, so I lay down quickly again. A dreadful noise was going on in the town, so I decided to go back beside a wall at the rear of the houses and try to reach "B" Squadron. As we started off I saw Pat, on foot, in the distance. He had hoped to shoot the Tiger from behind, but had met it coming back after knocking out the rest of R.H.Q. It fired once, killing his co-driver and gunner, but he and the driver managed to bale out unharmed. Machine-gunners fired at them from the first floor windows of the houses, but he ran to the R.S.M's blazing tank in which the wireless was still working and was able to warn "B" and "C" Squadrons, who were still in ignorance of what had happened. Then he went along the main road until he came to a corner and saw me in the distance. Here he was fired at by yet another machine gun and had to hide. Later, he managed to get back to "B" Squadron. The Tiger drove off undamaged, its commander waving his hat and laughing. Its armour was so thick that none of our Cromwell tanks had been able to knock it out.'

Harold Swain was a gunner in 65th Anti-Tank Regiment RA attached to 7th Armoured. 'We were told by our commanding officer, Major Gale, that we would *not* be going to Normandy as a Regiment, but we were being split up and sent over as reinforcements. So we were sent back to Aldershot for a few days for our jabs and our kit, then over to Normandy shortly after D-Day 1944. A few days later I joined the 65th Anti-tank Regiment, R.A. as a gunner, but although we had done our training on field guns and 6-pounder anti-tank guns, when I joined the 65th they had 17-pounder guns. I was then told that we were part of the famous 7th Armoured Division, or the Desert Rats. I felt very proud as I was a very young soldier of just twenty years of age.

'Our real first taste of action was at Villers Bocage, where the 7th Armoured made a bulge in the German lines, and they counter-attacked us. They had the Tiger tank, with the dreaded 88mm gun, which our tank regiments with Cromwells, were very wary of, as the 88mm was a very good gun. The Tiger tanks knocked out three of the four guns in our Troop, and we lost a lot of our comrades, either killed or taken prisoner, but we managed to survive.'

After withdrawing from Villers Bocage, Tracy-Bocage and Amaye by the 14th, the Division took up new positions east of Caumont, where they remained until the end of June, living in slit trenches beside their tanks, losing men steadily from the incessant shelling and mortaring, and in clashes with roving Tigers and groups of *Panzerfaust*, armed Panzer grenadiers and infantry. Jack Geddes of the CLY, now living in Lilli Pilli, N.S.W. Australia, supplies an account of this time:

'The shelling ceases and the twice delayed trucks of "B" Echelon arrive at last to service the tanks of "A" Squadron with petrol and ammo. We all work like madmen to unload the trucks lest trouble starts up again. You would be surprised at the amount of wood, wire and canisters the factory bods used to wrap a shell or two. It is quiet now and the trucks move off again. Hopefully I can crawl into my blankets beside the tank, which is my home, and which carries the proud name of "Alexander". It is a Sherman "Firefly" tank; one of the only four the Squadron possesses, which has the new British 17-pounder gun fitted, long barrelled and lethal. The other Fireflies, some scholar or clown has named Ajax, Achilles and Agamemnon. All the other Cromwell tanks in the Squadron have stubby 75s. I am the proud gunner, looking back on a career which already, over the years in the Western Desert and in parts of Italy, has progressed upwards from the two-pounder gun (pathetic pea-shooter) to a 17-pounder gun, a rise of 15 pounds, the only army promotion which I know.

'Now there is time for sleep, blissful sleep, and I quickly fall into the listless slumber of the very exhausted ... but I am awoken again when it becomes my turn to go out on sentry – two hours of walking about the quiet leaguer at night, when every minute drags. There is a flicker of fire still from the burning of a farmhouse from the West which, unfortunately, we set fire to, pouring crates of Browning bullets into the curtains and windows under the mistaken impression that the Germans were there. There is also the dull glow of twin fires burning on the skyline. During my sentry duty I could not take my eyes off these fires, for they flamed up and died down again; they changed colour and died down again, and would take on a new life when they seemed most dead, and we know that the tongues of flame had found an undiscovered box of Browning ammunition, a new shell to ignite.

'All of us knew that these were the two tanks of "2" Troop, which had been lost in the previous day's fighting, but time passes, and at last I can crawl back into the bedroll. I have taken off my boots and tunic top and put them by my head where I can find them in any panic which may arise. I have worn the same clothes for seven days running, as have we all, but I know that they must take us out of battle soon, for we are beginning to reach the limit of our endurance. We must come out of battle to lick our wounds and re-equip. God! ... but in Normandy the days are long. It is still summer – the long evenings stretch for ever and the nights are too short, but at least I must have fallen asleep because when I awoke the fires had died down and the night is dark and cold. I can feel the wind in my face and the dew on my hair as it blows under the long flat hull of the tank "Alexander", and there is a wonderful God-given silence. I can hear the wind whistling gently at the rear of the tank which houses the aerial engine of many cylinders. I can hear it as it plays among the bogie wheels, gently, of this monster Alexander. In the silence, friend and foe sleep. Well, almost silence, almost sleep, but I can hear the scraping of the sentry's boots as he walks among the assembled tanks, tommy gun in hand, and I know too that the turret watchers are in their tanks.'

On 30th June the Division was withdrawn to an area near Jerusalem for a rest and refit: casualties in the Division during their first three weeks in France exceeded 1100 men, and some changes had to be made.

It has to be said, and it might as well be said here, that by most accounts 7th Armoured did not function too well at this time. The Division seemed to have lost some of its old flair and push, and to have become sluggish. Accusations of 'stickiness' appear in several accounts, a reluctance to push ahead in the face of opposition. One account relates that although General Erskine reported 'No serious difficulty in beating down enemy resistance,' the Division only lost four tanks yet made very little progress on 10th June, and fared little better on the 11th. Then on the 13th came the fight at Villers Bocage, which was a shambles. General Dempsey said, 'The attack by 7th Armoured should have succeeded. I went to see Erskine and told him to get moving.'

There were probably several reasons for this lack of flair. Most of the men in 7th Armoured had now been fighting steadily for three years and had become very cautious old soldiers. The bocage terrain was unfamiliar and not at all what they were used to, even after their time in Italy. Colonel Duncan Riddell, who had served with 7th Armoured in the Western Desert, and who was then serving with the currently more thrusting 11th Armoured Division, is sympathetic to their plight. 'They were an experienced division; perhaps too experienced. They had seen a lot of war and a lot of death. Most of the other units, unlike 7th Armoured and 51st Highland Division, had spent the war training in the U.K. To units like the 11th Armoured and 15th Scottish, to give a direct comparison, war was still an adventure, and they were eager for the fray – for a while at least. 7th Armoured and the 51st Highland had long since realized that war is a nasty, bloody business.'

Sergeant Bobby Bramwell MM also puts the situation in perspective. 'Three years in the desert was not the best preparation for the bocage. We'd had no training for this jungle country ... it was that close, and not tank country at all. We couldn't deploy and were stuck in roads. Think about that.'

These points have to be made, but need not be laboured, and Lt.-Col. Mike Carver, then of 1 RTR, and now a Field Marshal, completely disagrees with them. 'That is utter, absolute cock! If the CLY had not been thrusting ahead at Villers Bocage they would never have got into trouble. I reject those charges completely. The bocage isn't tank country, but 7th Armoured were ordered to fight there and that is what they did.'

Major General Verney, who came over from the Guards Tank Brigade to take command of 7th Armoured some weeks later, has left an account of how he found 7th Armoured.

'A great many of the officers and men were war weary, and there was no large-scale system of relief, and it was owing to this that they made a very poor showing in Normandy. Looking back, it is quite easy to see that there ought to have been considerable changes. Whole units, particularly in the Infantry Brigade, should have been exchanged for fresh troops who had spent the last few years training in England. In the desert the fighting had generally been fluid and certainly since Alamein in October 1942, had consisted in the pursuit of a retreating enemy. In Normandy, they met an enemy who had no intention of retreating, and was determined to drive them back into the sea.

'There is no doubt that familiarity with war does not make one more courageous. The infantryman can find opportunities for lying low at the critical moment, the tankman can easily find a fault with his engine or with his wireless, and this disease spreads rapidly. The commander who finds his men getting canny soon loses confidence and becomes nervy himself. If he also happens to have done a lot of fighting, and especially if he has been brewed-up in his tank once or twice, he gets slow and deliberate and is quite unable to take advantage of a situation that requires dash and enterprise, two elements particularly important in an armoured division, which exists to quickly exploit a favourable situation.

'Even more important, both the 7th Armoured and the 51st Highland, were a law unto themselves and seemed to think they need only obey those orders which suited them. Before the Battle of Caumont, for example, I had been warned to look out for the transport of 7th Armoured on the road. Their march discipline was non-existent. They greatly resented the criticism they received, and it was a severe shock to 7th Armoured when General Erskine was removed. In the Armoured Brigade there were several troubles, and many men in the tank crews had done more than their fair share in the war. The 1st and 5th Tanks were no longer having a go and the Brigade Commander was dead tired. The Inniskillings, on the other hand, were a fresh regiment who only came out to France in July and for dash and enterprise they set an example to the others. The Rifle Brigade was in a bad way. In the Goodwood Battle in July they had a very bad time, and 131 Infantry Brigade had had a lot of losses and their state was the worst of all. In the 1st/6th Queens, admittedly the hardest hit battalion, the strength of the four Rifle Companies on the 6th August was eight, fifteen, forty and fifty-five respectively of all ranks, instead of over a hundred men in each company. The consequence of this was seen during my first week in command, when we had over a hundred and twenty cases of desertion.

'The obvious answer to all this was to put in a large number of fresh men or to take the Division out for a long rest. Neither course was feasible. The British Army was so short of men that at the end of August an Infantry Division had to be disbanded and its men distributed among other units. Taking 7th Armoured out of the line was tried, but they were required back almost as soon as they got out. In any case this was a palliative, not a cure.'

Seventh Armoured certainly had its ups and downs over the next few weeks, as we shall see, but they soon got going again and were back to their old form by the time the Battle of Normandy ended. Seventh Armoured were not closely involved in the next attempt to break out from the beachhead, 'Operation Epsom', where the three fresh divisions of 8th Corps, including 11th Armoured, thrust South on a line west of Caen. 'Epsom' lasted for a full week – from 26th June until 1st July – but managed to push the bridgehead south as far as the River Odon, at considerable cost in lives, losing over 4,000 men. Having tried twice to the west of Caen, Montgomery now switched his weight to the left side of the city and tried again, with 'Operation Goodwood' on 18th July.

Seventh Armoured Division went into action again on 17th July, as one of three British armoured divisions deployed for 'Operation Goodwood'. This took place on the plain south-east of Caen, and 'Goodwood' became, and remains, one of the most controversial battles of the entire Normandy campaign. The controversy centres on the objectives for the operation, which have been interpreted either as an all-out thrust on Falaise, and Montgomery's main attempt to break the German defences, or simply as an attempt to draw all the German armour east, onto the British front, and so enable the Americans to break out in the West around St Lô, and go careering off to Brittany and the Loire.

Montgomery's Operational Directive, however, seems to leave little room for argument. The objectives of 'Goodwood' were, he stated: '(1) To engage the German armour in battle and write it down to such an extent that it is of no future use in battle. (2) To gain a good bridgehead over the Orne, through Caen, and so improve our position on the east flank. (3) Generally to destroy German equipment and personnel.' The directive continued, 'A victory on the eastern flank will help us gain what we want on the Western flank.' He also added, however, that if all went well, '8th Corps can then crack about as the situation demands.' This seems a reasonable aside, for no one can tell how a battle will turn out, and had the German front crumbled, Montgomery would have been foolish not to push on and take advantage of the situation. However, this last sentence has since been taken as evidence of an original intention to advance on Falaise. When the British did not do this, accusations of failure began to fly about among the Allied Command.

'Operation Goodwood' involved passing all three armoured divisions, 11th Armoured, the Guards Armoured Division, and lastly 7th Armoured, across the River Orne, and although the country east of the Orne was more open than the bocage, there was a great shortage of intact, suitable bridges. This, in turn, meant that the three divisions had to advance in columns of brigades – one after the other – hardly the ideal formation for three mobile armoured divisions mounting a surprise attack.

Seventh Armoured moved up from Jerusalem on 17th July and concentrated north and north-west of Caen, greatly cheered by the temporary return to the Division of the 11th Hussars. Led, as in the good old days, by the 11th Hussars, the Division crossed the Orne bridges on the 18th and soon met the enemy at Cuverville, where the 5th RTR had a stiff fight, losing six tanks while 11th Armoured Division lost more than a hundred. On the next day, 19th July, in the midst of serious traffic congestion and plagued by severe shelling, 5th RTR met Tiger and 75mm gunned Panther tanks at Bourguebus, which the 5th Tanks occupied on the 20th. On the same day the CLY reached the Caen-Falaise road near Bras. The weather then broke with torrential rain turning the ground to mud, so the Division then concentrated near Demouville, where they remained for the next eight days, being heavily shelled for most of the time. 'Operation Goodwood', then ground to a complete halt before the entrenched defences and artillery of the Bourguebus Ridge.

On 25th July the Division took part in 'Operation Spring', in support of the 2nd Canadian Corps, who were attempting to force a path down the Caen-Falaise road, but from the 26th to 28th they were again in defensive positions near Tilly-la-Campagne, enduring long hours of shelling. On the 29th the 4th CLY, much depleted after Villers Bocage, was transferred from 7th Armoured Division to the 4th Armoured Brigade – now an independent brigade and commanded by Brigadier Mike Carver, late of the 1 RTR. There the 4th CLY were amalgamated with their sister regiment, the 3rd CLY into the 3/4th CLY. By now, the Americans had broken out in the West, and 7th Armoured left 11 Corps on 28th July and returned to 30 Corps back at Caumont in the *bocage* country.

The next Normandy operation involving 7th Armoured, at the end of July 1944, was 'Operation Bluecoat'. Before that began the Division was reinforced by the 5th Royal Inniskilling Dragoon Guards, the famous 'Skins', who came to replace the 4th CLY. Among them was

Tony King: 'We were told that our role was to replace the 4th County of London Yeomanry (which had suffered such heavy casualties on the battlegrounds around Caen that it was no longer operational) in the 7th Armoured Division – the Desert Rats – joining the 1st and 5th RTR as the main armoured units in the 22nd Armoured Brigade, with the 8th Hussars as the Division's reconnaissance unit, and the 11th Hussars – the Cherry Pickers, with their unique cherry-red berets – as forward reconnaissance, equipped with armoured cars. The only vehicles the Skins had brought from England were some 3-ton trucks loaded with kit and stores, and we collected mainly new Cromwell tanks from a huge equipment compound near Bayeux and set about preparing them for battle.

'Two sources of amazement to newcomers to the beachhead were the fabulous amount of vehicles and stores which had already been shipped over through the Mulberry Harbour and the casual way in which they had been dumped in fields without camouflage – cocking a snook at the Luftwaffe which, by then, had been overstretched and depleted by heavy losses so as not to pose much of a threat. Nevertheless, our first encounter with enemy action was a night raid by fighter bombers dropping small 50lb bombs and anti-personnel bombs on our "laager" (a term borrowed from South Africa, meaning a camp defended by wagons), one of which landed on the hull of our tank, with a tremendous detonation but causing no damage. Unluckily, our gunner (the only crew member who had not experienced civilian bombing raids) was completely unnerved by this episode, which made us all feel a bit jittery, and he was immediately replaced the next morning in the interests of crew morale.

'Ironically, the regiment's first casualties were not as a result of German shots fired in anger. While we were waiting to be re-equipped, a bathing party to the coast was organised and some swimmers were caught out by the strong undertow; rescue attempts resulted in the loss of the Padre, one other officer and a trooper, and I shall never forget the sight of their heads bobbing on the waves as they drifted out to sea, eventually to disappear. Although we fired our revolvers in the air we were unable to attract the attention of a passing fishing boat, and all we could do was to stand and watch helplessly. Another pointless tragedy occurred when our new tanks were being commissioned for action, loaded with ammunition and filled with petrol. A turret-mounted machine gun was accidentally fired and a trooper standing on the hull of the next tank was shot dead. This accidental firing was not an uncommon occurrence, since the trigger mechanism of both the main gun and the machine gun was foot-pedal operated. All it needed was a steel-tipped ammo boot to slip on the steel turret floor when the safety catch had been carelessly left disengaged and br-r-p or bang, as the case may be. Fortunately, accidental firing of the big gun was less common, since it was seldom loaded until enemy action was imminent. When it did happen, however, it was quite likely to take parts of the crew commander or wireless op/gun loader with it on the unexpected recoil within the very confined space of the turret.

'So, at long last, Lance-Corporal King AC, otherwise affectionately known to his mates as "Abie" (due to some trace of Semetic features inherited from my paternal grandmother) went into action as driver to Lt. Maurice Fitzgerald, Officer i/c 3rd Troop, A Squadron, with Cockney Jimmy Hewitt as wireless operator/loader, Ginger Hutchinson (a tough Geordie whose real forename I never knew) as replacement gunner, and Wally Gent, a quiet type from somewhere in the Midlands as co-driver and front machine gunner, in a Cromwell hung about with loose track plates (to help deflect 88mm armour-piercing shells fired from German Tigers and Panthers, which our standard armour plating was no match for and which had a faster muzzle velocity and longer range than our 75mm – very confidence inspiring!), ration boxes and bedding rolls, for which there was no room inside the tank or in the inadequate external storage bins fixed to the hull.

'I cannot honestly say that I recall anything of our first engagement with the enemy in those first few confused days of my real war, but some of the things most firmly imprinted upon my memory in the breakout from the bridgehead, the Falaise Gap, and the 'swan' up towards the Belgian border by the end of August are as follows:

'Watching in horror, a tank from another troop "brew up" instantly after a direct hit from an 88 and the frantic efforts of the crew to escape the inferno. The gunner, sitting down in the turret, always the last to leave, did not make it (thin side armour to the hull, hundreds of gallons of high octane petrol in slab tanks either side of the engine and a mixture of fuel and oil sloshing around the sealed bottom plates, often below the turret floor made an incendiary combination). Helping to pull a tank driver out of a tank which had gone over a mine. The impact had broken both his legs and the only way to get him out through the narrow hatch was to haul on his webbing shoulder straps, after injecting an ampoule of morphia and crushing between his teeth a chloroform ampoule wrapped in gauze, both standard issue in the crew's first-aid kits. Gaping in astonishment at the degree of devastation caused by bombing and subsequent artillery barrages to little towns like Villers

Bocage, where Army bulldozers were trying to locate the former streets under the enormous mounds of rubble.

'Listening in awe to the sheer volume of sound from a dawn barrage by 25 pounder artillery behind our position, the shells howling over our heads to soften up the enemy positions before our main attack and, later, watching the bewildered German troops, some only boys, emerge from fox holes and ditches with hands raised in surrender to our infantry support. Snatching quick meals of tinned meat and veg., heated in billy-cans on our petrol-fuelled pressure stoves, or balancing sardines on hardtack biscuits as an even quicker energy-restorer, with the ever-lasting brews of thick, sweet tea and – a special treat while in Normandy – the occasional binge with a ripe Camembert (spooned from its container) and a bottle of Calvados. Puzzling over the luke-warm welcome we received from the people of Normandy, for whom we thought we should be welcome liberators, forgetting at the time that German occupation there was not too rigorous and that the suffering caused by the US Air Force and other Allied operations in the area was severe; in the main only the ladies of the town in places like Bayeux and Caen extended the welcome mat!'

On 30th July the Division was ordered forward to Caumont, where they were finally rejoined by the 11th Hussars who remained with the Desert Rats until the end of the war. The Division went into action again, in thick mist, on the morning of 1st August, advancing towards Aunay-sur-Audon through 'terrible traffic congestion with 50th Division.' A Canadian officer is credited with one of the shrewdest remarks about the Normandy fighting: 'What beats me,' he said to a tank officer, 'is why we don't bring over one London bobby to control the traffic, and we'd be out of here in no time.' The 1/6th Queen's had put in a night assault on high ground east of Aunay, which was followed by a fierce German counter-attack on the afternoon of 3rd August. A battle then took place around Aunay, where both the Queen's infantry and the 5th RTR were severely cut up.

General Verney has left an account of this engagement: 'By now the weather was very hot and dry and it remained so until the end of the month. This made things pleasant, but there was one great incon-venience – dust. This was of a density that was indescribable and experts said it exceeded anything in the desert. Great clouds of red dust hung over every column of traffic, and to pull out was to risk collision with a vehicle coming the other way. The dust also drew shellfire, and along particularly bad stretches one could see notices saying, "Go slow, dust brings shells". During this hot weather, clothing departed from the regulations to a remarkable degree. The desert veterans were notorious for their clothing, corduroy trousers, light coloured shirts, and bright silk scarves round their necks. Tin hats were only worn by the Infantry Brigade and only then when they were actually in battle. The roads were so narrow and the country so broken that it was not possible to move the rest of the Division up through Aunay, but during the night of 6th/7th August, the 1st/7th Queens, who had been moved to this area, carried out a most excellent night attack which gained them a footing on the plateau by dawn at a cost of four officers and forty other ranks killed and wounded. They killed a great many Huns and took a hundred and forty-two prisoners. Supported by 1 RTR, the Queens remained on the top until the 10th August, but they found it impossible to advance although they successfully repelled counter-attacks intended to drive them off. In the meantime 50 Division were advancing on Mont Pincon.

'On the 8th August the Corps Commander wanted to launch two columns of tanks and infantry from 7th Armoured on Conde, which was over ten miles away. Neither column got started. As soon as they began to advance on the top of the plateau they met stiff opposition, and the country was too thick for tanks. The Inniskillings, who led the left column, tried hard and lost several good officers, including the Adjutant and a squadron leader. About the 7th, 43 Division cleared Mont Pincon, and General Horrocks, now commanding 30 Corps, established an OP for himself on the top. This was on the forward slope and must have been visible for miles. He used to send for his Divisional Commanders to come up and confer with him there, and a more unpleasant drive it would be hard to imagine. The road up was frequently shelled and it was considered wise to park the cars on the reverse slope and then run to reach the pit. General Horrocks was one of those rare people who was stimulated by being shelled, rather as some are stimulated by a good gallop. It was nice for him being made like that but no fun for his companions.

'By the evening of the 9th we had cleared the crest by Mont Pincon and La Vallée, when all except the Inniskillings and the two RHA regiments were taken out of the line for a fortnight's rest. One summer evening, I attended a performance of a good concert party led by George Formby, the Lancashire comedian and banjo player, which went on until about dark. Formby told me it was their tenth performance that day and they had been on the go since early in the morning. Next day, just after lunch, the Hun put a salvo of shells into the field where I had my caravan. One man was killed and three wounded by this long-range artillery, for we could not hear the shells coming.'

General Verney's account takes us ahead of time, so we must return briefly to the start of the battles for Caumont and Mont Pincon. Seventh Armoured were still not doing so well, but then neither were the other two divisions of 30 Corps, the 43rd and the 50th. Everyone was finding it very difficult to make any headway in this close country, so ideal for defence and so strongly defended with mines, roving Tigers and Panthers, and strong detachments of enemy infantry, all well supported by artillery and mortars. Hard eyes were now resting on 7th Armoured and General Dempsey now demanded more vigorous efforts. Then, following an order to 'Get on or get out,' the axe finally fell on the higher ranks of 30 Corps. The Corps Commander was replaced by Lt-General Horrocks, now recovered from his wounds, and, as we have seen, Brigadier G.S. Verney came over from the Guards Tank Brigade to replace General Erskine. Brigadier Hinde and many other officers of the Division – more than a hundred in all – were also sent home or posted to other commands, a shake-up that shook the entire Division. Meanwhile, Operation Bluecoat continued with 30 Corps advancing on Mount Pincon.

The 11th Hussars attempted to find a way through Villers Bocage, which had been reduced to rubble by the RAF. In spite of this and a plentiful supply of mines, the 11th Hussars made their way round the town, making a way for the Inniskillings and one of the Rifle Brigade companies. With steady pushing from above and dire warnings of the consequences of any sign of 'stickiness', the Division now started to move with something like its old dash, probing forward down every possible road, track and avenue. On the 5th, the 22nd Armoured Brigade advanced no less than fourteen miles through the bocage to Bonnemaison, reaching an open plateau south of the next major physical obstacle, Mont Pincon (365m), which lay three miles due south of Aunay. Easy, direct access, even to the foot of Mount Pincon, is prevented by a deep wooded valley, then thickly sewn with mines. This was a task for the sappers and the infantry, so the Queens and the Divisional Sappers spent the night of the 6th and most of the 7th August lifting mines, being heavily shelled all the time. The Queen's Brigade assaulted the enemy positions in the valley on the night of 8th August, and on the 9th and 10th the Division advanced round Mont Pincon, which was left to the 50th and 43rd Divisions, and advanced on Conde. During this 'Bluecoat' operation the three battalions of the Queen's Brigade were almost continually in action and had lost almost a thousand men, or one third of their strength, since the start of 'Goodwood', just three weeks before. All ranks were nearing exhaustion and their problems were compounded by the fact that reinforcements were now in short supply. By 1944, all Britain's available manpower was now fully committed to the war, and the only way to reinforce one British division was to break up another one, and distribute the men among undermanned units.

On 10th August, some of the Division moved back to rest, although the 'Skins', the Artillery and the 11th Hussars were attached to other formations for a while and so continued in the line.

During the second week of August, the Allied Armies, British, American and Canadian, managed to pin the bulk of the German forces into an area which became known as the Falaise Pocket. Fighting desperately, the Germans managed to keep the flap of the pocket open while a number of units escaped, but massed artillery and the relentless strike of the Allied Air Forces did awesome execution among the rest. The Falaise Pocket became a charnal house of burning tanks and vehicles, dead and injured men and, since the Germans were still using horse transport, hundreds of dead horses.

Llewellyn Davies was a fitter in the REME, attached to the Light Aid Detachment of the 5th Royal Inniskilling Dragoon Guards, and recalls this time: 'The Skins were mopping up and moving round the Falaise Pocket to head for the Seine. Somewhere in Normandy I had done some repairs on a Cromwell, and I wanted to test it for a mile or so. The driver of a Cromwell is down in the front and only has a hole, about ten inches in diameter, to see through, practically only straight ahead. The crew commander or someone up in the turret guides him by means of the intercom radio. My "mate", the electrician, became my guide. Having guided me out of the field by radio, I set off, quite happily, down the road on test, until I felt my mate hitting me on the head, getting me to stop! The intercom had packed up, and he had been shouting to me to pull out. The tank tracks had picked up yards of field telephone wires from the edge of the road. We pulled all the broken wire off the tracks and threw it in the ditch, turned the tank round and headed back very quickly. Turning into the field, I ran over and flattened our L.A.D. sign. The Skipper saw this and raised hell with me, so I did not report anything else. I felt sorry for the Signals blokes who had lost all that wire.

'By now we were used to the smell of burnt property, trucks, tanks and the stink of dead cattle with their legs sticking straight out in the air. The 7th Division and others were getting closer to the Seine with lots of action on the way. The German Panzerfaust carried by one

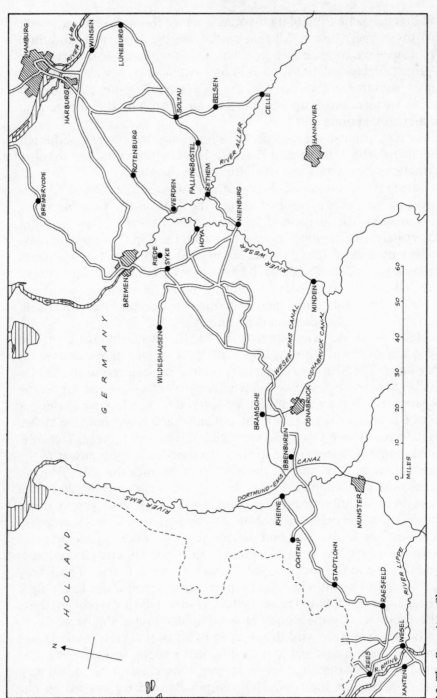

13 The Pursuit to Ghent

infantryman took its toll on tanks. The charge would pierce the tank armour with the blast spreading inside, maiming or killing the crew. The German 88mm gun was, perhaps, a tank crew's most hated opposition artillery and could also be used against aircraft. They fired about 20 lbs of solid shot, which could and did sometimes go in one side of a tank and out the other side. I actually saw a kaputt tank like this.'

On 15th August, while this carnage was going on near Falaise, to the south, General Verney was ordered to round up his Division and join the 1st Canadian Army under General H.D.G. Crerar, for an advance to the Seine on the northern border of Normandy, a distance from Caen of some sixty-five miles. The German front was collapsing and 7th Armoured was on the move again, sweeping forward across the Norman *campagne* towards the Seine and the countryside of Picardy.

Between the Orne and the Seine, the Norman countryside is not like the *bocage* south-west of Caen. The countryside is open and rolling and the main feature here is a series of rivers, none very wide, but all quite wide enough to pose problems and provide an aggressive enemy with a secure defensive position. The Divisional advance began on 17th August, led as ever by the 11th Hussars and the infantry of the Queen's Brigade supported closely by the tanks of the 8th Hussars. The German Luftwaffe was now again active, though only by night, while the Allied Airforces operated continuously by day, in support of the advancing armies. Soon after the advance began, British aircraft accidentally strafed the tanks of the 8th Hussars, causing more than twenty casualties. The River Vie was crossed near Livarot on the 18th, and the town was captured on the morning of the 20th, when the 6th Queen's and the Sappers were greeted by thousands of citizens waving flowers and bottles of wine. The bridge over the Vie was then strengthened and the tanks of the 22nd Armoured Brigade were over that afternoon, and advancing on the River Touques, on the road to Lisieux. A bridge was then found intact and the advance continued on the 21st in spite of mines and periodic attacks from small parties of enemy troops and tanks, including one from elements of the 12 SS Panzer Div. with Tigers.

The town of Lisieux was strongly held and the Germans held out until early on the 23rd, before surrendering. Meanwhile, skirting the town, the 7th Queen's had posted some troops forward to the banks of the Orbiquet, while street fighting continued in Lisieux. Derrick James Watson of the 1/5th Queen's again:

'21st/22nd/23rd August 1944: The Battle for the town of Lisieux. We were much depleted by the fighting in what was described as the

Battle for Caen, where we were opposed by no less than four Panzer Divisions, three Infantry Divisions and a large number of 88s. We prepared for an attack on Lisieux, the 1/5th Queen's now commanded by that splendid man, Jock Nangle, now promoted to Lt.-Colonel. We had the support of the Inniskilling Dragoons (the "Skins"), fresh out from England and full of the traditional dash of the Cavalry. The Cromwells led the way through the streets of the town, firing their Besas into the houses as they went. D. Coy, commanded by Major Pat Henderson, followed in single file on either side of the street, followed in turn by me carrying an armful of Battalion signs (55), which I was to plant to show the way to the following troops. However, at the first bend in the High Street the leading Cromwell "brewed up" – only one of the crew escaping – and Major Henderson was severely wounded by a direct hit from a mortar bomb. Orders came to withdraw from the town, the exits being covered by road blocks covered by Spandaus and panzerfaist and mortars and shellfire, causing heavy casualties. The town was then to be heavily stonked by the medium regiment, the results being devastating but the result meant any further advance by the tanks was impossible. Later that evening I was approached by our Australian M.O., Captain Moore, who explained that he had ensconced his RAP in a house on the edge of the town, close behind the battalion. In the late afternoon, when it was dusk, the troops came marching back and he noted first A Coy, the B, then C, then D. "It dawned on me," he said, that he was in *front* of the Battalion and shouted to Sgt "Jumbo" Wicks, the RAP Sgt. and now an Usher in the House of Lords, to "... pack up – we're moving back." He reproached me, saying, "I know I am a non-combatant, but do the Gunners on both sides know that!"

'Next day I was on reconnaissance on the right flank, to find a way round for the tracked vehicles. First I found a Scotsman lying on the ground with a great hole in his back. I assumed he was from the 51st Highland Division, who were out there somewhere. While I bandaged him up with a field dressing, he explained that he and his mates were made prisoners – he tried to run away and got shot in the back. Although he repeatedly called for help, no one came, and he was going to write to Sir James Gregg about it. I brought the stretcher bearers who took him to the RAP, where he later died.

'Continuing my reconnaissance up a steep slope and across a large open space in the middle of which was a very high, ramshackle barn, I saw a shape peering out of the doorway. I drew my revolver and started to stalk the building, until a man emerged making friendly signals with a bottle, and calling out something like, '*Francais*'. It was a local farmer taking shelter with his wife and three small children. He assured me there were no Germans anywhere around, and it certainly was all peace and quiet – quite unreal. I told him to stay there today, but tomorrow he should leave, and in sign language indicated that the tanks might be coming through and he and his family must lie very low. I went back to report that the way was clear and was told to direct a Sherman with a 17-pdr. I warned the commander about the barn and the French family and watched the Sherman crawl jerkily up the steep slope, when suddenly a large, bulky object fell off the back. With the tank poised on the crest of the slope, I saw the officer alight and recover his bed-roll! Having got his priorities right, he proceeded on his task, whatever that was. Fierce fighting by ourselves and the 51st Highland Division cleared the town of the anti-tank guns and panzer-faust, and although there were still snipers in the Cathedral, the town was virtually ours by 4pm on 23rd August.'

The 11th Hussars managed to make their way through the town on 24th August and 22nd Brigade soon followed, enjoying a ten-mile run to the River Risle down the main Route National between groups of cheering Frenchmen. When they got to the river all the bridges were down, but after an advance of twenty-six miles in two days, everyone was in top form and searched at once to find a way across the river, aided in the approach by that most useful machine, the Divisional bulldozer, which cleared the rubble from the bombed streets and shattered villages, filling in craters to let the advance continue. The Inniskillings found a bridge near Montfort and the Scout Troop found another in fairly good state at Pont Authou, a mile upstream. The Inniskillings drove the enemy from Port Authou and the rest of 22nd Armoured Brigade came across that afternoon.

For the next three days the Division pushed on across the rolling wooded country between the Risle and the Seine, taking many prisoners but fighting a series of sharp little actions against small pockets of the enemy. On the evening of the 28th the Division reached the Seine by the Foret de Bretonne. They had come a long way, physically and spiritually, in the last few weeks, and were again in top fighting form. Ahead now lay the frontiers of France and Belgium, and beyond that Holland and Germany itself. The war in Europe had just seven months to run.

13

Belgium and Holland

SEPTEMBER–DECEMBER 1944

> War is at best barbarism.
> Its glory is all moonshine.
> Only those who have neither
> fired a shot nor heard the
> crying of the wounded could
> think otherwise. War is hell.
>
> *William T. Sherman*

The Battle of Normandy ended for 7th Armoured when the Division reached the Seine on 28th August. On 31st August they began a whirlwind advance that would carry them across Northern France and up to Ghent and the port of Antwerp, an advance reminiscent in all but terrain of their days of glory in the Western Desert. In six days the Division covered a distance of some 220 miles, overcame countless enemy positions and captured 10,000 prisoners and a vast amount of material.

At the start of this campaign, the Division came under the command of 12 Corps (Lt-General N.M. Ritchie), and was concentrated near Le Neubourg, south of Elbeuf, on the west bank of the Seine. By now the Division, like the rest of the British Army, was becoming seriously short of both men and equipment. The 22nd Armoured Brigade had lost a third of their Cromwells, while the three battalions of the Queen's Brigade were each the equivalent of two companies short.

On 30th August the Divisional force expanded when the 4th Armoured Brigade, now under Brigadier Mike Carver, together with the

Royals and the 10th (Medium) Regiment, Royal Artillery, came briefly under command. These three units were already fighting north-east of the Seine, and their situation gave the Division a bridgehead over the river for their advance on Ghent. The Division then surged forward on a two-brigade front – 4th Brigade and Royals on the right, 22nd Brigade and 11th Hussars on the left, with the Queen's Brigade in reserve. The Divisional History records a particular debt to the men of 67 Coy RASC which, when ordered to establish a refuelling point for the tanks on the far side of the Seine, did so by putting in seventy-two hours of solid driving and going without sleep for ninety-six hours – how they stayed awake can only be wondered at. It should again be pointed out that while the action part of the Divisional story inevitably concentrates on the 'teeth' arms of the tank and infantry units, the Division could not have functioned without the RASC, the Sappers of the Royal Engineers, the signallers and the RAMC Medics, all the support elements essential to an armoured division in war.

The advance began before dawn on 31st August in driving rain, and with immediate traffic congestion, as the entire Division, hundreds of tanks, scout cars, armoured cars, bren-gun carriers and lorries had to file carefully across just two bridges over the Seine. It took ten hours for the 3rd RHA to cover the first eighteen miles, but once the Division was across the river and able to deploy, the speed of the advance soon picked up. By nine in the morning the leading troops of the 11th Hussars were halfway to the Somme, cheered on by the populations of every town and village, but already beginning to bump into small parties from the German rearguard, armed with spandaus and panzerfausts. Lt. Hunt and several men of the 11th Hussars were wounded or killed in these encounters.

The Inniskillings of 22 Brigade made a run of seventy-two miles on the first day of the advance, and had been on the road nineteen hours before they met the enemy at Abancourt, a strongpoint eventually cleared by the Rifle Brigade. The 4th Armoured Brigade almost reached the Somme on the 31st, meeting scattered pockets of enemy resistance on the way, but getting up to the river by dawn on 1st September. Derrick Watson of the Queen's recalls this period:

'We were told that our Armoured Cars and Tanks were advancing on Ghent and were urgently requiring the infantry for protection. Accordingly, Lt. Col Nangle ordered the battalion to be prepared to move off at first light the following morning. Driving his jeep with me as escort/navigator, we set off as darkness fell. About midnight I knocked up a Belgian householder to ask the way, (I thought at the time that this was a funny way to fight a war!) and also to enquire if there were any Germans about. He was most incensed at being disturbed from his slumbers, although he did give the information that the Germans were *kaput*, confirmed that we were in Belgium, and slammed the door in my face. Further on in the countryside we came to a fork in the road, tossed a coin, and decided to take the right-hand road. Those following, some time later, took the left fork and ran headlong into a stranded Tiger tank. All but the leading vehicle were able to reverse and make their escape, but next morning Reconnaissance found the Tiger, which had been set on fire, and no sign of our vehicle, which had presumably been captured together with its occupants. We continued our drive without further incident and next day the Battalion liberated Ghent in triumph.'

The Somme crossing proved difficult. Every bridge but one in the Divisional area had been blown up, and the surviving one at Hangest collapsed under the last tank of the first squadron of the Scots Greys to cross. The Royals and 44th Royal Tanks of 4th Armoured Brigade finally got across near Amiens, and a Bailey bridge was flung across the river by the Divisional Engineers of the 4th Field Squadron R.E., near Picquigny, five miles to the west. The advance continued to the next river obstacle, the Authie, where the Division met stiffening resistance from German units, from companies up to battalion strength, putting in attacks from the east. The Division was now so far ahead of Corps HQ that wireless contact was lost. On 2nd September, 4th Armoured Brigade and the Royals reverted to the command of 12th Corps. Seventh Armoured Division had now run off its maps but the advance went on, much of it at night, the Division forging ahead fast to 'bounce' the enemy out of his defensive positions before they could be properly prepared.

Rex Wingfield was with 'A' Company 1/6th Queen's. 'The "Swan" to Ghent continued, fanning out over the Pas de Calais. We were ordered to spray any V1 sites we saw. The authorities seemed a little scared of the Doodlebugs. A strange rumour spread that orders had been issued that no prisoners were to be taken on the sites. We saw plenty of the sites, but no movement on them and prisoners very wisely did not claim the distinction of belonging to them ... they'd heard the rumour too.

'Our triumphal procession continued. Liberation was becoming almost monotonous – only the girls were different, thank goodness! Jock was looking very battered by now. One or two of us were being careful in towns, as we had face wounds sustained during the welcome. Fruit travelling at an approaching speed of forty-five miles per hour is very painful. That we didn't mind very much, but when bottles of wine began to sing through the air too, we skulked at the bottom of the truck. At the next town we were ready. As we slowed in the main square, the trucks sprang into action. Battered liberators appeared above the sides of the truck and opened a barrage of fruit, cigarettes, soap, chocolate and toilet rolls on the crowd. Our barrage mowed swaths of havoc, but our fire was as nothing to the stuff that came sailing back. Somebody started on the wine-bottle racket again, so, with a despairing volley of tinned Compo rations, we withdrew to prepared positions behind the sides of the truck. Safely seated on the floor, with our backs to the sides, we watched the various items sail over our heads to be fielded by the men on the other side. We in turn caught their "overs". When the shower of missiles died down, the girls boarded and fell into the laps of the waiting consumers. I believe a man did try to come in – once!

'We crossed the Belgian frontier. The first big town we came to was Oudenarde. Our trucks stopped in the square by the beautiful Town Hall. Belgian civvies in hundreds came pouring into the square, the girls gay with outfits of the Belgian national colours – red, yellow and black. It must have been quite a shock to them to see TCVs pull up opposite the Town Hall – empty! As they moved away in disappointment, berets slowly appeared above the sides. They rose higher and higher. Furtive eyes peered out and swivelled slowly round the square. A sudden roar came from the interior: "Look! A 'Gents', a real live 'Gents'!" The TCVs erupted into a flood of khaki which foamed and swirled round the municipal lavatories. Ah! The Bliss!

'We were fêted and kissed to death, but were reproached for not showing ourselves at first. We explained. This time the civvies helped us to pack our truck scientifically. A despatch rider appeared. The Belgians sensed what that meant for they began wailing "Good-bye". We rolled onwards.

'We had come from the Seine almost non-stop. For mile after mile we had rocked and swayed to the high-pitched whine of the four-wheel drive. Our whole world was the roof and metal sides of the truck. For hour after hour, day after day, we had slumped in a half-doze in our seats, rifles knocking against our knees, respirators and big packs swinging from the roof bars; all our meals were taken in the truck and all our nature calls had to be performed over the side of the truck or standing sleepily on the mounting-step with an equally sleepy comrade hanging on to our webbing straps to stop us from falling into the road. We played cards, dozed and smoked as the wheels sang on. We were tired.

'The truck stopped. We jerked awake, instinctively gripping our rifles.

We sensed that this was real trouble. "O.K. Debus! We've caught up with the tanks. The road's mined and we want some snipers flushed!"

'We jumped down in battle kit and stretched ourselves after the long trip. Opposite was a sign informing us that we were at Melle on the outskirts of Ghent. The Major turned to me. "Right-ho, Wingfield! You've commanded a section before. Take eight men down this road till you come to a wood, turn right and go down to the canal. Keep to the towpath, under cover as far as possible. If the cover peters out, come back to the road. Your job is to locate and deal with snipers and, if possible, find out the enemy strength on the other side. Sergeant Harris, take the other eight and clean the snipers out of that wood. You'll find a tank and a Belgian civvy to act as a guide. Move off in ten minutes."'

On 2nd September the 1/5th Queen's captured a flying-bomb site and took 400 prisoners. The 8th Hussars and the 5th Queen's crossed the Authie and advanced on Frévent and St Pol, before bumping into a large enemy force, which was eventually pushed back by the weight of 22 Brigade. At one time on 2nd September, units of the Division were involved in small battles and fire-fights on an eighteen-mile front. Petrol was now the main problem in maintaining the rate of advance, but the indefatigable RASC drivers still kept going, bringing up constant replenishment for the ever-thirsty tanks and armoured cars.

North of Frévent the Division left Picardy and on 3rd September entered the flat coal-mining country of Artois, west of Lille. This region is seamed with pits, narrow roads and canals, linking small mining towns and villages. General Verney therefore requested permission to switch his advance through the more 'tankable' country east of the Lille, while still heading for the Divisional objective, Ghent. The 11th Hussars found and crossed an intact bridge over the Aire Canal at Hinges, while a carrier patrol of the Queen's reached Bethune just in time to rescue a contingent of the French *Maquis* fighters besieged by Germans in the town jail. The rest of the Division was now concentrated around St Pol, from where the Inniskillings found an intact bridge over the La Bassée canal at Cambrin, which the Germans were about to demolish. The Skins drove off the enemy and established a small bridge-head over the canal with A Company of the Rifle Brigade and their own C Squadron.

On 4th September, General Verney received orders to make a final dash across the Franco-Belgian frontier for Ghent. The Division was now consuming 70,000 gallons of petrol a day, over seventy tanker-loads of fuel, and it was therefore decided that nothing larger than a composite brigade could be kept going all the seventy miles to Ghent. This 'Ghent Force' was therefore made up of the 11th Hussars – it was now quite unthinkable for 7th Armoured Division to go anywhere without the 11th Hussars – HQ 22 Armoured Bde, 5th RHA, the Inniskilling Dragoon Guards, 5th Royal Tanks, the 6th Queen's, and 'A' Company, the Rifle Brigade. This Force struck out for Ghent on the afternoon of 4th September 1944. Harry Upward was with the 5 RTR during this advance:

'Daybreak came at about 4.30 am, and though tanks spent the night in close leaguer, we moved out at first light, getting about three hours sleep a night, with a spell on guard as well. Night was when you refuelled and re-armed. I think a Sherman did about one mile to the gallon, and we refuelled out of jerry-cans and lived on dry rations, keeping close contact with the Queen's and the Rifle Brigade. We carried infantry on our tanks, and had Canadians as well, during our advance into Belgium. On the swan up to Ghent we were going up to a hundred miles a day or thereabouts, a bloody long way, and it was hard to keep awake. It's hard work driving a tank across country, and easy to lose a track. At night we would dig a pit and then drive the tank over it – it's dangerous to get under a tank for a kip on soft ground, for it can settle on you. Anyway, we had a great reception from the Belgians – cheering, bottles of wine. My battalion of the 5th Tanks took Ghent and later on we got a little plaque for it, but I lost mine afterwards.'

As far as Carvin there was no opposition and the Brigade really tore along, to cheers from the frantic locals. The Cromwell tanks were fast enough to keep up with the wheeled vehicles, and the very ground shook as the tank columns roared past. Within two hours the Brigade had crossed the frontier from France into Belgium, and met with an even more tumultuous reception from the local people; the tanks and trucks soon filled up with flowers and fruit and bottles of wine and brandy, a number of men receiving slight injuries from well-meant but mis-aimed bunches of grapes.

General Verney's account includes this happy time. 'We crossed the frontier into Belgium and except for one blown bridge, at Warcoing, had a clear run through. Our reception in Belgium exceeded even the tremendous scenes we had already experienced in France. It was quite unforgettable and most inspiring. I, for one, was beginning to get very tired; in fact, that morning was the first one on which I really did feel tired even before going out, but the reception we received from people of all classes put new life into one and made one feel that one could still pull out a bit more.

'The Belgians seem to go in for the largest flags in the world, and the number of flags per head of the population must also be the largest in the world. Besides flags on every church and almost every house, there were numerous banners strung across the roads – "*Vive les Anglais*", "Welcome", "Well Done", and other such greetings. At many places, also, were boards with chalk or paint inscriptions on them in the same vein, and one that said, "You are quite welcome".

'Every vehicle was pelted with flowers, apples and pears, most of them being extremely hard and unripe and one had to take no little care dodging these well-meant tributes. This greeting was kept up for several days, and many thousands of apples and pears must have been given away. To stop was fatal – the vehicle was instantly surrounded and boarded, hands were shaken, faces kissed, flowers and fruit poured in.

'For the first time since the African Campaign, the Division was to be used in its most successful role, the break-through, unhampered by pockets which could not be by-passed. Certain aspects of this type of action we had already glimpsed – the cheering crowds, the proffered drinks, the flowers, kisses, the energetic if sometimes tiresome Partisans, but in front of us had always been enemy forces, usually comparatively well equipped, who were acting in obedience to an organised command.

'From now on until Ghent, we had left behind the dust and stench of the beach-head, the never-ending Artillery fire and the over-crowded roads, for a war in which the Tanks or Armoured Cars could get on or round, through virtually undamaged towns and villages. True, there was much fighting to be done, but it was fighting for which we were well equipped, and the opposition was such as we could either overcome with our own weapons or else outmanoeuvre by our superior mobility.'

The advance was finally halted at dusk near Audenarde, (or Oudenarde), after an advance of fifty miles, where the armies snatched a few hours sleep before resuming the advance at dawn. A small German force was met at Nazareth, eight miles outside Ghent, but once this force had been overcome, a curious incident developed on the outskirts of the city, involving the German Commander, General Daser, and Lt-Colonel Holliman, Commanding Officer of the 5th RTR.

First, a civilian appeared under a white flag and said the German garrison wished to surrender. Then a German officer appeared and said that he and his C.O. would like to surrender. This C.O., a Major, then said that his General would *probably* surrender with the entire garrison. An argument then developed because the General would only surrender to an officer of equal rank. Lt-Colonel Holliman, commanding 5 RTR, therefore tried to pass himself off as a General, but this plot failed when one of his men accidentally addressed him as 'Colonel'. Brigadier Mackeson then came up and the haggling continued, with Brigadier Mackeson pointing out that he was 'almost' a general. The German General then announced that his Corps Commander had ordered him to fight on. Fortunately, his forces had already started to withdraw to the northern outskirts of the city, so the historic heart of Ghent was spared the inevitable destruction caused by street fighting. At dawn on 5th September the 11th Hussars and tanks of the Inniskilling Dragoon Guards entered Ghent from the east, beating off attacks from roving parties of Germans retreating from the centre, which, however, was still reported to be 'stiff with Germans'. In spite of this, and some opposition from snipers and pockets of infantry, by 20.00 hours that day the bulk of the Division had entered Ghent and parked their tanks outside the Town Hall.

The next three days were spent clearing away pockets of resistance around Ghent, and preparing to defend the city from counter-attack, for the Division's situation was still precarious. There was continual shelling during which a lorry containing men of the Queen's was hit, and much time was spent eliminating snipers and mortar fire from the docks area, while the Sappers of the 4th Field Squadron, busy repairing a bridge at Wetteren, were set upon by a company of Waffen SS, whom they beat off with the assistance of their Inniskilling drivers, killing twenty-four and taking ten prisoner. South of Ghent lay a large German force, the 15th Army, which, in spite of some several maulings, could still muster eleven depleted divisions. Their commander, General Von Zangen, seemed determined to concentrate his force around Audenarde and fight his way out to the east and back to Germany, a move which would take them through both 7th Armoured Division and the communications of 11th Armoured Division. The 11th Hussars therefore kept the 15th Army under very close observation while the Engineers blew every bridge over the River Lys. On 6th September, thwarted in their original intention, the 15th Army changed its direction and withdrew north, across the Scheldt.

Meanwhile, the widely scattered units of 7th Armoured began to concentrate on Ghent. As the units arrived, the Division gradually spread out to the east of the city, and there was sporadic fighting all along the River Scheldt, until 11th September, when the Polish Armoured Division arrived to take over the area.

Derrick Watson again: 'After a delightful ten days in Ghent we marched out on 7th September 1944, to continue the war. There was

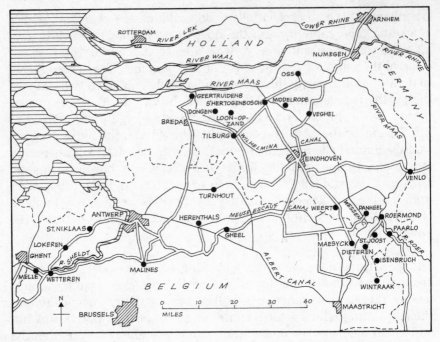

14 Holland

much cheering from the citizens and some weeping from the young
women, two of whom ran beside their loved ones in the ranks for some
yards before dropping back, breathless and weeping. The Official History
of the Division reads as follows:

7 Sept–10 Nov 1944:   Mopping up operations in Belgium &
Holland.
10 Nov–1 Feb 1945:   Operation Blackcock.

'During the above operations we suffered many casualties and took
many prisoners. When Major Russell Elliott was killed by a shell which
hit a tree under which his slit trench HQ had been dug, I was promoted
to Major to take over "A" Coy by Lt-Col Ian Freeland, a fine soldier from
a family of soldiers. Both his father and his grandfather had been
generals and his brother was another Lt.-Colonel.'

Seventh Armoured then moved east to Malines, south of Antwerp,
where there was little room for tanks or armoured cars to manoeuvre,
although the snipers of the Queen's Brigade came into their own. Snipers
of the 7th Queen's, operating near Herenthals, claimed a 'bag' of sixteen
Germans killed and four wounded on 21st September alone. The Divi-

sion's casualties in the previous month had largely fallen on the infantry of the Queen's and the Rifle Brigade, a number of anti-tank gunners and mortar men had to leave their heavy weapons and be sent into the line armed with rifles. The Division was not directly involved in the Arnhem fighting, but some time after that battle there was one memorable incident when an old officer of the 8th Hussars, a parachute Brigadier at Arnhem, returned to the welcoming arms of 7th Armoured Division.

Brigadier Shan Hackett, late of 'C' Squadron 8th Hussars, had been wounded at the Battle of Arnhem and hidden by a Dutch family until he was able to escape.

'I made my way down the Waal in a canoe, and came to a quay at the edge of the river, where I saw a tall, angular figure standing there in the dark. This turned out to be Tony Crankshaw of the 11th Hussars – it would have to be the 11th Hussars, wouldn't it? He had a bottle of whisky under his arm. "Hello, Shan," he said. "Welcome back." I went to sleep that morning in the CO's bed. That night I had dinner with Monty. We had oysters ... the best meal I'd had in months. Monty had a theory that anyone who would stand up to him would not be daunted by the King's enemies.'

During October, the Division held the line west of the town of S'Her-togenbosch, and then gradually moved into position along a line from Veghel, south of s'Hertogenbosch, south and east to the River Maas. Here they occupied a static front of some fourteen miles. This was a period which put a great strain on the Division's already slender resources, with a steady stream of killed and wounded, especially among the infantry. Life consisted of a relentless round of day and night patrols in flat, wet, polder country, any rest period disturbed by sporadic mortaring and shelling. The one bright spot was the fact that the town of Oss contained a huge supply depot for the German Army, stuffed with meat, bacon, butter, cheese – food that no one had seen much of in the last five years. The Dutchman in charge of this depot was said to issue supplies to the British Army in the morning and the German Army in the afternoon, quite happy to supply anyone with anything he had, provided they signed for it. The town telephone lines were also intact, and it was often possible to ring towns behind the German lines and ask the citizens what was going on – an unusual but quite effective form of reconnaissance.

At the end of October, orders arrived to clear the enemy away from the Maas and advance towards Emelhuen. The division was ordered to pass through the 51st and 15th Divisions by s'Hertogenbosch and advance into Holland to the mouth of the River Maas at Geertruidenberg, an advance of some thirty miles. This was through thickly wooded country at first, giving way to polder country, large fields divided by dykes, a difficult country for tanks but ideal for defence.

The advance began at 0400 hrs on 22nd October 1944 with heavy artillery fire in the known enemy positions followed by the advance of the Queen's Brigade, supported by the 8th Hussars and by flail and 'Crocodile' flame-throwing tanks. The enemy line consisted of village strongpoints manned by infantry and artillery, all surrounded by minefields. The Division lost four tanks of the 8th Hussars and had sixty casualties during the day, but by that night the 7th Queen's gradually cleared Middelrode and took 130 prisoners. On the 25th the Division crossed the river and on the 29th captured Loon-op-Zand, after a stiff two-day fight. The 11th Hussars and the 1/5th Queen's, with 8th Hussar tanks in support, at once pressed on in bitterly cold weather over icy roads for Dongen, where they received 'the best welcome in Holland,' but a warmer one from a group of Germans with tank and artillery support. Still meeting pockets of resistance, the Division moved up to the banks of the Maas. The advance had taken a week and cost the Division twenty-two tanks and over 100 men, but they had pushed on as ordered and taken nearly 900 prisoners.

The Division had a quiet ten days on the Maas, but this rest, like most of the others, was not to last. The first days of November saw little contact with the enemy, and the troops could be warmly billeted in Dutch houses when not on outpost duty or overhauling their Cromwell tanks and other equipment. The Allied Armies, American, Canadian and British, had now been on the move for four months, and with France, Belgium and much of Holland free of the enemy, the time had come for a short pause, before the final push into Germany.

Then, on 10th November, the Division moved to the east and took up fresh positions along the Maas and the Wessen canal in 'unattractive country, sodden with water and abounding with mines,' where their outposts were manned by the Queen's, the Rifle Brigade, and the ever-vigilant 11th Hussars, who were now wearing their new multi-zipped winter clothing, known to the troops as 'zoot-suits', a real boon in this bitter winter weather.

On the 14th, the Division took a small but costly part in an operation to clear the enemy away from east of Weert, when the 1/7th Queen's and 'C' Squadron of the 8th Hussars were ordered to seize a lock on the canal at Panheel. The attack was met with fierce resistance and intense artillery fire, and in forty-five minutes all but one of the Queen's officers were killed or wounded. Total losses, killed and wounded, exceeded thirty men, a hard and shocking blow to an already depleted infantry battalion.

Rex Wingfield of the 1/6th Queen's recalls the reaction of the infantrymen in battle: 'It is a fact that no normal man is not scared by the *thought* of action. Any man who won't admit that he's scared is either a liar or a B.F. The strange thing is that the waiting for action is frightening, but once the battle or the patrol starts, fear vanishes. The clue is that word Action. In battle so much is happening at once, you're so busy that you haven't time to be scared. You haven't even time to think. You do things instinctively. But at night or in some pause in the battle, you have got time to think. Then you have time to think of what has happened, the mate you saw go down, the tank which brewed up, the shell which stuck into the ground two feet away from you and failed to go off. At the time they happened, the events of the day were vague. They had nothing to do with you. Now you begin to try to work them out. When Ted fell, did he try to break his fall? If he did it probably meant that he was only wounded, but if he seemed to sag at the neck, knee and ankle, you know what that meant. You look into the dusk. A solitary man is digging a trench. You watch him carefully. If he digs slowly and apathetically, you know his mate is dead. You call him over and he drops in beside you and your mate. Silently you hand him a fag. Silently he lights it. The smoke curls up. You don't speak, but he knows that all of you are mourning a mate together. All the wishing in the world won't bring him back. You console the survivor as best you may. Within a few minutes you remember some incident in which the dead mate looked ridiculous. That may seem callous, but it's the Infantry way of mourning. By next morning all is normal. You can't mourn all the time, but the night is first. The night guard duty is a lonely time. You are alone with your thoughts.'

The serious shortage of manpower in 7th Armoured was now compounded by the 'Python' order by which all men who had served overseas for five years could be returned to England, or if they volunteered to return, could still have an extended leave. This order meant the virtual end of the Queen's Brigade, which was now seriously under strength anyway. The three Queen's Royal Regiment battalions were now formed into one; the 1st/5th Queen's and the 131 Infantry brigade was made up by the addition of the 9th Durham Light Infantry and the

2nd Bn., the Devonshire Regiment. Other long-standing members of the Division, like the 11th and 8th Hussars and the RHA also lost a good number of their most experienced men. There was also a change in command. General Verney went to command an armoured division in Italy and General L.O. Lyne arrived from the 50th Division as Divisional Commander. The replacement situation throughout 21st Army Group was so serious that the 50th Division was disbanded and its men sent to make up the numbers in other formations. Among those arriving at this time was Ronald Mallabar of the 9th Bn., the Durham Light Infantry.

'I attained the age of eighteen on 25th July 1942 and was required to register for military service. When I did so I expressed a preference for the Army. Eventually I was ordered to report, on 3rd December 1942, to a Primary Training Wing at Gallowgate Camp, Richmond, North Yorkshire. There, recruits underwent six weeks basic training, together with intelligence and aptitude tests to establish which branch of the service would benefit from their presence.

'Unlike the other recruits who swarmed about Richmond in civilian clothes, I arrived wearing a smartly pressed battledress uniform, the sleeves of which showed obvious signs of having recently borne a Lance-Corporal's stripes. No one ever asked me about the reason for my uniform or my martial skills, so they never learned about my service as a volunteer from the age of sixteen in the Home Guard. When I joined the Army I had to take my uniform, minus stripes, with me. Incidentally, by this stage of the war, the Home Guard was not the 'Dad's Army' joke it is sometimes thought to be. It certainly taught me enough to make my entry into the Army completely painless.

'I was told that it had been decided I would be an asset to the Royal Corps of Signals and that was where I was going. This was not at all what I had in mind and faces turned white when, probably for the first time, someone said, "I'd rather go into the infantry, if you don't mind." After waiting outside I was eventually told that I could go into the Infantry only if I went as a Regimental Signaller. I accepted. Only later did I learn that if I had gone into the Royal Corps of Signals I would have been taught communications skills and been classed as a trades-man, with enhanced pay. As a Regimental Signaller I had to be able to do a dozen jobs while enduring the horrors of the infantry. No extra pay.

'I landed in Normandy with my battalion as part of 162 Independent Infantry Brigade, but after a few weeks the brigade was broken up to provide reinforcements for the depleted 50th (Northumbrian) Infantry

Division. As I was born in County Durham, I was glad to join the 9th Battalion, who were fighting at a place called Hottot. After fighting around Normandy and into Belgium, I was wounded in the opening stages of Operation Market Garden (the Arnhem "do"), and was flown to England in a returning Dakota. When I returned in November 1944, 50 Div had gone and 9 DLI was part of the 7th Armoured Division.

'At first, being in battle was quite enjoyable. I was doing an interesting job, for which I had been trained. Life was hard and uncomfortable, but I was young and strong and felt invulnerable. Although people were being killed, it was all rather unreal. Ignorance is bliss, but my outlook began to change when I was wounded for the first time. I realised that I was not immortal and each time I saw a friend die I grieved, but I was grateful that it was not yet my turn. I began to rejoice, as each dawn broke, to realise that I had survived another day.

'After being wounded for a second time, my attitude underwent another change. I came to believe that for me the war would only end when I was killed. By this time the 9th Battalion had become my whole life and everything else seemed unreal. When I was away from the battalion, even in hospital, I fretted to be back. I was obsessed by the idea that my comrades needed me with them and that I was letting them down by my absence. I missed hearing a Geordie voice calling out, "Howway, me bonny lads, get forward. Your mates are up there!"

'Back in action, I continued to go forward, not because I was brave, but for a variety of other reasons, chiefly pride. I would rather have died than shown fear. Also I felt that I had a duty to be with my friends, supporting them as they walked, ran or crawled towards the people who were trying to kill them. It is my belief that we kept going because none of us was prepared to be the one who showed that he was afraid. We never thought about the fact that we were doing the fighting, while for every one of us there were nine or ten soldiers who would never hear a shot fired in anger. The only comment I ever heard was, "If we survive this, don't try to tell anybody about it, because they won't understand."

'If the battalion was my universe, the Colonel (in this case Lt.-Colonel John Mogg, later General Sir John Mogg) was God! He was universally admired and with his cry of "Crack on!" was the ideal man to command a mechanised infantry battalion. For me he established his position as deity one night when we were dug-in and under heavy fire. It should have been pitch dark, but the area was illuminated by our ammunition truck, which had been hit and was burning furiously. As I crouched in my trench, fiddling with my radio, I heard a voice say, "Keep your head down, son!" I looked up to see Colonel Mogg strolling about in front of the trenches, swinging his walking stick, apparently oblivious of the tracer bullets which were weaving trails of light about us.

'If my respect for the Colonel knew no bounds, my opinion of officers in general was more ambivalent. Because of my position as a Signaller, I was always close to the officer, and because he relied on me a great deal we had a degree of mutual respect and friendship. However, I was appalled by the class distinction which prevailed between the officers and the "other ranks". For example, no matter what the situation, there had to be an "Officers' Mess", be it only a barn or a corner of a wrecked building. I was always amazed at the way in which the officers' whisky and gin rations managed to reach our front line positions.

'It was universally believed, rightly or wrongly, that most officers would do anything to get themselves decorated. This may have been an exaggerated point of view, held by men who were constantly being led into danger. However, I remember being annoyed when attending an "O" Group or conference at which a pending company attack was discussed. Officers were saying things like, "Let me have this one Colonel, Geoffrey had the last party!" Party! I knew that someone had to do it and that they were only going through their officer routine, but they were talking about people getting killed.

'In Holland, in the bitter winter of 1944/5, I enjoyed the comfort of a scrounged "tank suit". This was, as the name implies, issued only to members of tank crews. It was a one-piece garment like a flying suit, made of showerproof material and warmly lined. It was liberally supplied with useful pockets and, by a cunning arrangement of zip-fasteners, could be converted into a sleeping-bag. Worn over my uniform, this kept me quite cosy until, during one of my enforced absences, someone scrounged it.

'I was also the fortunate owner for a time of two sleeveless leather jerkins. I was wearing one when I was wounded in January 1945 and it was ruined by being covered in blood. I lost the second jerkin one day while advancing on foot along a forest track in Germany. At this time we were pestered by lone Germans who travelled about on pedal cycles or on foot, carrying a Panzerfaust, the German equivalent of the bazooka. These people would hide until a suitable target appeared, fire the panzerfaust (literally, "armour fist") and pedal away. On this occasion, the Bren Carrier accompanying us was hit by a man lurking among the trees. The crew were killed and the vehicle burst into flames. As the German made his run, he was hit by a burst of fire and fell wounded. Immediately, that strange compassion of the infantryman came into play and, with our friends' bodies burning beside us, I was prevailed upon to take off my jerkin and cover the wounded German to keep him warm. That was the last I saw of it.

'We even scrounged from the enemy. It was my practice to carry a German Schmeisser machine pistol, which used the same 9mm ammunition as our own awful Sten guns and, in my pouches, two German grenades, which were much lighter than our No. 36 grenades. These were "egg" grenades, and not the celebrated potato-mashers, which would have looked rather ostentatious stuck in my belt, which was the way the Germans carried them. On one occasion, when I was wounded and capture seemed imminent, I got rid of this enemy weaponry pretty smartly, on the assumption that I would have received short shrift if found in possession of it.

'Enough about scrounging ... a small anecdote .... We entered a German village, just vacated by the enemy. About midnight I found myself alone, watching the road along which they had retreated. It was pitch dark. I could see a red glow in the sky, but that was not unusual. Suddenly, I heard the sound of a bugle and a German voice shouting. The sounds grew nearer until I could hear the sound of heavy boots on the road. Visualising a desperate counter-attack by a fanatical SS Battle Group, I cocked my rifle and jumped into a ditch. A figure came into sight, running towards me. In the dark I could make out the familiar coal-scuttle helmet and jack-boots. The man was shouting and blowing fanfares as he came. I took aim, then made out what he was shouting: *"Die Wurstfabrik brannt!"* He was not the leading member of an enemy horde, but an old man calling out the volunteer fire brigade of old men and boys because the sausage factory was on fire. He did not see me in the ditch as he passed and never knew how close he came to ending his life on that road.

'On 9th January 1945, I took part in an abortive night raid by A Company at a village called Isenbruch, in deep snow. I never found out the purpose of the raid, although the talk was that it was to snatch some German VIPs from a house. I judged that the raid was important from the fact that four signallers accompanied the rifle company, instead of the usual one, the only time in my experience that this occurred. The raid was preceded by an artillery barrage along the whole front, to confuse the enemy. Shortly after we moved off, we found that our creeping barrage was creeping too slowly and the shells were falling short and exploding among us. The only way we could escape was by running forward and jumping into a dyke which ran across our front. It was about six feet deep and six feet wide and half full of water. We had to break the ice as we jumped in and then stand up to our waists in freezing water. As the shells were still exploding about us, I began bellowing into my microphone, "Lift the stonk one hundred." This was Signalese for "Kindly move your barrage one hundred yards further forward." After my second shout, someone pressed the muzzle of his revolver into my face and hissed, "Jerry is just over this dyke. If you don't shut up I'll blow your head off." I shut up. Fortunately, my appeals soon had their effect and the shells began falling further ahead.

'We scrambled out of the dyke and found to our horror that it was not the Germans who were just over it, but their minefield, which they had quickly laid by the simple expedient of laying the mines on the ground to be covered by the heavily falling snow. Immediately men were being killed or losing their legs, and within a few minutes we had suffered so many casualties that we were obliged to give up and withdraw without ever seeing a German.

'I later heard that the following morning the Company on the right of the Battalion had opened fire on a figure crawling in the snow in front of their positions. They had ceased firing when the figure began singing the DLI's Geordie anthem, "Blaydon Races". A patrol brought the man in and he turned out to be a Private from the raiding company, who had crawled all night, right across the battalion front, minus a leg. The bitter cold had stopped him from bleeding to death, but the poor fellow died soon afterwards.'

On 16th December 1944, the German army struck hard across the Ardennes in the operation known to history as The Battle of the Bulge. Seventh Armoured were not involved in this battle, which petered out under Allied air attack when the skies cleared on Christmas Day. While the Germans were battling east towards the Meuse and being repulsed by the American Army, 7th Armoured were training their reinforcements, servicing their vehicles and coping with the cracking winter cold which froze tank tracks to the ground and made ungloved hands stick to the chill metal of turrets and guns. It all seemed a far cry from the deserts of North Africa in the New Year of 1945, as the Division waited for orders to advance into Germany for the last stage of their long march from Alamein.

14

Germany

13TH JANUARY—8TH MAY 1945

War's a game which, were their subjects wise,
Kings would not play at.

William Cowper

Operations began for the men of 7th Armoured on 13th January 1945 when they took part in 'Operation Blackcock', a move designed by 12 Corps to clear the enemy away from territory up to the River Roer. Ronald Mallabar of HQ Coy 9 Bn Durham Light Infantry:

'The 7th Armoured Division had been holding static positions in Holland throughout the winter, but in January 1945 it was time for Operation "Blackcock", the clearing of the German Army from the West bank of the Roer. This kicked off with the order, "9 DLI will attack and capture Dieteren". It was to be a purely infantry operation, for the simple reason that our front was traversed by an unbridged canal. We would have to cross the canal and advance to take our objective, then hold it until engineers had constructed a bridge, so that tanks and other vehicles could follow to support us. We were even ordered to wear our steel helmets instead of the woolly hats we normally affected.

'We moved off in the early morning of 16th January. It was bitterly cold and the ground was covered in thick snow. The fog was largely of our own making, being caused by our smoke screen freezing in the air and refusing to disperse. Because of this, although the whole battalion was moving forward, I could only see the few men nearest to me.

'As a regimental signaller attached for the time being to a rifle company, I carried on my back a No. 18 radio set weighing 56 lbs.

261

This, of course, displaced my pack, which was slung on my left side beside my bayonet. My water bottle was on my right side and my entrenching tool slung below my belt at the back. The ammunition pouches on my chest and the bandolier of fifty cartridges over my shoulder completed the hundredweight of equipment under which I trudged. Of course, I also carried my rifle and on my head I wore the hated new model helmet. We all knew that these helmets were unlucky. Besides, they looked awful, being in appearance a cross between a Russian and a German helmet. I had disposed of my old-fashioned one when I was wounded four months previously and bitterly regretted it. I was constantly reminded of the helmet's presence by the sound of my vertical rod aerial rattling against its brim. I was also beginning to feel very hot as I was wearing several layers of warm clothing, topped by a greatcoat and a leather jerkin.

'When the enemy's shells began to burst among us I was reminded of how cold it really was, despite the fact that I was streaming with perspiration. I noticed with some surprise that the lumps of earth thrown up by the exploding shells were frozen hard and because of the waterlogged nature of the Dutch soil, composed largely of ice.

'A signaller in the infantry laboured under a number of disadvantages. Foremost, he was a prime target for snipers, because to eliminate him played havoc with the battalion communications. He also had the serious problem, because of the chattering in his headphones, of being unable to hear what was going on around him. He had, perforce, to keep his eyes darting about in order not to miss seeing what his comrades were doing. They, of course, could hear various unpleasant noises which caused them to throw themselves to the ground. our signaller, on seeing this, would follow suit, always a little late! When he hit the ground, he encountered another disadvantage – half a hundredweight of radio in its brass case shot forward along his back, hit him on the back of the head, knocked his helmet over his eyes and winded him. This was why, on the occasion of this brief bombardment, I chose to take my chances and remain on my feet.

'We were soon in the village and, after a brisk fight, the surviving Germans withdrew. I entered an empty house, dumped my radio on the floor and sat beside it. A series of loud explosions just outside caused me to throw myself flat against the wall. I got up again, somewhat relieved, when I found that the racket was caused by riflemen exploding anti-personnel mines in the hope of loosening the hard-frozen earth sufficiently to enable them to dig trenches.

'A message came over the air from battalion headquarters, ordering everyone to listen for enemy tracked vehicles which were supposed to have put in an appearance. We were glad to do so – if German tanks got in among us we would have a hard time. Naturally, we convinced ourselves that we could hear the familiar roar, clank and squeak approaching, but no tanks materialised.

'The next message I received was equally alarming. Enemy machine-gunners had got behind us and put a stop to the bridge-building by firing along the canal. My company was to send a platoon back to deal with them. I accompanied the platoon as it trudged back through the village. The lieutenant led the way, followed by myself, and behind me a dozen riflemen in single file, of whom, because of the fog, I could only see the first two. Before we had left the village, I saw the lieutenant throw himself to the ground and draw his revolver. I too crashed into the snow, with the usual unpleasant results. We lay like this for a while, then up got the officer and took a few more steps, only to dive again. Once more I followed suit, unable to see much, but beginning to feel rather sore and breathless. Up we got again, only to repeat the process for a third time. Thoroughly fed up, I crawled through the snow towards the officer. As I drew close, I got the impression he was sobbing, but when I lay alongside him, I could see that he was shaking with laughter. Being in no mood for hilarity, I snarled at him, "What the hell is going on?" I honestly thought he had gone off his head. He could not reply for chortling, but took hold of his water-bottle and shook it in my face. The contents had frozen and lumps of ice clanked against the sides of the metal container. As he explained when he recovered, it sounded exactly like a rifle being cocked and each time he heard it he had thought that he was about to fall victim to a sniper, hence his diving exhibition. I passed the word back to a relieved platoon and we continued our walk.

'We reached the canal without incident and patrolled along it for a few hundred yards. There was no sign of the enemy, so we set off back towards the village. On the way we passed a German sub-machine gun lying on the ground. Normally, this would have been picked up by someone for his personal use as they were in great demand, but we left this example because it had its careless former owner's bloody fingers mangled in the breech mechanism. We then saw a dead German lying face down in the snow. The top of his skull had been sliced off and lay in front of him like the lid of a box, still hinged by the skin of his forehead. I noticed, without emotion, that his brain looked just like a walnut in its half-shell.

'We had just reached the village when I heard the thumping sound of a mortar battery opening fire and I knew somehow that this time I was for it. I turned to face a farm building on my left, and dropped to my knees just as one of the bombs exploded right behind me. I felt a crash at the back of my head and was blown against the wall. My leather jerkin immediately turned red and glossy with the blood that was pouring down my face and running off my chin. Still on my knees, I imagined myself lying face down in the snow with the top of my skull sliced off. What had happened was that the blast had been taken by the soles of my boots, my entrenching tool, my radio and my helmet. My "unlucky" helmet was split from top to bottom, but it and my radio had saved my life. A bomb splinter had passed between the rim of my helmet and the top of the radio, and hit me in the back of the head. The blood was mainly from my left ear, where the splinter had emerged.

'I was patched up with field dressings and passed on to an Advanced Dressing Station, where a doctor examined me and said cheerfully, "Hello! You're the fellow with five holes from one bullet." This was news to me, so I asked him what he meant. He explained that my splinter had entered the back of my head and reappeared just behind my ear, making two holes. It had then hit the back of my ear and come out at the front, making two more holes. It had then clipped a piece off the little lug at the front of my ear and this was claimed as the fifth hole. I was a celebrity! Twenty years later, a lady doctor at my local hospital removed a small piece of steel helmet from my head. She was German!'

Sergeant Bertram Vowden recalls this time with 8th Hussars: 'On Thursday, 4th January 1945, I went for the usual briefing and began to get the idea that we were re-grouping. On 6th January I went as relief for the Squadron's Quarter Master Sergeant and found that we were really going to move, but on the following Monday we were told to move to Wintraak, about half a mile from the German border. The weather was grim and we were sleeping on the wet floor of a derelict café; outside it was bitterly cold and snowing.

'The following day I went with a 15cwt lorry to draw the Squadron's rations, and skidded into a ditch, taking half an hour to dig ourselves out. At the Troop sergeant's conference we were told we would be moving yet again and the next day, Thursday, 11th January, we knew we were going to Gheel for six days and were warned on security.

'At Gheel we were put into good billets and hoped we would be staying there for a while. I slept in a real bed that night ... it was lovely! Next day came, and with it a long drive to Maastricht, and we drew rations from a place called Dilson. The roads were extremely dangerous for driving. On 14th January we were working hard on stores in the QMs lorry. Tanks were busy, checking on their guns and rations for action. The following day the tanks were camouflaged. It was still cold and snowing, and that day we suffered a bad accident, when the Divisional Armourer was checking over the stock in the lorry and examining the Webleys and Smith and Wesson's .38 revolvers. These had been deposited by men called from their tanks to go on a short leave, and they had to leave their arms, of course, under wartime conditions and as a precaution against the old problem of familiarity breeding contempt. However, one gun was left in the lorry with six full chambers, and when it was picked up the armourer must have put pressure on the trigger, because it fired and killed his mate.'

Derrick Watson again: 'In the closing stages of Operation Blackcock, A Coy were ordered to occupy Paarlo, a village on the banks of the River Roer. I had under command a tank from 1 RTR, a Vickers Heavy Machine Gun Section, and a wireless link to the rear. We also had to manhandle bridging to cross the dykes, which lay between Aadenburg and Paarlo. We approached the village in the late evening and to our great relief the tanks were able to stay with us, causing a German forward post to be hastily abandoned, leaving behind a Spandau and a large amount of ammunition. The ground was frozen hard, so we abandoned the idea of digging in.'

Lt. Max Baker and his platoon occupied a large four-storey building in the main street of Paarlo, overlooking the river. During the night of 29th/30th, about fifty German troops crossed the River Roer in assault boats. Verdon Bisley of Lt. Baker's platoon recalls what follows: 'Late in the evening there was a sudden barrage and then a terrific bang upstairs, and two men were brought down, blinded by a bazooka rocket which had blown in the lookout window. Cpl. Dennis took them to the cellar for safety.'

Derrick Watson: 'At this time I received a last message from the Wireless Operator: "Get some help up here quickly." In an attempt to relieve them, I took two sections from another platoon and we started crawling towards the house. A German whom we thought was wounded, started crying, "Please, friends, come and help me," but when we stood up a Spandau opened up and wounded the Lance Corporal beside me. We withdrew to the protection of a tank, which opened a brisk, continuous and effective fire on the Spandau, and on another one which replied. At this stage it was clear that the Germans were in part occupation of the house and also occupying the ground between the house and my Coy HQ.'

Meanwhile, Verdon Bisley was carrying out a spirited battle from the top of the stairs, watching the front door, the entrance to the cellar, where Cpl. Dennis was guarding the wounded, and the window on the landing which overlooked the river, when the front door was blown in. Verdon heard the Germans shouting and charging, and grenades came through the window. Corporal Dennis in the cellar kept the enemy at bay from behind a steel curtain, which was repeatedly hit by grenades thrown by the Germans. Each time a grenade was thrown in, Dennis replied with a burst from his Sten-gun.

Verdon Bisley continues his account: 'As time passed, my ammunition was running out, the Bren-gunners came down and took most of mine. I found a phosphorus grenade in my pocket, pulled the pin and threw it down the stairs. Grenades came through the window in reply, the bombardment got worse and I was thrown against the wall but not seriously injured. Three of us were in the hall when we heard a voice outside say in a sort of German accent, "Out! Out! Run! Run!" We just said, "Yes, you bastard," and fired. Fortunately we did not hit him because it was one of our own officers, a Czech who had just joined us, later known as Robert Maxwell, who now owns newspapers. With this, Major Watson came in the front door and said, "Who wants medals?" but all we wanted was the ammunition he had brought, and to this day I believe that the battle for the house and the safety of the men below was saved by the phosphorus grenade I had thrown. Cpl John Melmoth, who led one of the sections which lifted the siege of the house, still recalls the warm welcome he received from the beleaguered garrison.'

Derrick Watson again: 'In conclusion, I had to return hurriedly to my forward Coy HQ after we had lifted the siege of the house, because my tank opened up again, the bullets whizzing overhead. I climbed up on the tank and saw the Germans in full retreat through the woods on the other side of the river. I gave the Tank Commander a box of Bren ammunition from our store, as he preferred to use a Bren rather than his Besa, and then laid down a barrage on the retreating Germans to bring the battle of Paarlo to a satisfactory conclusion.'

For Operation Blackcock, the Division took under command the 8th Armoured Brigade and the 155 Infantry Brigade, and later on, 1 Commando Brigade. Their initial advance was held up by terrible traffic congestion on the few suitable roads. The weather was bitterly cold, with constant snow flurries, but the attack duly began on the 13th with a preliminary advance by the 1st/5th Queen's, supported by Flail tanks and artillery. Then came several days of hard fighting, across canal after canal, through village after village, up to St Joost, which was stoutly defended by German parachute troops who inflicted many casualties on the 8th Hussars, the Durhams and the Rifle Brigade in house-to-house fighting, in which Colonel Holliman of the 5th RTR was killed.

R. Godwin again: 'The weather improves and we are mobile again in mid-January. We advance and arrive in St Joost, bottled up in a small road junction with the infantry. My tank at this time is new to me, a Sherman Firefly, with the long barrelled 75mm gun. The rest of the troop are in Cromwells. We are now using this tank as close support tank to the troop and we are supposed to deal with any big stuff we might encounter. The St Joost area is strongly held by three companies of German parachutists, who are young and fanatical, and the Crocodile flame tanks are just about to put in an attack, although the light is fading fast. The enemy is resisting house by house as the flames reach out to them, and we sit tight in our tank, being heavily mortared throughout a long and sleepless night. We are still in the thick of things and around 5 am start to get some sort of breakfast in readiness before my troop are ordered out to relieve another troop of infantry holed out overnight in a farm near the village. After all these years of fighting, the strange feeling comes over me that this is the day.

'It is very misty as we turn off up the farm track and position ourselves around the farmhouse. As we arrive and the other troop withdraws with the infantry on their tanks, we are suddenly under fire. Six Jerry self-propelled guns appear. My officer backs into the barn and I am backed into a pile of manure – everything has happened so fast. I see my first shot seemingly pass through and under the leading tank. Then a shot hits the farmhouse three yards away. We reload and fire, but nothing happens – a faulty shell or striker. Jock has already opened the breech and tells me the cap has been struck. I throw the shell clear of the turret and decide to pull the tank round the side of the farmhouse. Unfortunately, one Jerry tank has gone round the other side already. An armour piercing shell hits us square in the turret. I am severely wounded in the chest, back and left leg by splinters from the turret as the shell came through, but the shell has taken poor Jock squarely in the chest. It is more than twenty years before I rid my memory of his screams. The gunner, and Pete the driver, have bailed out. I am still struggling as the plug on my headset won't part, but I manage to throw it off, get out, and run to the farmhouse wall before I collapse. Pete dashes to the tank for the first-aid box and gives me morphine, and I am lifted onto the engine plates of the Troop corporal's tank. We set off across the field, and as I am facing the rear I can see the Jerry tank swinging his gun on to us, and shout to the Corporal to weave about. Before Jerry can get a sight on, we are on the track and onto the road for St Joost. Fortunately for me, the MO sees the problem and saves my life. The largest piece of shrapnel had gone through the rib cage, cut the diaphragm and left me drowning in my own blood. The MO tells me later that had it been the First World War I wouldn't have made it.'

The enemy were gradually pushed back to the Roer, covering their retreat with mines and machine-gun nests, but by the end of the month 'Blackcock' was judged a success. The Division then held the ground gained and the main activity, until the middle of February 1945, was patrolling by men from 1st Commando Brigade, who carried out a number of raids across the Maas. Meanwhile, the Allied armies moved up to the Rhine, and by early March stood poised to cross into Germany.

On 21st February, 7th Armoured were pulled out of the line and sent back a hundred miles to train for the Rhine crossing, 'Operation Plunder'. For this operation, 7th Armoured, as part of 12 Corps, were to cross the Rhine at Xanten and Wesel, going over just behind the assault forces as soon as Bailey bridges could be slung across the river. The Division would then exploit eastwards towards their final objective, the great city of Hamburg, which lay just 190 miles away to the north-east. The initial assault across the Rhine on the 23rd/24th March 1945 at Wesel was supported by the guns of 3rd and 5th RHA, and three days later, on the morning of the 27th, the 11th Hussars led 7th Armoured across the Rhine.

Those who have followed the story of the 7th Armoured Division this far, will have noticed the growing importance of the infantry element, as the Division left the desert and continued to fight the war across the close country of North-Western Europe. The war had only five weeks to run when 7th Armoured crossed the Rhine with the 11th Hussars in the van, closely followed by the infantry and the sappers.

Ronald Mallabar continues the story: 'For the crossing of the Rhine in March 1945, I was assigned to the duty of Second-in-Command's Radio Operator. This promised to be an exciting assignment, as the 2 i/c spent a good deal of time racing about in front of the battalion in a jeep, reconnoitring the line of advance.

'While I was fitting the big No. 19 radio set into the jeep and checking it over, the 2 i/c, Major Scott, approached, accompanied by his driver. They greeted me, and the Major inspected the jeep which was to be home to the three of us. During the bitter winter in Holland, the driver, like all of his fellows, had dispensed with the folding canvas roof of the

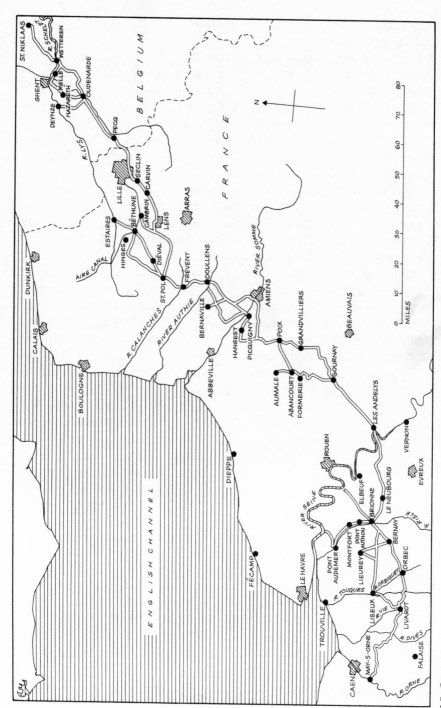

15 Germany

jeep and transformed it into a saloon by constructing a box-like body out of scrap metal, wood and canvas. There had been intense rivalry between the drivers as to who could produce the most luxurious vehicle and our driver was particularly proud of his efforts. He assured us that we could look forward to a fairly comfortable time, whatever the weather. "Fine," said Major Scott, then turned to me. "Do you require anything done with the jeep?" "Yes," I said, with a wave of my hand. "I want all of this off." The driver went berserk, but the Major shushed him and asked me to explain. I pointed out that he and the driver would be sitting in the front, each near an exit, while I would be cooped up in the back. When the inevitable emergency arose, I would be trapped in a flimsy box, with no means of escape. I already wore two wound stripes on my sleeve and was in no hurry to add to my collection. I felt sorry for the protesting driver, but Major Scott ended the discussion with, "He wants it off," and the jeep was soon once more a regulation vehicle.

'When we crossed the Rhine my elation at attacking the Fatherland was tempered by the sight of the body of a British parachutist hanging in the trees on the German side of the river. For some reason it seemed more poignant than the heaps of dead I had already seen. We advanced through Germany against varying resistance. My association with Major Scott was short-lived, as by the end of March he had been wounded and his place in the jeep was taken by the battalion Adjutant.

'The entrance to Stadtlohn was partially blocked by a typical obstacle of the period. This consisted of two parallel rows of stout logs, embedded in the ground and extending halfway across the road. Between the rows of logs was a huge wooden drum, full of earth, which was rolled out so as to block the rest of the road. There was just room for the jeep to squeeze through and we entered the town. We saw that it consisted of two long parallel streets which, apart from the church tower, had been completely flattened by bombing. It felt quite lonely driving along the ruined street. Halfway back along the other street, the jeep was struck by a hail of machine-gun fire from the church tower. My headphones, which I had laid on top of the radio were shattered and the driver's rifle was splintered in its rack in front of him. I rolled over the back of the jeep and into a convenient bomb crater, thanking God and Major Scott for allowing me to have my way over the boxed-in jeep.'

Tony Rampling was another 7th Armoured soldier who took part in the Rhine crossing. 'The roads and tracks and fields leading to the banks of the River Rhine were packed with vehicles of all descriptions, waterproofed and amphibious, all waiting for dusk. Artillery fire was going overhead, softening up the enemy. Everyone was very tense, not knowing what to expect on the other side; the engines of vehicles were running for what seemed like hours. I think everyone wanted to make sure they wouldn't conk out on the way over.

'Our team of six, manning a DUKW, followed the infantry, and our brief was to find a suitable sloping bank that the Sherman tanks could negotiate on their arrival. Then at dawn we were to indicate the landing place with red and green lamps. The tanks, being waterproofed and with high canvas sides and propellers, swam over, and on reaching land the sides were dropped down and they were off in action. The Royal Engineers seemed to have a Bailey bridge in operation very quickly, and I remember seeing my brother coming over in his Scout car. We found some German cars and travelled in those to catch up with the Regiment.'

The towns and villages on the east bank had been shattered into rubble by heavy bombing, and the advance was therefore slow, but with the 11th Hussars in the van, leading 22 Armoured Brigade forward, the Division made its way to the north-east, fighting every yard of the way to the River Ems. On the way the 11th Hussar History records that Colonel Wainmann threw away his map-sheets as the Regiment advanced, as an indication that the 11th Hussars would never retrace their steps. In this fashion 7th Armoured advanced towards the town of Rheine on the River Ems.

The Germans were on their home ground now, and every hamlet was defended, committing the Division to an endless round of actions against small groups or roving companies of enemy infantry equipped with anti-tank guns and *panzerfausts*, sometimes supported by one or two Tiger tanks. Even now, with the end of the war in sight, the Germans continued to fight with skill and determination, exacting a toll for every mile of ground surrendered.

The Division crossed the Ems on 3rd April, through the 11th Armoured Division's area, and captured the town of Ibbenburen after a stiff fight against snipers, many of them officer-cadets and NCOs from the local tactical training school. Here the Durhams took very heavy casualties, and tank commanders, sitting, heads exposed, in their turrets, were particularly vulnerable when giving close support to the infantry in the streets of the town. Robert Davey and Frank Barnes were Platoon Commanders in the 2nd Battalion the Devonshire Regiment:

'Our Brigade was instructed to take a town by the name of Rheine, which had a big aerodrome near the Dortmund-Ems canal. We were to take a ridge by the name of Ibbenburen, which was very ably defended by Hitler Youth Officer Cadets from Hannover. Each Platoon had an

RASC lorry but the leading Platoon was carried forward on tanks. When we met resistance we left the vehicles behind and went on with or without tanks, depending on the countryside. We spent a lot of time sitting on the back of the tanks going in, and the only snag was that you could not hear anyone firing at you for the noise of the engines and the tracks. One man was kneeling between my knees, speaking to me, I had my back to the turret, and the next moment he fell dead. When the company went in we followed our own creeping barrage, and when we got to the heights we had to winkle out the cadets who were well dug-in. They had been badly shelled but they were really tough. Afterwards, when we were collecting the wounded, I found one boy under a bush, who spoke perfect English and asked me if the stretcher bearers had gone. I said, "Yes," and he said, "In that case I'll die." It was just as well he did. He was very good looking but had no arms or legs.'

The advance was now speeding up. On 5th April, led by 1 RTR and the 2nd Devons 'with "A" Squadron in the lead, flat out, guns blazing,' 22nd Armoured Brigade reached the Weser at Hoya, where the bridge was blown up just as the leading tank of 1 RTR was about to cross. Another intact bridge was found at Verden, but when the 8th Hussars arrived they found it strongly defended. The Division then swung north towards Bremen. There was fierce fighting all the way, at Riede and Syke and Wildeshausen, a small town west of Bremen, which fell on 10th April.

Little of this fighting involved large numbers of troops, but the actions were still fierce and desperate, and the enemy sometimes appeared in considerable force, as at Syke, where three companies of infantry, supported by two Tiger tanks, put in a fierce counter-attack against C Squadron of the 11th Hussars, a company of the Rifle Brigade and a battery of the Norfolk Yeomanry, and there was a stiff fight before they were driven off. On the next night a strong party of SS Troops infiltrated into Wildeshausen, and a fierce fire-fight broke out in the town centre around midnight, the enemy destroying four tanks and some lorries before they were driven out. Leaving Bremen to fall to troops of the 3rd Infantry Division, 7th Armoured swung south to cross the Aller at Rethem on 14th April. The Rethem position was stoutly defended by German marines, who put up stiff resistance for four days before they were subdued. From the Aller, the Division had ten days of fighting through Soltau and Fallingbostel, where they liberated the large British POW camp, a compound containing a number of 7th Armoured men, some captured long ago in the Desert, some more recently in the

Normandy campaigns. Other units of the Division, like Ricky Hall's RASC Company, also had cause to see the terrible sights at the concentration camp at Belsen, which had been overrun by the 11th Armoured Division.

Rick Hall again: 'You could smell Belsen from miles away. I had been with 7th Armoured all the way from the desert, and seen a lot of sights in that time, but never anything like that. We had to take disinfectant in because they had typhoid and all manner of diseases and were burying the dead in great pits with bulldozers. If people ask you if the war was worth it, I can tell you that no one who saw Belsen could ever have been in any doubt about that.'

Germany was now falling apart, but the German Army kept on fighting. On 17th April, the Inniskillings and the infantry of 155 Brigade took Soltau, needing the support of flame-throwing Crocodile tanks to clear enemy snipers from the rubble-strewn streets and houses. The Division then drove the enemy before them up to the River Elbe at Harburg, and now had two remaining tasks; to cut the Bremen-Hamburg autobahn and so cut off German troops of the 1st Parachute Army retreating from Bremen, and then clear the wooded country to their rear, between Harburg and Soltau, which was thick with still truculent enemy troops. This done, they would take Hamburg.

Harry Upward was still driving his Firefly tank in the 5 RTR: 'The war was almost over now, but you couldn't ease up. Advancing from Ghent, I used to drive with the hatch open, rather than trying to see through the visor or the periscope, but for some reason I decided to let my seat down and close the hatch ... and a second later a 105mm hit the front of the tank and took big lumps out of the armour and the gun. That should have told me my luck was in – or runnng out!

'Somewhere near Luneburg, only a day or two before the war ended, the whole Squadron was advancing across this open plain, and we were at the rear, with our big gun. Then we stopped while the tank commander went ahead for a recce on foot, and as we pulled back to go ahead, we got a direct hit from an 88mm. It was quite an experience. I had the hatch up ... there was this great concussion ... a flash and a bang to make your teeth ache ... and the tank was on fire ... just like that. Thank God the gun was positioned to the front or I would not have got out, but as it was, we all got out and I was the only one hurt, with burns on my hands and face. They took me to a hospital in Brussels and that was the end of my war. I don't regret it, and the Germans were all right – just like anyone else. As for the crew, we were like a family.'

Bertram Vowden also remembers that the fighting went on until the very last minutes of the war. 'We had reached a small village and the German defenders had withdrawn, leaving a log-built roadblock to slow down our tanks' advance. One troop moved quickly through the centre of the village, found no enemy and confirmed it was all clear for us to go and replenish. My small convoy started to go forward when there was a burst of machine-gun fire. About six or more Germans had taken up cover at the side of the road near the roadblock, and as one of our tanks approached, with the officer observing all around him for any movement and with head and shoulders out of his turret, the Germans had fired and he had been killed. When I arrived the Germans were lined up with hands on heads, but the one who was identified as firing the fatal shot at the officer had himself been shot by one of the dead officer's crew. The officer was the last casualty we suffered, as shortly after we moved in and accepted the surrender of Hamburg, and for us the war was finally over.'

By 20th April the woods between Bremen and Hamburg had been cleared, but many of the enemy SS paratroopers, submarine crews and reservists had withdrawn into Hamburg and seemed prepared to make a fight of it. The full weight of 7th Armoured was therefore deployed against the town, with heavy artillery concentrations preceding an all-out attack by tanks and infantry. Hamburg had suffered considerably from attacks by the RAF, and on 29th April a deputation of citizens came into the 7th Armoured lines under a white flag and discussed the surrender of the town. General Lyne sent a message back to the German Commander, General Wolz, demanding the immediate surrender of the city and pointing out that unless this demand was met forthwith, the entire weight of Allied arms would be turned against him.

Corporal David Fyffe of 7th Armoured HQ recalls the surrender: 'I was a Scout Car driver, but the only thing of note that happened to me was at the close of activities, when my officer, Lt. Peter Linguard, was given the task of going into Hamburg to bring out a German officer whose task was to arrange for the meeting of the advance party of the German Generals surrendering to Monty on Luneburg Heath.

'I found it a bit nerve-wracking to be one of the only two British soldiers slowly creeping into Hamburg. I can tell you that there wasn't a single soul to be seen in the streets until we arrived at our destination.'

On 1st May the news of Hitler's suicide came through on the BBC, and on 2nd May General Wolz arrived at Divisional HQ to discuss the arrangements for the surrender, which was taken by Brigadier Spurling on the afternoon of 3rd May. Later that afternoon, the 11th Hussars led 7th Armoured into the ruins of Hamburg, and on 8th May 1945 the German Army surrendered. The long march of 7th Armoured Division was almost over.

For the next two months the Division stayed in the Hamburg area, sorting out prisoners, helping to clear up the inevitable mess in the city itself and dealing with the tens of thousands of displaced persons who were roaming the ruins of Nazi Germany, attempting to find their way home. Then, in July 1945, the Division was directed to move to Berlin, firstly to join the Occupation Forces there, and secondly to take part in the great Victory Parade through the city on 21st July.

Signaller Mallabar of the 9th Durhams went with the Division on this last stage of the journey: 'The arrival of the Division in Berlin was a great personal thrill. The city was, of course, in ruins, thanks to the efforts of RAF Bomber Command and the Red Army. Of the buildings left standing, many were in a dangerous condition, with the adjacent footpaths fenced off with wire in case of falling masonry.

'Later in my stay, I became aware of some worrying traits. The most notable was that the Germans were convinced that this was only a lull in the war, and that soon the Allies would re-arm them and together we would invade Russia. They seemed to have an infinite capacity for self-deception.

'When the war ended we were warned to be on the alert for personal attacks by German partisans, as had happened in the countries occupied by the Nazis. The Germans were terrified of 'Die Russen', and told gruesome tales of the period after the cease-fire, when they were apparently given licence to do as they liked. Apart from wholesale looting and violence, "raped eight times" was a typical report. There was a problem with them coming into the British sector with lorries and looting houses. We were obliged to operate mobile patrols to combat this.'

The last act of this long-running drama took place on 21st July 1945, when 7th Armoured paraded past Winston Churchill down the Charlottenburg Chaussée in Berlin, a parade led by the 3rd Royal Horse Artillery and the Armoured Regiments, the 8th Hussars and the incomparable 11th Hussars, who drew a special cheer from those ranks of the Division who watched them roll past. Then came the Sappers, the Royal Engineers, and the Infantry, the Queen's, the Durhams, and representatives of all the other elements of this great Division, which had fought in victory and defeat, from 1939 to the last days of the war, and marched to the ruins of Berlin from the desert of Alamein.

Later that day, Winston Churchill met the men of the Division and spoke some words that they would treasure:

> I have, not for the first time, had the pleasure of seeing your troops march past, which brings to my mind many moving incidents of these last, long fierce years .... It is a march unsurpassed in all the story of war so far as my reading of history leads me to believe. May the fathers long tell the children about this tale. May you feel that in following your great ancestors you have done something of good to the whole world, which has raised the honour of your country and of which every man should be proud.

There is, however, one final tale, a small incident which somehow typifies the strong spirit of the 7th Armoured Division. Eric Johnson, of the 2nd Royal Gloucestershire Hussars was captured in the battles around Gazala in 1943. Nearly two years later, accompanied by three other ex-POWs, he was walking home across the flat countryside of East Germany, pushing an old handcart.

'This contained our few belongings, half a sack of somewhat frosted potatoes and about five kilos of coarse flour, loaded by a farmer after we had given him twenty cigarettes. Thus we came towards Wurzen.

'Late that night we found a narrow footbridge across the River Mulde, and there we left the old handcart. It had served us well but was too wide to cross that bridge, but our last act before gaining our freedom was to get out the broken-bladed claspknife we carried, and on the one sound leg of the handcart we cut and scraped a symbol ... the Jerboa badge of the 7th Armoured Division. We left the handcart on the riverbank, its shafts pointing forlornly into the air, but one day some kindly disposed historian will record that place as the most easterly point in Europe reached in the war by that renowned and widely travelled rodent.'

Floreat Jerboa!

Selected Bibliography

The Crucible of War (The Western Desert 1940) by Barrie Pitt (Johnathan Cape, 1980).

Armoured Crusader: General Sir Percy Hobart by Kenneth Macksey (Hutchinson).

The Eleventh at War by Dudley Clarke (Michael Joseph, 1952).

Take These Men by Cyril Joly (Constable, 1955).

The Tanks – A History of the Royal Tank Regt (2 vols) by Basil Liddell Hart (Cassell, 1959).

The Rifle Brigade in the Second World War by R.H.S.W. Hasting (Gale & Polden).

Desert Rats at War by George Forty (Ian Allan, 1975).

Wavell, Scholar and Soldier by John Connell (Collins, 1964).

With Rommel in the Desert by Heinz Schmidt (Harrap, 1950).

The Rommel Papers, edited by B. Liddell Hart (Collins, 1964).

Auchinleck by John Connell (Cassell, 1959).

African Trilogy by Alan Moorhead (Hamish Hamilton, 1949).

Tobruk by Michael Carver (Batsford, 1969).

Alamein by Michael Carver (Batsford, 1962).

Pillar of Fire by Ronald Atkin (Sedgwick & Jackson, 1980).

The Desert Rats: A History of 7th Armoured Division by Major General G.L. Verney (Hutchinson, 1954).

The Only Way Out by R.M. Wingfield (Hutchinson, 1955).

A Short History of 7th Armoured Division 1943–45 by Michael Carver (Privately published 1947).

Out of Step by Field Marshal Lord Carver (Michael Carver) (Hutchinson, 1989).

Winged Dagger by Roy Farran (Fontana, 1954).

Road to Victory (Winston S. Churchill 1941–45) by Michael Gilbert (Heinemann, 1989).

History of the 2/7th Bn. The Queen's Royal Regiment by Roy E. Bullen (Bisley, 1958).

Alamein by Philip Warner (William Kimber, 1979).

Rommel's War in Africa by Wolf Heckman (Granada, 1981).

The Battle for North Africa by John Strawson (Batsford, 1969).

The Galloping Third by Hector Bolitho (John Murray, 1963).

The Desert Generals by Correlli Barnett (William Kimber, 1960).

Brazen Chariots by Robert Crisp (Muller, 1959).

Rommel as Military Commander by Ronald Lewin (Batsford, 1968).
Rommel by Brigadier Desmond Young (Collins, 1950).
The Desert War by Alan Moorehead (Hamish Hamilton, 1963).
Montgomery by Alan Moorehead (Hamish Hamilton 1946).
7th Armoured Division by John Sanders (Squadron Pubs. 1977.
British Tanks of the Second World War (The Tank Museum, 1956).
Tanks of Other Nations (Germany) (The Tank Museum, 1969).

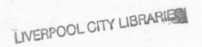

Index

Abbassia 31, 32, 33
Acroma 69
Afrika Korps 43, 61, 65, 67, 79, 116, 134, 136, 138
Agedabia 61, 100, 101, 102, 171
Agheila 167
Alam Halfa 109, 133–40, 149
Alem el Fakhri 78
Alexander, Field Marshal ix, 132, 144, 145, 160
Alexandria 31, 33, 59
Anderson, General 180
Anderson, Sgt. Jock 88
Antelat 57, 67, 171
Ariete, the 66, 86, 87, 98, 99, 127, 130, 134, 161
Arras 8, 9
Ashworth, Lt. 202
A9 tanks 35
Auchinleck, General Sir Claude 79, 80, 82, 101, 102, 107, 126, 129, 130, 131, 132
Aunay-sur-Audon 236
Austin, Allan, 116–18, 137, 148–51
6th Australian Division 39, 55
9th Australian Division 61, 67, 68–9

Bainbridge, John (Tank Corps) 20–22, 32
Baker, Lt. Max 265
Balbo, General 39, 40
Barce 57
Bardia 48, 51, 55, 56, 61, 166, 170, 171
Barrow, Hugh Major (RHA) 92–4
Barton, Jimmy 93
Battipaglia 198
Battleaxe, Operation 72–9, 80
Bayeux 216, 234
Beda Fomm 55, 57, 59, 60, 61, 65, 66, 69

Beech, Harry (RA) 181
Beeley, Rifleman 92
Bell, Len 42
Beurat 167, 178
Benghazi 32, 33, 57, 60, 63, 65, 68, 69, 103, 115, 141, 171
Beresford-Pierse, Lt.-Gen. 72, 78
Bergonzoli, General Annibale 55, 56, 60
Big Willie 6
Bilsborough, Walter (RASC) 120
Binks, Col. (4th Armoured) 59
Birley, Lt.-Col. 20, 86, 116, 124
Bir el Tamir 129
Bir Hacheim 69, 106, 108, 110, 111, 112, 113, 115, 116, 119, 122, 123, 124, 125
Bir Harnet 113
Bisley, Verdon 265, 266
Bismark, Major-General Georg von 138, 142
Black, Frank (RHA) 92
Blackcock, Operation 261, 265, 266
Black Watch 97
Blood, Harry (RASC) 114–15
Bluecoat, Operation 233
Boer War (1899–1901) 3
Bovington Camp 20
Bradbury, Teddy 96
Bradley, Lt. Col. 7
Bramwell, Sgt. Bobby (CLY) 184, 219, 230
Buckledee, Harry (11th Hussars) 43–4
Bucknall, General 208
Bulge, Battle of the 260
Buq-Buq 49, 53, 54, 60

Caen 216, 232
Cairo Cavalry Brigade 29
Cairo Brigade 39

279

Cambrai, Battle of 10, 11
Cameron Highlanders 52
Campbell, Brigadier Jock 41, 48, 89, 92, 94, 96, 98, 103
Capua 198, 201, 203
Capuzzo, Fort 42, 46, 47, 69, 71, 72, 73, 74, 75, 77, 89, 92, 99, 124, 166, 170
Cardigan, Earl of 18
Carr, Brigadier 144
Carter, Frederick (RASC) 105
Carver, Field Marshal Lord 13, 14, 22, 35, 131, 140, 151, 200, 220, 230, 233, 244
Castel Benito 167
Caumont 236, 238
Caunter, Brigadier J.A.L. 37, 57, 59
Cheers, Stan (6 RTR) 77
Churchill, Winston 5, 37, 63, 79, 82, 84, 107, 131, 132, 141, 167, 184, 193, 275–6
Clark, George (KDGs) 64–5, 200
Clark, General Mark 204
Clay, Captain (RGH) 80–81
Cloudsley-Thompson, J.L. 226
Cole, Lt. George 182–3
Combe, Brig. John 46, 54, 57, 59, 68
Combeforce 57
Conie, Jock 77
Cooper, Ray (22nd Armoured Brigade) 164, 167, 180, 206
Cotton, Lt. Bill 219, 222
County of London Yeomanry (The Sharpshooters) 13, 81, 90, 98, 226
Cranley, Lt.-Col. Lord 223
Creagh, Major-General Michael O'Moore 37, 49, 77, 78
Creagh, Mrs 37
Creek, Lt.-Col. John 187
'Cromwell' tank 16, 207, 209–10
Crusader, Operation 80, 82, 115
'Crusader' tanks 14, 16, 50, 72, 81, 87
Cunningham, Lt.-Gen. Sir Alan 82, 89, 99
Currie, John 93
Custance, Brigadier N. 174, 177
Cyrenaica 28, 29, 33, 38, 39, 40, 54, 57, 61, 65, 71, 82

Daba 147, 161, 163, 168, 169
Dardanelles 3
Daser, General 250

Davies, Llewellyn (REME) 239
Dean, Major 'Tinny' 22, 49, 51
Dempsey, General 230
Derna 57, 60, 72
Desert Air Force 39
Dunkirk 3, 28
de Salis, Lt.-Col. 92
Digby, F. W. (2nd RTR) 59–60
Drury, A. (Ted) (RASC) 172–3
Duce, Trooper (8th Hussars) 209

Eassie, Lt.-Col. 68
East, Col. Lance 155, 156
Eisenhower, General Dwight 163
El Adem 68, 69, 84, 112–13, 115, 125, 126, 171
EL Agheila 61, 63, 66, 69, 174, 175
El Alamein 11, 33, 109, 115, 118, 126, 128, 130, 132, 133, 141–2, 163–79
El Duda 97, 112
El Gubi 86, 87, 95, 98, 101, 110, 112, 114, 116
Elles, Lt.-Col. Hugh 8, 9, 10
Elliott, Major Russell 168, 169, 252
Ellis, Sgt. Harry 166–7, 203, 208
Elsington, Lt.-Col. W. R. 182
Emmett, 'Ticker' 45
Epsom, Operation 232
Errington, Col. 183
Erskine, General 160, 180, 203, 209, 220, 230, 231, 238
Experimental Armoured Force 12, 13

Falaise 232, 241
Falklands War 5
Farran, Lt. Roy (3rd Hussars) 185
Fawcett, Major 67
Finnigan, Barney 74
Firefly tank 207
Flanagan, A. (2nd Royal Tanks), 20, 60
Flers, Battle of (1916), 7, 8
Fletcher, Lt. 113–14
Fox, Capt. 68
Frapwell, J.I. (RGH) 115–16
Free French Forces 51, 106, 125, 133, 147, 148, 156
Freeland, Lt.-Col. Ian 252
Fuka 169
Fuller, Major J.F.C. 8, 9, 10, 11, 12, 13, 16, 65
Fyffe, Cpl. David 274

Gabr Saleh 86, 89, 98
Gallipoli 3
Gambut 115
Garnett, Lt. 215
Gatehouse, Brigadier Alec, 78, 81
Gazala 106–28, 148
Geddes, Jack (CLY) 228
Geneifa 169, 182
George V 10
George VI 198, 208, 220
Gerawla 31, 41
Ghent 248–51
Gillman, Neville (4th CLY) 17–18, 95–6,
    103–4, 126–7, 134, 136–40, 153–4
Godwin, R. (RGH) 19–20, 86–7, 90–91,
    99–101, 207, 267–68
Goodwood Operation 232, 233
Gordon-Finlayson, Lt. Gen. Sir Robert 30
Gott, Brigadier W. H. E. ('Straffer') 29, 37,
    48, 69, 70, 71, 82, 103, 104, 132
Graziani, Marshal Rodolpho 41, 42, 48
Grazzanise 201
Gregory, Major Desmond 188
Grey, Ronald 69
Guderian, General 12, 14
Gunn, Lt. Ward 94

Hackett, General Sir John 'Shan' 18,
    108–9, 135–6, 253
Hafid Ridge 74, 76, 77
Haig, General Earl 8, 12
Halfaya Pass 33, 71, 72, 74, 78, 79,
    82
Hall, Rick (RASC) 17, 75–6, 95, 120,
    170, 187, 273
Hamburg 268, 273, 274–5
Hankey, Lt.-Col. Maurice 3, 5, 6
Harding, Field Marshal A. F. 140, 142–6,
    147, 148, 151, 152, 157, 158, 173–4,
    160, 167, 168, 169–82
Haslam, Ron 54, 70
Hayes, Lt. 155–6
Heavy Armoured Brigade 30
Hill, Ken (50th RTR) 37
Himeimat 137, 139, 140, 142, 147, 151,
    152, 158
Hinde, Brigadier 180, 221, 238
Hindenberg Line 10
Hitler, Adolph 13, 28, 65, 84, 274
Hobart, Major General Sir Percy 14, 22,
    29–30, 32, 36–7, 55, 207, 208, 215

Hoggarth, Peter (1/7th Queen's) 196,
    202
Holliman, Lt.-Col. 250
Holt Caterpillar Tractor 6
Homs 195
Honey tank 81
Horrocks, General 136, 142, 145, 151,
    158, 187, 198, 204, 237
3rd Hussars 54
7th Hussars 29, 30, 46, 47, 53, 81, 91
8th Hussars 18, 29, 30, 47, 54, 89, 97,
    113, 234
11th Hussars (Prince Albert's Own) 'The
    Cherrypickers' 13, 15, 18–19, 29, 30–
    32, 38–9, 42–8, 54, 57, 59, 61, 69–
    70, 98, 103, 161, 170–71, 174, 186,
    195, 198, 208, 233–4, 236, 238, 251,
    253, 268, 274

4th Indian Division 39, 41, 49, 52, 53,
    72
Ireland, John (RTR) 121–3
Italian Littorio Armoured Division 129
Italian 10th Army 39, 40, 47, 56, 59, 60

jerboa 37–8
Jerboa Strollers 173
Johnson, Eric (RGH) 276
Jones, Lt.-Col. B. S. 185

King, Tony 234
King's Dragoon Guards (KDGs) 57, 61,
    81, 123, 131
King's Royal Rifle Corps (KRRC) 29, 30,
    31, 46, 69, 89, 91
Kingsford, Lt. Pat 156
Kirkpatrick, Capt. Jimmy 204, 205
Kirkham, Major Harry (RTR) 22, 49–52
Kitchener, Lord 6
Knott 'Granny' (Driver) 51, 52
Koenig, General 106, 125, 133, 136,
    158

12th Lancers 13, 15
Lassman, Herb (RHA) 41–2, 104–5
Lawrence, T. E. 3
Leese, Gen. Sir Oliver 132, 176
Lewis, Sergeant Alec 30, 41
Libya 3, 19, 65, 69, 86
Liddell Hart B. H. 5, 12, 16, 30, 65
Light Armoured Brigade 30

Lindsay, Col. 200
Lisieux 241
Lloyd George, David 5
Loman, Fred 119–20
Loos 3
Lungershausen, General 151
Lyne, General L. O. 256

Maadi 43
Mackeson, Brigadier 251
Maddalena, Fort 32, 45, 46, 115, 170
Mallabar, Ronald (Durham Light Infantry) 256–60, 261–4, 268, 270, 275
Malatti, General 52
Malines 252
Malta 80
Marmon Harringtons 69
Mark I (A9) tank 14, 16, 30
Mark II (A10) tank 13, 14, 16, 30
Mark III (A13) tank 14, 210
Mark IV tanks 17, 210
Mark VI tank 13, 14, 29, 30, 35, 46, 50, 61, 72
'Matilda' tanks 13, 16, 48, 49, 52, 71, 72
Maxwell, Robert 266
McCreery, General 144, 204
McEwan, Lt. Keith 223
Mechili 69, 72
Medenine 181, 184, 186
Mersa El Brega 66, 67, 173, 174
Mersa Matruh 29, 33, 36, 38, 42, 60, 67, 69, 118, 127, 129, 148, 163
Messervy, General 77, 103, 109, 112, 115, 124, 125, 130
Messe, General 149, 190
Mikelia 60
Miles, Major 73
Milne, General 12
Milner, Gerald (RASC) 119
Mogg, General Sir John 257–8
Montgomery, Gen. Bernard 132, 133, 136, 137, 141, 145, 147, 160, 170, 186, 207, 208, 232, 253
Mont Pincon 237, 238
Morrison, Col. 41
Muir, Captain 116, 124
Mussolini, Benito 28, 41, 63
Msus 57, 103

Neame, General Philip 66, 67, 68, 72
2nd New Zealand Division 39

4th New Zealand Reserve Co. 55
Nibeiwa 49, 52
Normandy 215–43
Norrie, Lt.-Gen. 82, 98

O'Connor, General Richard 38, 39, 46, 47, 48, 56, 66, 68
OMAHA beach 215
Oss 253

Page, R. G. (KDGs) 65, 97
Palmer, Major 126
Panzer Divisions 14, 16, 64, 65
Panzer Grenadiers 27
Parish, Lt. 67, 68
Parker, Sgt. 'Sniffy' 169
Parkin, Sgt. 'Sniffy' 155
Paschendaele 10, 11
Pavitt, 'Foxy' 183
Payne, Guy 88
Percival, Corporal J. 146–7
Phelps, Lt. 68
Phillips, Capt. M. B. 68, 125
Picardy 3
Pile, General Timothy 81
Pimple, the 59
Pivot Group (Support Group) 30
Pollard, 'Snub' 46
Pope, Brigadier 28
Powell, Reginald (Royal Tank Corps) 19, 77–8
Prosser, A. S. (11th Hussars) 18–19, 43
Pyman, Lt.-Col. H. E. 109

Qattara Depression 33

Rabia 53
Rampling, Tony (7th Armoured) 270
Ramshaw, L/Cpl. Bob 44
Reid-Scott, 2nd Lt. 54
Renton, General 140, 144
Riddell, Colonel Duncan 55, 68, 114, 124, 185, 230
Ridgway, Captain Mickey 119
Ritchie, General 103, 111, 244
Roberts, Maj.-Gen. G.P.B. 22, 135, 144, 168, 179, 180, 207
Roberts, Sgt H. 4
Roddick, Brigadier, 145
Rogers, 'Dingle' 52

Rommel, Field Marshal Erwin 43, 63, 64–7, 69, 71, 76, 78–82, 84, 86, 89, 91, 95, 97–9, 102–3, 108, 110–11, 123, 126–7, 131–6, 142, 148, 151, 163, 166–7, 174, 180, 184
Roy, Cpl. 33
Royal Armoured Corps 15, 23
Royal Army Service Corps (RASC) 29, 55, 56
Royal Artillery 13
Royal Engineers 13, 181
Royal Gloucestershire Hussars (RGH) 19, 81, 86
Royal Horse Artillery 29, 30, 46, 52, 54
Royal Hussars 18
Royal Naval Air Service (RNAS) 3
Royal Tank Corps 12, 13, 15
Royal Tank Regiment 10, 29, 30, 31, 33, 37, 48, 49, 51, 54
Russell, Brigadier H. E. 37

Salerno 196, 198, 204
Scafati 198
Sciones, Major R. I. 75
Sfax 186
Sidi Ali 75
Sidi Aziez 170
Sidi Barrani 33, 40, 42, 48, 49, 52, 56
Sidi Bish 59
Sidi Omar 75, 77, 82, 86
Sidi Rezegh 80–101, 126
Sidi Saleh 57
Sidi Suleiman 75
Sirte, Gulf of 57
Siwa Oasis 33
Smail, Col. (11th Hussars) 203, 208
Smith, General Sir Cecil 37
Smith, Major C. M. 30
Smith, Sgt. Maj. 43, 44
Smith, S. G. (11th Hussars) 64
Smith, T. T. (KRRC) 48–9
Sofafi 49, 53, 75, 78
Soluch 171
Sollum (Egypt) 19, 31, 33, 38, 42, 54, 67, 69, 72, 115
Somerset Light Infantry 13
Somme, Battle of 3, 7, 8, 10
South African Armoured Car Regt. 81, 123, 124
Spring, Operation 233
Stumme, General 142

St Valery 64
Sueter, Commodore Murray 3, 6
Suez Canal 29
Swain, Harold (65th Anti-Tank Reg. RA) 228
Swinton, Lt.-Col. E. D. 6, 7, 8, 12

Tank Brigade 13, 14
Tank Corps 7, 10, 11
Tarhuna 176, 177
Taylor, G. W. (S.A. Armoured Car Reg.) 120–21
Territorial Yeomanry 15
Tilshead Camp, Salisbury Plain 13
Tobruk 38, 48, 56–7, 63, 65, 67–71, 82, 84, 86, 89, 101–2, 114, 118–19, 123, 125, 129, 141, 169, 171
Torch, Operation 142
Towns, Sgt. Gibson (Tony) (RGH) 87–8
Trevor, Major Bill 116
Tripolitania 29, 61, 63, 66, 69, 82, 84
Tripoli 60, 62, 63, 64, 66, 80, 167, 168, 177, 178, 180, 204
'Triton' 6
Tummar, East and West 49, 52
Tunis 180–91
Turner, Brigadier C. E. F. 151, 157–60, 178–9

Unaike, Col. 124
Upward, Harry (RTR) 249, 272
UTAH beach 215

Valentine tank 81
Verney, General 111, 230, 236–7, 238, 241, 248, 249, 256
Vickers Medium Tanks 13
Villers-Bocage 219, 221, 222, 223, 224, 225, 226, 227, 238
Villers-Bretonneux 11
Vowden, Bertram 218, 264–5, 274

Waddington, Lance-Sergeant 151–2
Wainmann, Major 203, 208, 271
Waites, Arthur (7th Hussars) 15–16, 22, 33
Watkins, Sgt. 32, 40
Watson, Derrick (1/5th Queen's) 154, 168–9, 182, 223, 241, 245, 251–2, 265, 266

Wavell, General Sir Archibald 38, 42, 48, 49, 52, 56, 57, 60–61, 63–4, 67, 71, 72, 79
Werncke, Major (Panzer Lehr) 225
'Whippets' 11
Whistler, Brigadier 201
Whitlock, Capt. 67, 68
Willis, Major 126

Wilson, General Sir Henry Maitland 36, 38
Wingfield, R. M. xiii, 246, 255
Wittmann, Captain Michael 223
Wolz, General 274

York, J. W. (Queen's Brigade) 164
Ypres 3, 9